Ancient Records from North Arabia

NEAR AND MIDDLE EAST SERIES

1 *The Mosaic Tradition*
F.V.Winnett

2 *Safaitic Inscriptions from Jordan*
F.V.Winnett

3 *History and Chronology of the Eighteenth Dynasty of Egypt: Seven Studies*
Donald B.Redford

4 *Oral Formulaic Language in the Biblical Psalms*
Robert C.Culley

5 *Jewish and Mandaean Incantation Bowls in the Royal Ontario Museum*
W.S.McCullough

6 *Ancient Records from North Arabia*
F.V.Winnett and W.L.Reed

Ancient Records from North Arabia

F.V.WINNETT and W.L.REED

with contributions by

J.T.MILIK and J.STARCKY

University of Toronto Press

Printed in Canada by
University of Toronto Press
Toronto and Buffalo
SBN 8020-5219-3

This study of some of Arabia's antiquities
is respectfully dedicated to

HIS MAJESTY FAYṢAL ibn ʻABD AL-ʻAZĪZ ibn
ʻABD AR-RAḤMĀN ĀL SAʻŪD
KING OF SAʻUDI ARABIA

Preface

Prior to the beginning of the twentieth century only fifteen Europeans are known to have visited northern and central Arabia.[1] The smallness of their number was compensated to some extent by the acuteness of their powers of observation, and they gave the outside world excellent descriptions of the physical features of those parts of the country which they saw and of the life and customs of their inhabitants.[2] Several of these explorers, notably Charles M. Doughty, Charles Huber, and Julius Euting, were interested in the antiquities of Arabia as well and not only described the ruins they encountered but copied hundreds of ancient inscriptions which they found engraved on the rocks. Most of the inscriptions were, however, mere graffiti from which little information of a historical character could be extracted. As a result, scholars were unable to reconstruct from them even an outline of the history of the northern and central parts of the peninsula in ancient times.

With the dawn of the twentieth century a new era in Arabian research began as an increasing number of Europeans entered the country. Between 1908 and 1914 the Czech scholar Alois Musil carried out a series of important explorations in the northern Ḥijāz and Najd which added greatly to our knowledge of those regions. He also brought together all the references to North Arabian places and tribes which are to be found in Assyrian, Hebrew, Greek, and Latin sources.[3] Musil's work marked an important step forward but many areas of obscurity still remained. The most notable contribution to our knowledge of ancient North Arabia was made by two French Dominican scholars, A. J. Jaussen and

1/See R. H. Kiernan, *The Unveiling of Arabia* (London, 1937), D. G. Hogarth, *The Penetration of Arabia* (New York, 1904), and *Handbuch der altarabischen Altertumskunde*, ed. D. Nielsen (Copenhagen and Leipzig, 1927).

2/See especially W. G. Palgrave, *Narrative of a Year's Journey through Central and Eastern Arabia, 1862–63* (London, 1865), C. Guarmani, *Northern Najd* (Eng. trans. by A. D. Carruthers, London, 1938), and C. M. Doughty, *Travels in Arabia Deserta*, I and II (Cambridge, 1888).

3/See his *The Northern Ḥeǧâz* (New York, 1926), *Arabia Deserta* (New York, 1927), and *Northern Neǧd* (New York, 1928).

R. Savignac. In the course of three expeditions in 1907, 1909, and 1910 they carried out an exhaustive examination of all the monuments and inscriptions surviving above ground at, or in the neighbourhood of, the oases of Tabūk, Madā'in Ṣāliḥ, and al-ʻUlā. They also paid a hasty visit to Taymā'. Their work was done with such accuracy and such meticulous attention to detail that their report, *Mission archéologique en Arabie*, I (Paris, 1909), II (Paris, 1914), remains the foundation-stone on which all future research into North Arabia's past must rest. Mention should also be made of Bernhard Moritz's visit to al-Qurayyah in 1906 and to the Ḥijāz in 1914,[4] to Douglas Carruther's journey to Taymā' in 1909,[5] and to Henry Field's explorations, described in his *North Arabian Desert Archaeological Survey, 1925–50*.[6]

With the rise of King ʻAbd al-ʻAzīz (better known as Ibn Saʻūd) to a predominant position in Saʻudi Arabia in 1924, the barrier which had hitherto existed between Arabia and the Western world, and which had hampered scholarly research, began to disappear. H. St. J. B. Philby was able to travel about extensively, and he described in detail many parts of the peninsula which had previously been unknown to scholars, or largely unknown.[7] American oilmen and engineers also entered the country to aid in developing its resources. More important for historical research was the invitation extended in 1951 by the king to two of the foremost authorities on pre-Islamic Arabia, Professor Gonzague Ryckmans and his nephew, Professor Jacques Ryckmans, of the University of Louvain. Accompanied by Philby and Captain Philippe Lippens, they explored the area between Jiddah and Najrān and then northward to Riyadh (ar-Riyāḍ). A popular account of the expedition has been published by Lippens,[8] but most of the inscriptions recorded (reported to number over 10,000) have not yet appeared.[9]

Our own expedition was an outgrowth of a long-cherished interest in Arabia and its history, and a growing awareness of the important role which the peninsula

4/B. Moritz, "Ausflüge in der Arabia Petraea" (*Mélanges de la Faculté orientale de Beyrouth*, 3 [1908], pp. 403–12) and *Arabien* (Hanover, 1923).

5/*Arabian Adventure* (London, 1935).

6/Papers of the Peabody Museum of Archaeology and Ethnology, Harvard University, vol. 45, no. 2 (Cambridge, Mass., 1960). Most of the places visited by Field lie in that part of the North Arabian desert which extends beyond the border of modern Saʻudi Arabia. See also Field's *Bibliography on South-western Asia* (3 vols.; Coral Gables, Fla., 1953–6) and *Bibliography: 1926–1966* (Ann Arbor, Mich., 1966).

7/See especially *The Heart of Arabia* (2 vols.; London, 1922), *Arabia of the Wahhabis* (London, 1928), *Sheba's Daughters* (London, 1939), *Arabian Highlands* (Ithaca, 1952), and *The Land of Midian* (London, 1957).

8/*Expédition en Arabie centrale* (Paris, 1956).

9/The Islamic Arabic texts have been published by A. Grohmann; see *Expédition Philby-Ryckmans-Lippens en Arabie, 1951–52*, IIe partie, Textes épigraphiques, tome 1, *Arabic Inscriptions* (Louvain, 1962).

had played in the economic, political, and religious life of the ancient Near East. It was with the hope of obtaining a clearer understanding of that role that we laid plans for a North Arabian expedition and applied to the Saʿudi Arabian government for permission to enter the country. Our application was approved, and in the spring of 1962 we were granted visas valid for one month from the date of entry. The time allowed was not as long as we had hoped for, but we decided to make the most of our opportunity, and less than a month after receiving the visas we were on our way out of ʿAmmān.

We had three objectives in mind: first, to visit as many of the North Arabian oases as possible and discover what ancient monuments still exist above ground; secondly, to collect samples of ancient North Arabian pottery which might indicate the cultural relationships of the oases with the outside world; and thirdly, to search for ancient inscriptions. We had no intention of doing any excavating. With the limited amount of time at our disposal this would have been quite impossible in any case. But there was an even stronger reason for refraining: in our application to the Saʿudi government we had stated that it was not our intention to engage in excavation or to remove any antiquities from the country; we wished simply to conduct an archaeological and epigraphical survey. We did hope, however, that the information obtained might pave the way for the opening up of archaeological work in Saʿudi Arabia at some future date. Up to the present no such activity has been permitted by the government except for some clearances undertaken by R. LeBaron Bowen and F. S. Vidal of the Arabian American Oil Company (Aramco) at Jāwān near Qaṭīf on the Persian Gulf.[10]

The carrying out of the expedition was made possible only by the co-operation of several institutions and a great many persons. We are under a special debt of gratitude to Mr. Thomas C. Barger, then President of Aramco, and to Mr. William R. Chandler, President of the Trans-Arabian Pipe Line Company (Tapline), for the support which they gave to the project from the very beginning.[11] They endeavoured to assure its success by associating with us an experienced desert traveller and competent Arabist in the person of Dr. F. S. Vidal, a member of Aramco's

10/See R. LeBaron Bowen Jr., *The Early Arabian Necropolis of ʿAin Jawan* (*BASOR*, Supplementary Studies, nos. 7–9; New Haven, 1950), and F. S. Vidal, "A Pre-Islamic Burial in the Eastern Province" (published in the Mecca monthly magazine *Al-Manhal*, Shaʿban 1375/April 1956, pp. 546–53 [in Arabic]). Dr. Vidal dated the tomb to *ca.* 50 A.D. He informs us that a carbon-14 test carried out several years later at the University of Pennsylvania gave a date between 60 B.C. and 124 A.D.

11/Mr. Barger's interest in Arabia's past is of long standing. Winnett recalls with pleasure that it was Mr. Barger who entrusted him with the publication of a Himyarite inscription discovered in 1945 (cf. *BASOR*, no. 102 [1946], pp. 4–6).

Arabian Affairs Division at Dhahran. Without Dr. Vidal's assistance the expedition would have accomplished far less than it did; it might even have come to grief.[12] Mr. Barger also loaned us one of Aramco's best Sa'udi guides, Sārī ibn Mukhaylīl. Sārī had travelled extensively in the northwestern part of the peninsula and came originally from the Wādī as-Sirḥān, one of the regions we hoped to visit.

We are also deeply indebted to the late W. A. Campbell, a former Vice-President of Tapline, for the encouragement and assistance which he gave, also to Messrs. John Sabini and David Dodge of the same company. They generously placed at our disposal three Dodge Power-Wagons, two of them brand new, the other almost so. They also provided us with two Sa'udi driver mechanics, Muḥammad ibn Sulṭān and Muḥammad ibn Fahad.

Others who rendered valuable assistance were Mr. Hanna Franjieh, Tapline representative in 'Ammān, who helped us in our negotiations with the Sa'udi Embassy there, and Messrs. Dale E. Garrison and Harry F. Hopper, Government Relations Representatives of Tapline at Turaif and Badanah respectively. Nor should be neglect to mention the assistance of Mr. G. A. Linabury and Mr. J. H. Arnold.

Winnett expresses his thanks to the Canada Council and to the University of Toronto for financial assistance which made it possible for him to participate in the expedition. He is also deeply indebted to Mrs. Hughdene Ponick for her unfailing patience in typing and retyping various drafts of the manuscript, and to Miss Lorraine Ourom of the University of Toronto Press for her careful editing of it. Reed acknowledges his indebtedness to the College of the Bible (now the Lexington Theological Seminary), Lexington, Kentucky, for granting him sabbatical leave and to the American Association of Theological Schools for granting him a fellowship for study abroad. We are both indebted to Professor A. H. Detweiler, of Cornell University, at that time President of the American Schools of Oriental Research, for the encouragement and official backing which he gave to our enterprise. We are also grateful to Abbé Jean Starcky and J. T. Milik for undertaking the decipherment of the Nabataean inscriptions found by the expedition. Their scholarly contribution has greatly enhanced the value of the present volume.

Finally we wish to thank the Sa'udi Arabian government for its friendly co-operation, and to record our grateful appreciation of the cordial reception everywhere accorded us in Arabia. From *badawī* to *amīr*, one and all extended to us that hospitality for which the Arab people are so justly renowned. It is our

12/We are indebted to Dr. Vidal for a number of excellent photographs, especially the colour photographs, and also for reading the manuscript and making numerous suggestions for its improvement.

hope that the new light which our expedition has been able to throw on the ancient history of their land will be some return at least for all the kindness they showed us.[13]

This work has been published with the help of grants from the Humanities Research Council of Canada, using funds provided by the Canada Council, and from the Publications Fund of the University of Toronto Press. The cost of publishing the plates was generously borne by Aramco.

February 1969

W.L.R.
F.V.W.

13/A preliminary report on the expedition appeared in *BASOR*, no. 168 (1962), pp. 9–10.

Contents

LIST OF COLOUR PLATES

Abbreviations

AAA	*Annals of Archaeology and Anthropology* (Liverpool)
AASOR	*Annual of the American Schools of Oriental Research*
AfO	*Archiv für Orientforschung*
AJA	*American Journal of Archaeology*
AJSL	*American Journal of Semitic Languages*
Ak.	*Akkadian*
Albright, *Dedan*	W. F. Albright in *Geschichte und Altes Testament* (Albrecht Alt Festchrift, Tübingen, 1953), pp. 1–12
Albright, *Massa'*	W. F. Albright, "The Biblical Tribe of Massa' and Some Congeners," in *Studi Orientalistici in onore di Georgio Levi Della Vida*, I (Rome, 1956), pp. 1–14
ANET	*Ancient Near Eastern Texts Relating to the Old Testament*, ed. J. B. Pritchard (2nd ed.; Princeton, 1955)
Ar.	Arabic
Aram.	Aramaic
ASOR	American Schools of Oriental Research
Beeston, *Desc. Gram.*	A. F. L. Beeston, *A Descriptive Grammar of Epigraphic South Arabian* (London, 1962)
BA	*Biblical Archaeologist*
BASOR	*Bulletin of the American Schools of Oriental Research*
BOr	*Bibliotheca Orientalis*
BSG	*Bulletin de la Société de géographie* (Paris)
BSOAS	*Bulletin of the School of Oriental and African Studies*
Caskel, *LL*	Werner Caskel, *Lihyan und Lihyanisch* (Arbeitsgemeinschaft für Forschung des Landes Nordrhein-Westfalen, Heft 4. Abh.; Cologne and Opladen, 1953)
CIS	*Corpus inscriptionum semiticarum*
Cl. Ar.	Classical Arabic
CRAIBL	*Comptes-rendus de l'Académie des inscriptions et belles-lettres*
D	Dedanite
DM	R. Dussaud and F. Macler

Dougherty, *Nab. and Bel.*	R. P. Dougherty, *Nabonidus and Belshazzar* (New Haven, 1929)
Dougherty, *Sealand*	R. P. Dougherty, *The Sealand of Ancient Arabia* (New Haven, 1932)
Doughty, *Doc. épig.*	Charles M. Doughty, *Documents épigraphiques recueillis dans le Nord de l'Arabie* (Paris, 1884)
Doughty, *Travels*	Charles M. Doughty, *Travels in Arabia Deserta* (3rd ed.; London and New York, vol. 1, 1921, vol. 2, 1923)
Dussaud, *Penetration*	René Dussaud, *La Pénétration des Arabes en Syrie avant l'Islam* (Paris, 1955)
EDAr.	D. H. Müller, *Epigraphische Denkmäler aus Arabien* (Vienna, 1889)
EL	Early Lihyanite
Enc. of Islam	*Encyclopaedia of Islam*
ERE	*Encyclopaedia of Religion and Ethics*, ed. James Hastings (New York, 1908–26)
Eut.	Julius Euting
Euting, *Tagbuch*	Julius Euting, *Tagbuch einer Reise in Inner-Arabien*, I (Leiden, 1896), II (Leiden, 1914)
Gl.	Eduard Glaser
GJ	*Geographical Journal*
Gr.	Greek
Grimme, *Neubearbeitung*	H. Grimme, "Neubearbeitung der wichtigeren Dedanischen und Liḥjanischen Inschriften" (*Le Muséon*, 50 [1937], pp. 269–320)
Grohmann, *Arabien*	A. Grohmann, *Arabien* (Munich, 1963; Handbuch der Altertums Wissenschaft, 3. Abt., 1. T., 3. Bd., 3. Abschnitt, 4. Unterabschnitt)
H	Hijazi type of Thamudic
Hadr.	Hadrami
Hal.	Joseph Halévy
Harding, *NST*	G. L. Harding "New Safaitic Texts" (*Annual of the Department of Antiquities of Jordan*, I [1951], pp. 25–9)
Haussig, *WM*	H. W. Haussig, *Wörterbuch der Mythologie*, I (Stuttgart, 1962)
Hava	J. G. Hava, *Arabic-English Dictionary* (Beirut, 1921)
Heb.	Hebrew
Höfner, *Altsüd. Gr.*	Maria Höfner, *Altsüdarabische Grammatik* (Leipzig, 1943)
HTIJ	G. L. Harding, *Some Thamudic Inscriptions from the Hashimite Kingdom of the Jordan* (Leiden, 1953)
Hu.	Charles Huber
Huber, *Journal*	Charles Huber, *Journal d'un voyage en Arabie, 1883–84* (Paris, 1891)
HUCA	*Hebrew Union College Annual*
IB	*The Interpreter's Bible* (New York and Nashville, 1952–5)
Ibn Dor.	*Ibn Doreid's genealogisch-etymologisches Handbuch*, ed. F. Wüstenfeld (Göttingen, 1854)
IDB	*The Interpreter's Dictionary of the Bible*

IEJ	*Israel Exploration Journal*
ILN	*Illustrated London News*
Jamme, *Doc. sud-arabe*	A. Jamme, "Documentation sud-arabe I et II" (*Rivista degli Studi Orientali*, 38 [1963])
Jamme, *Notes*	A. Jamme, *Notes on the Published Inscribed Objects Excavated at Ḥeid bin ʿAqîl in 1950–51* (Washington, D.C., 1965)
Jamme, *Pièces épig.*	A. Jamme, *Pièces épigraphiques de Ḥeid bin ʿAqîl* (Louvain, 1952)
Jamme, *TS*	A. Jamme, *Thamudic Studies* (Washington, D.C., 1967)
JAOS	*Journal of the American Oriental Society*
JBL	*Journal of Biblical Literature*
JEA	*Journal of Egyptian Archaeology*
JNES	*Journal of Near Eastern Studies*
JRAS	*Journal of the Royal Asiatic Society*
JRCAS	*Journal of the Royal Central Asian Society*
JRGS	*Journal of the Royal Geographical Society*
JS, *Mission*	A. Jaussen and R. Savignac, *Mission archéologique en Arabie*, I (Paris, 1909), II (Paris, 1914)
JSOR	*Journal of the Society of Oriental Research*
L	E. Littmann
Lane	E. W. Lane, *Arabic-English Lexicon* (London, 1863–93)
Lih.	Lihyanite
Littmann, *Saf. Insc.*	E. Littmann, *Safaitic Inscriptions* (Leiden, 1943)
Littmann, *SI*	E. Littmann, *Semitic Inscriptions* (Princeton, 1905)
Littmann, *TS*	E. Littmann, *Thamūd und Ṣafā* (Leipzig, 1940)
Littmann, Voc.	Vocabulary of E. Littmann, *Safaitic Inscriptions* (Leiden, 1943)
LL	Late Lihyanite
Luckenbill, *AR*	D. D. Luckenbill, *Ancient Records of Assyria and Babylonia* (Chicago, 1926–7)
Min.	Minaean
MS	Milik-Starcky
Musil, *Ar. Des.*	Alois Musil, *Arabia Deserta* (New York, 1927)
Musil, *N. Ḥeǧâz*	Alois Musil, *The Northern Ḥeǧâz* (New York, 1926)
Musil, *N. Neǧd*	Alois Musil, *Northern Neǧd* (New York, 1928)
MVAG	*Mitteilungen der Vorderasiatischen Gesellschaft*
N	Najdi type of Thamudic
Nab.	Nabataean
OLZ	*Orientalistische Literaturzeitung*

Palgrave, *Narrative*	William G. Palgrave, *Narrative of a Year's Journey through Central and Eastern Arabia, 1862–63* (London, 1865)
Palm.	Palmyrene
PEQ	*Palestine Exploration Quarterly*
Ph.	H. St. J. B. Philby
Philby, *Midian*	H. St. J. B. Philby, *The Land of Midian* (London, 1957)
Pirenne, *Paléographie*	Jacqueline Pirenne, *Paléographie des inscriptions sud-arabes*, tome 1: *Des origines jusqu'à l'époque himyarite* (Brussels, 1956)
Qat.	Qatabanian
QDAP	*Quarterly of the Department of Antiquities in Palestine*
R	W. L. Reed
RB	*Revue biblique*
RÉS	*Répertoire d'épigraphie sémitique* (Académie des inscriptions et belles-lettres, Paris, 1914–)
RNP	G. Ryckmans, *Les Noms propres sud-sémitiques* (Louvain, 1934–5)
Ry.	G. Ryckmans
Ryckmans, *L'Institution*	Jacques Ryckmans, *L'Institution monarchique en Arabie méridionale avant l'Islam* (*Ma ʿîn et Saba*) (Louvain, 1951)
Ryckmans, *Notes épig.*	G. Ryckmans, "Notes épigraphiques" (*Le Muséon*, 50 [1937], pp. 323–37)
Ryckmans, *Religions*	G. Ryckmans, *Les Religions arabes préislamiques* (2nd ed.; Louvain, 1951)
Sab.	Sabaean
Saf.	Safaitic
Salmoné	H. A. Salmoné, *Arabic-English Dictionary* (London, 1890)
SAr	South Arabic
Sav.	Savignac
SBWA	*Sitzungsberichte der Akademie der Wissenschaften in Wien*, phil.-hist. Klasse
SE	Südarabische Expedition
Sourdel, *Cultes*	D. Sourdel, *Les Cultes du Hauran à l'époque romaine* (Paris, 1952)
Starcky, *Palm.*, *Nab. et Arabes*	J. Starcky, "Palmyréniens, Nabatéens et Arabes du Nord avant l'Islam," in M. Brillant and R. Aigrain, *Histoire des Religions*, IV (Paris, 1956), pp. 201–37
Syr.	Syriac
T	Tabuki type of Thamudic
Tham.	Thamudic
vdB, *HT*	A. van den Branden, *Histoire de Thamoud* (Beirut, 1960)
vdB, *ID*	A. van den Branden, *Les Inscriptions dédanites* (Beirut, 1962)
vdB, *IT*	A. van den Branden, *Les Inscriptions thamoudéennes* (Louvain, 1950)
vdB, *TTHE*	A. van den Branden, "Les Textes thamoudéens de Huber et d'Euting" (*Le Muséon*, 69 [1956], pp. 109–37)
vdB, *TTP*	A. van den Branden, *Les Textes thamoudéens de Philby*, I and II (Bibliothèque du *Muséon*, vols. 39 and 41; Louvain, 1956)

Wehr	Hans Wehr, *A Dictionary of Modern Written Arabic*, ed. J. Milton Cowan (Ithaca, 1961)
WH	F. V. Winnett and G. L. Harding, Collection of unpublished Safaitic texts
Winnett, *Notes*	F. V. Winnett, "Notes on the Lihyanite and Thamudic Inscriptions" (*Le Muséon*, 51 [1938], pp. 299–310)
Winnett, *Study*	F. V. Winnett, *A Study of the Lihyanite and Thamudic Inscriptions* (Toronto, 1937)
WR	Winnett-Reed
Wright, *Ar. Gram.*	W. Wright, *A Grammar of the Arabic Language*, 3rd ed., I and II (Cambridge, 1933)
WSIJ	F. V. Winnett, *Safaitic Inscriptions from Jordan* (Toronto, 1957)
Yāqūt	Yāqūt, *Muʿjam al-Buldān* (Beirut ed., 1376/1957)
←	Direction of writing

I Journal

W.L.REED and F.V.WINNETT

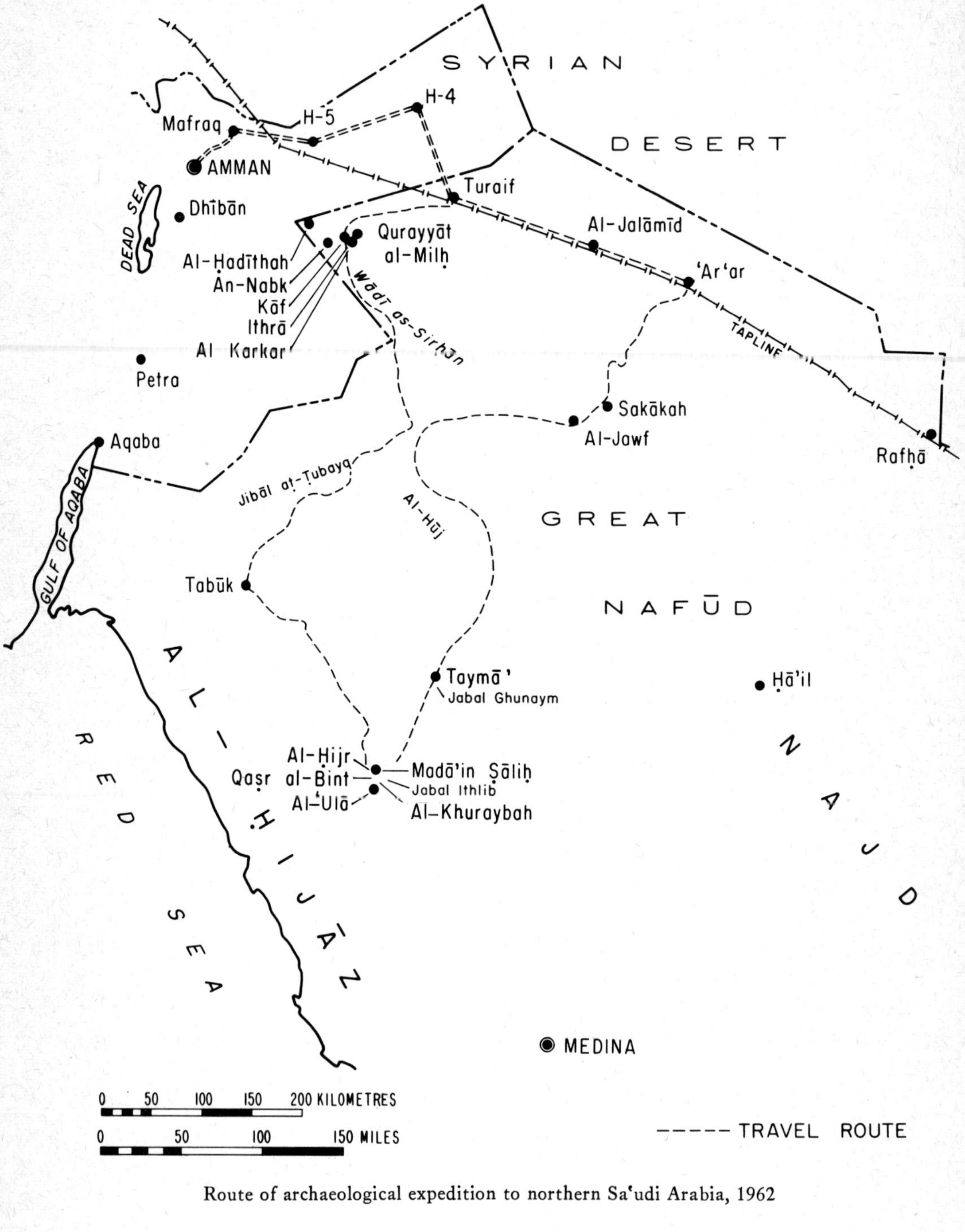

Route of archaeological expedition to northern Sa'udi Arabia, 1962

Every student of Arabian history who visits the Near East feels the lure of the great Arabian desert, that vast expanse of territory which so few Westerners have seen and about which so much remains to be learned. When Winnett was serving as Director of the American School of Oriental Research in Jerusalem, Jordan, in 1950–1 and in 1958–9 he made several journeys into the Jordanian desert under the tutelage of Mr. G. Lankester Harding. The discovery of over four thousand pre-Islamic Arabic graffiti made him eager to venture farther afield in the hope of finding other ancient Arabian records. Hence in 1958–9 he made some preliminary inquiries regarding the possibility of undertaking an expedition into the Arabian peninsula itself. Reed, who succeeded him as Director of the Jerusalem School, took up the idea and pushed the matter further. He also sailed down the Red Sea and visited the ports of Jiddah and Aden. Finally, as a result of his efforts, the Saʿudi Arabian Government, in the spring of 1962, kindly issued us entrance visas valid for one month from the date of entry.

We met in ʿAmmān and spent several days securing supplies and discussing our plans with the Saʿudi Arabian Embassy. Then on the morning of April 27, 1962, we set out in Reed's Volkswagen Camperbus for Turaif, one of the pumping-stations on the Trans-Arabian Pipeline (Tapline) in Saʿudi Arabia. Our route lay along the Baghdad highway as far as H-4,[1] where we turned south and headed across the open desert. The entire journey of 231 miles took thirteen hours.

The town of Turaif is set down in the midst of the naked desert, a fact which was impressed on us as all day long the wind whipped sand and dust into our faces. Before the establishment of the pumping-station in 1950, there was nothing there. Now there is a small town of modern, air-conditioned bungalows, a community centre with cinema, restaurant, and recreational facilities, a school, a swimming-pool, and company store. South of the residential area is the industrial section containing the pumping-station, oil tanks, garages, repair shops, and company offices. An Arab town has grown up outside the compound.

1/See map.

At Turaif we were joined by Dr. F. S. Vidal, who had been assigned by the Arabian American Oil Company (Aramco) to accompany the expedition. Dr. Vidal is an anthropologist by training, a graduate of Harvard, speaks Arabic fluently, and has had first-hand experience of Arabian archaeology at Jāwān. These qualifications, plus considerable experience of desert driving, were to make him an invaluable member of our party (Fig. 1).

We were fortunate in having at our disposal the new series of excellent maps of Saʿudi Arabia published jointly by the Saʿudi Arabian Ministry of Petroleum and Mineral Resources and the United States Geological Survey. These consist of both geological and topographical sheets, scale 1:500,000, based largely on aerial surveys. The only map which had not yet been published was that for the Wādī as-Sirḥān area, but Vidal brought the work sheet for this map along in the hope that he would be able to check it and correct it, if necessary, by observation on the ground.

Our original plan had been to follow the pipeline road from Turaif to Rafḥā and then strike south along the Darb Zubaydah, the pilgrim road from Iraq, and follow it to Ḥā'il, then turn west to Taymā' and from there cut across to the Darb al-Ḥajj, the pilgrim road coming down from Syria. We believed, rightly or wrongly, that these two pilgrim roads were ancient caravan routes, and that by following them we might find many inscriptions left by the passing caravaneers. However, since our visas were good for only one month, and since it was necessary to allow for possible breakdowns and accidents, we decided to curtail our proposed itinerary considerably. Instead of proceeding eastward as far as Rafḥā, we decided to go only as far as Badanah, near ʿArʿar, and strike south from there to al-Jawf and Taymā'. From Taymā' we would proceed in a southwesterly direction to Madā'in Ṣāliḥ and al-ʿUlā, then turn back north to Tabūk, and from there head for the Wādī as-Sirḥān. This would allow more time to search for inscriptions and to examine any ancient ruins encountered.

Tapline had generously placed at our disposal three Dodge Power-Wagons and the services of two of their best driver-mechanics, Muḥammad ibn Sulṭān and Muḥammad ibn Fahad. The Power-Wagons were equipped with four-wheel drive and oversize tires for desert travel. One carried a generator and radio transmitter so that we might keep Tapline informed of our whereabouts. Each of the others carried two 50-gallon drums of petrol, two similar drums of water, and two spare tires, as well as camping equipment and food supplies. No attempt was made to take sufficient provisions for the whole journey since we counted on being able to secure fresh bread, meat, and some tinned goods in the oases through which we passed, and also fresh supplies of petrol.

On the afternoon of the 29th Mr. Dale E. Garrison of Tapline took us to see an ancient site called Dawqirah about twenty miles southwest of Turaif. The ruins are located on a tongue of land which projects into a large silt-flat (*khabrah*) about three by five kilometres in area, which is said to become a shallow lake after heavy rains. A reservoir lined with dressed basalt has been set within the *khabrah* in order to preserve at least some of the water from seeping away rapidly. Directly east of the reservoir are the ruins of three types of structures: (i) circles of uncut stones, (ii) a circular area piled up with stones, looking like a large grave, and (iii) a large building of which only the basalt foundation, about four feet wide, remains, the mud-brick walls having long since crumbled and been blown away. Along the east side of the remains of the courtyard a row of eight rooms can be discerned.

Henry Field[2] believed that the building was a Roman fort but Florence Day is inclined on the basis of architectural plan and pottery to date it to the Umayyad period.[3] It could have been either a military post or a caravansarai. We picked up some ribbed sherds which seemed to be either Byzantine or Early Arab, although they had been so polished by the sand and rain that it was difficult to identify them. This condition of sherds found on the surface of the desert poses a special problem for Arabian archaeologists.

The expedition left Turaif on the morning of April 30 (see Fig. 2) and headed for Badanah, another Tapline pumping-station 160 miles to the southeast. The first half of the journey lay across flat, gravel-strewn desert of a type which the Arabs call *ḥamād*. Then the terrain changed, becoming dissected by an intricate network of drainage courses. This region is called al-Widyān. No sign of life was observed, apart from a few men working on the pipeline road, until we entered the *wādī* leading to Badanah. Then black Bedouin encampments and herds of grazing camels began to appear. The largest encampment had seventeen tents, and the herds numbered from fifteen to about a hundred animals.

The town of Badanah is another man-made oasis in the heart of the desert and is in many ways a replica of Turaif. Mr. Harry F. Hopper, who was in charge of government relations, took us to meet Amīr ʿAbdallāh ibn ʿAbd al-ʿAzīz ibn Musāʿad, Governor of the Northern Frontiers. The Amīr resides in the Arab town of ʿArʿar, which has sprung up in recent years about a mile from Badanah. He received us cordially, stated that the central government had informed him of our impending visit, and wished us success.

Following our audience with the Amīr, we went on a tour of ʿArʿar. We were surprised at its wide streets, at the presence of traffic policemen on duty, and at the evidence of town planning. The principal street has a boulevard down the

2/*JRCAS*, 1951, pp. 188–9.

3/See Henry Field, *North Arabian Desert Archaeological Survey*, 1925–50, appendix F (Papers of the Peabody Museum of Archaeology and Ethnology, Harvard University, vol. 45, no. 2; Cambridge, Mass., 1960). Florence Day (*op. cit.*, p. 159) would identify it with Muqaddasi's station *at-Turaif*. For a ground-plan of the main structure, see Field, p. 126.

FIGURE 1 (From left to right) F. S. Vidal, Muḥammad ibn Fahad, Sārī ibn Mukhaylīl, Muḥammad ibn Sulṭān

FIGURE 2 The expedition preparing to leave Turaif

middle, planted out with young trees. The population of ʿArʿar is estimated at about ten thousand. Outside the town at the time of our visit was a camp of twenty-seven bus-loads of Iraqi pilgrims who were on their way to Mecca, for this was the season of the *ḥajj*. These were the first of many pilgrims we were to encounter in the course of our journey.

The following day, May 1, we started the second lap of our journey, making for the oasis of Sakākah, 110 miles to the south. The road leads through a broad *wādī* known as Wādī ʿArʿar but which farther on is called Wādī Muʿtadil. Many cairns could be discerned atop the ridges bordering the *wādī* but we did not stop to examine them. Shortly after entering Wādī Muʿtadil a violent dust-storm descended upon us and we were engulfed in what the Scripture calls the "howling wilderness" (Deut. 32:10).

The only settlement encountered on the way to Sakākah was the tiny village of ash-Shuwayḥiṭīyah. After enjoying the hospitality of the local Amīr, Nāṣir by name, we pushed on till near dark and camped in a basin in the hills a mile or so off the road.

Before setting out in the morning, Vidal tried to establish radio contact with Turaif and inform Tapline of our whereabouts, but the transmitter broke down. It remained useless for the rest of the journey, but fortunately it was found possible at the larger oases, through the kindness of the Amīrs, to send messages over the excellent wireless network of the Saʿudi Arabian government so that Tapline's Turaif office was always kept informed of our whereabouts.

The country through which we were now passing contained a number of rocky outcrops and we began to keep a sharp look-out for inscriptions. Finally, at a large outcropping called al-Qalʿah ("the fortress," Fig. 3), about four miles from Sakākah, we made our first find, eleven Thamudic graffiti[4] and about the same number of Nabataean,[5] as well as a petroglyph showing seven ostriches (Fig. 4), creatures which have become extinct in Arabia only in recent years. Hand-copies as well as photographs were made of most of the inscriptions encountered, since a rock surface is seldom smooth and a photograph rarely shows every detail. Furthermore, an inscription may be partly or entirely in the shade and the resulting photograph anything but clear.

We arrived in Sakākah around ten in the morning. The oasis, with its green palms, was a delight to the eye after the dreary waste we had been through (Fig. 5). Amīr ʿAbd ar-Raḥmān as-Sudayrī received us cordially and gave us permission to move about freely and to take all the pictures we wished, a privilege which H. St. J. B. Philby had not enjoyed on his visit in 1923 and which explains why he did not see the remarkable petroglyph mentioned below.

The most impressive structure in Sakākah is an old fort, Qaṣr Zaʿbal, crowning

4/See below, Thamudic inscriptions nos. 1–11, pp. 74–7.
5/See below, Nabataean inscriptions nos. 1–14, pp. 142–4.

a high sandstone hill on the northern edge of the oasis (Fig. 6). Constructed of stone and mud-brick, it is now in a somewhat dilapidated condition, although one of the round corner towers is quite well preserved. The fort is said to be about 120 years old, but it may stand on the site of a much earlier structure since we know from the Muslim geographer Yāqūt[6] that Sakākah was in existence in the thirteenth century A.D. In view of the fertility of the oasis one would have expected it to have had an even earlier history. It is now larger than al-Jawf and politically more important, the Amīr of Sakākah being over the Amīr of al-Jawf. George A. Wallin,[7] the first European explorer to visit these parts (1845), noted the importance of Sakākah in his day but he does not seem to have set foot in it, nor does William G. Palgrave (1863),[8] nor Carlo Guarmani (1864),[9] though both refer to it. The first Westerners to see it seem to have been Charles Huber[10] and Julius Euting[11] in 1883. It was later visited by Alois Musil[12] in 1909 and Philby[13] in 1923.

From the *qaṣr* one gets an excellent view of the oasis and the surrounding desert. As one gazes over the countryside he cannot fail to be impressed by the seeming precariousness of existence in these Arabian oases, ever encompassed, as they are, by the forces of drought and death.

West of the *qaṣr* is another, small sandstone hill called Burnus. Its upper western half has been cut or worn away leaving a broad platform in front of a rock face. On this rock face was a drawing depicting thirteen or fourteen female (?) figures about twelve inches high, with arms upraised and wearing what appear to be tasselled head-dresses (Fig. 7). The head-dresses are represented by a horizontal line from which several short lines, usually nine in number, project downward. A few animals, of uncertain identity, are also depictod We dubbed the drawing "the Dancing Girls," but it may depict a prayer scene.[14] In view of the Muslim attitude to the representation of the human figure, there can be little doubt that the drawing dates from the pre-Islamic period. One can only be grateful that there has been enough local regard for this antiquity to save it from destruction at the hands of some iconoclast. Any possible potency for evil which it may possess has been effectively neutralized by the inscription at the lower left: "There is no god but God."

6/Yāqūt, III, (Beirut ed.), p. 229, says that Sukākah (as he calls it) is one of the villages of Dūmat al-Jandal but that Dūmah is better fortified and its people sturdier.

7/See *JRGS*, 24 (1855), pp. 151–2.

8/*Narrative*, I, p. 61.

9/*Northern Najd* (Eng. transl. by A. D. Carruthers; London, 1938), pp. 58, 89, 103.

10/*Journal*, pp. 43f., and Atlas, folio 4.

11/*Tagbuch*, I, p. 124.

12/*Ar. Des.*, pp. 274–80.

13/"Jawf and the North Arabian Desert" (*GJ*, 62 [1923], pp. 241–59).

14/For other representations of dancers, see van den Branden, *TTP*, II, pp. xxv–xxviii, and *HT*, pp. 80–4.

FIGURE 3 Al-Qalʿah

FIGURE 4 Inscribed rock at al-Qalʿah, depicting ostriches (Vidal photograph)

FIGURE 5 View of Sakākah from the *qaṣr* (fort)

FIGURE 6 The *qaṣr* of Sakākah. The arrow marks the location of the petroglyph shown in Fig. 7

FIGURE 7 Ancient petroglyph at Sakākah

Not far from this drawing was a peculiar inscription, half-Arabic, half-Nabataean in appearance, deeply engraved in the red sandstone rock (Fig. 8). Its interpretation is uncertain.

In the low ground about five hundred yards south of the *qaṣr* is a large step-well which has been excavated in the sandstone rock (Fig. 9). The Amīr referred to it as an "ancient pool." It is very similar to the famous "pool" at al-Jīb (ancient Gibeon) in Palestine in that it too has a staircase cut into the side, starting on the north side and circling clockwise towards the bottom. There is a rectangular cutting in the wall, under the stairs, and a much larger cutting below this again, but the purpose of these was not apparent. Because of the eroded condition of the steps and the absence of any protecting balustrade such as the well at al-Jīb has, we did not attempt to descend. The open cut is about twenty-five feet across and over fifty feet deep. We were told that about eighty years ago the inhabitants of Sakākah endeavoured to clean out the well and put it back into commision but very little water was found and the attempt was abandoned.

On the ridge to the west of the well a number of Thamudic inscriptions (nos. 12–23) and one Nabataean (no. 15) were found. Some of these had already been

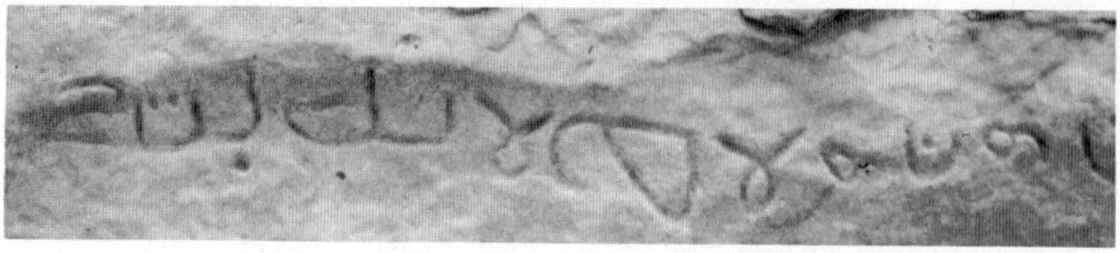

FIGURE 8 Inscription in curious script at Sakākah

photographed by Mr. Hopper of Badanah. They may be the work of passing nomads and hence cannot be used as evidence to prove that Sakākah was occupied by a settled population in pre-Islamic times.[15]

Amīr ʿAbd ar-Raḥmān informed us that there were ancient monuments to the south of Sakākah, so the following day we drove out to investigate. On the way we passed two oases, aṭ-Ṭuwayr and Qārah, visited by Huber[16] in 1883, by Musil[17] in 1909, and by Philby[18] in 1923. Several miles beyond Qārah, at a spot called by Muḥammad Sulṭān al-Madarah ("the town"), near the edge of the dunes of the great Nafūd, we found the monuments of which the Amīr had spoken. They turned out to be pillars,[19] six to ten feet in height, set up in the sand (Fig. 10). The pillars are arranged in clusters, usually with four to a cluster, although not all were standing (Fig. 11). The clusters appear to be set in a platform of irregularly shaped stones (Fig. 12), a feature which recalled some of the dolmens in Jordan. The surfaces of the pillars are scored with tribal marks but only one group of signs may be a Thamudic inscription.[20] The horizontal position of the inscription on the sloping pillar shows that it was inscribed after the pillar had tilted over. The clusters of pillars form a great irregular circle of approximately five hundred square yards, giving the impression of a large open-air sanctuary or, possibly, a burial-ground.[21] No settlement now exists in the immediate vicinity, but a mile and a half to the north is a hill where our guide said some pottery and gold coins were found about four years ago. When we returned to Sakākah and reported our impressions of the site to the Amīr, he conveyed the further information that

15/For the sherds found at Sakākah, see p. 74 and Fig. 83:3, 5, 8.

16/*Journal*, pp. 44, 47, and *BSG*, 7e série, tome 5 (1884), p. 325; also Euting, *Tagbuch*, I, p. 130.

17/*Ar. Des.*, see Index, pp. 607 and 628. For a photograph of Qārah, see p. 304.

18/*GJ*, 62 (1923), pp. 241–59.

19/Some are undoubtedly sandstone (there is a Sakākah sandstone formation) and were probably brought in from the Sakākah area; others seem to be limestone, and could have been quarried *in situ* from the underlying calcareous duricrust (F. S. Vidal).

20/See below, Thamudic inscription no. 24, p. 81.

21/Palgrave (*Narrative*, p. 251) reported the presence of a sort of Stonehenge at al-ʿUyūn in the province of Qasīm but Philby (*The Heart of Arabia*, vol. 2 [London, 1922], pp. 140–1) claims this to be a figment of Palgrave's imagination. According to Dr. Vidal, the people of the area have no recollection of any such monument. In any case, the monument described by Palgrave was different in character from that seen by us.

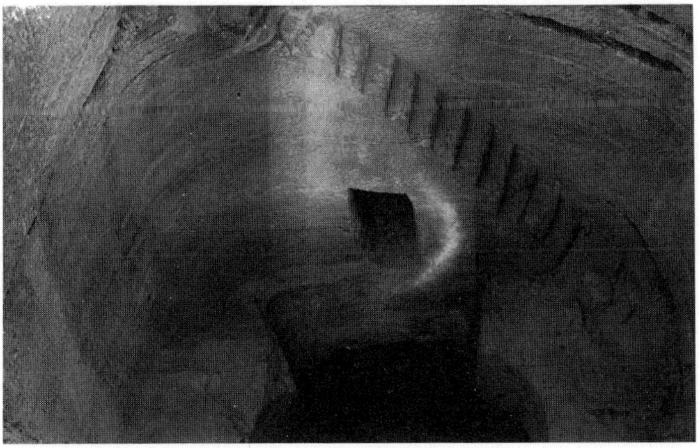

FIGURE 9 Step-well at Sakākah

at a place called Ghumayrah, a considerable distance east of Sakākah, there are plastered pools with stone-lined paths leading to them.

After restocking with petrol, we left Sakākah about three in the afternoon and headed for al-Jawf. Three miles from the oasis is a large outcropping of rock, the flat sloping surfaces of which bear twenty-four Thamudic inscriptions (nos. 25–48) and several drawings, the most notable of which is the figure of a lion (Fig. 13). Although lions are no longer to be found in the Arabian peninsula, the presence of numerous words for "lion" in Arabic and also the frequent representation of them in petroglyphs prove that they were once not uncommon there.[22] More Thamudic inscriptions (nos. 49–56) were found at a point not far beyond the preceding.

Shortly afterwards we came upon the trunk of a petrified tree, about eighteen inches in diameter and six feet long, broken into three parts (Fig. 14). It remains as a mute witness to an earlier pluvial period when this part of Arabia enjoyed a much heavier rainfall than it does today. We camped some distance off the road but during the night could hear the pilgrim buses rumbling by on the long journey to Mecca.

In the morning (May 4) we came to a tiny oasis called Muwaysin.[23] We had

22/The scepticism expressed by H. Kindermann in his article "Al-Asad" in the *Enc. of Islam*, new ed., regarding the existence of lions in ancient Arabia seems, therefore, to be unjustified. For other drawings of lions, see vdB, *TTP*, I, pp. 7–8 (quoting Philby); Littmann, *SI*, p. 107 and *TS*, pp. 116–17; *WSIJ*, no. 14. For reports of lions in lower Iraq as recently as forty years ago, see Wilfred Thesiger, *The Marsh Arabs* (London, 1964), p. 158.

23/See Huber, *Journal*, p. 48, and *BSG*, 7e série, tome 5 (1884), p. 325. Musil (*Ar. Des.*, p. 195; see also p. 304) speaks of al-Mwejsen as deserted, but it appeared to us to be inhabited now. Euting (*Tagbuch*, I, p. 124) calls it Mu'eizin.

FIGURE 10 Stone pillars in the desert south of Qārah

FIGURE 11 W. L. Reed standing beside the pillars

FIGURE 12 Showing platform in which the pillars are set

now reached the edge of the great basin known as al-Jūbah. A haze hung over the plain, but through it the palms of an extensive oasis could be discerned. This was the famous al-Jawf, the gateway to North Arabia (Fig. 16).[24] The oasis lies at the southern end of the great drainage basin known as Wādī as-Sirḥān. Since the drainage has no outlet, salt tends to accumulate and rise to the surface. This explained why the foreground appeared as a white, salt-encrusted plain. Al-Jawf used to be called Dūmat al-Jandal (lit. "Dūmah of the stones") and appears in the Old Testament simply as Dumah. In Genesis 25:14 (= I Chron. 1:30) Dumah is reckoned as one of the sons of Ishmael, the reputed forefather of the northern Arabs.[25]

In view of the important role which al-Jawf has played in Arabia's history, we hoped that important antiquities might be found there, and it was with feelings of some excitement that we gazed upon it. As we drove down into the basin, we recalled that through al-Jawf had passed practically all the European explorers of North Arabia. Wallin had stayed there for several weeks in 1845. Palgrave[26] had spent eighteen days there, Huber[27] and Euting[28] were there in 1883, Musil[29] in 1905, Captain W. H. Shakespear in 1914, Philby in 1923.[30] Some of the American oilmen have also been there but have left no record of their passing.[31] As we drew nearer we perceived that some of the palm groves looked neglected or even deserted (Fig. 15). The decline of the salt trade, the growth in importance of Sakākah, and the wars in the nineteenth and early twentieth century between the Rashīds of Ḥā'il and the Ruwālah are largely responsible for the present condition of the oasis. A number of the inhabitants have also been attracted northward to the new towns which have sprung up along the oil pipelines. Al-Jawf is a composite oasis, comprising several oases which have more or less coalesced. According to Palgrave the oasis was unwalled, but Philby claims to have found sections of an ancient stone wall. We observed no traces of such, although we made no special attempt to investigate the matter. We went directly to call on Amīr Muḥammad Nughaymish, and were pleased to find that our host of the previous day, the Amīr of Sakākah, was also present.

24/For the history of al-Jawf, see Musil, *Ar. Des.*, appendix VII; "Dūmat al-Djandal" (*Enc. of Islam*, new ed.); G. A. Wallin in *JRGS*, 24 (1855), pp. 139–58; and the references given by J. Starcky in *RB*, 64 (1957), p. 196, n. 1, and by R. Dussaud, *Pénétration*, p. 175.

25/The oracle in Isa. 21:11–12 which begins with the words "Watchman, what of the night?" may refer to Dumah, although the text is not above suspicion (see R. B. Y. Scott, in *IB*, V, p. 288).

26/*Narrative*, pp. 46–89.

27/*Journal*, pp. 48ff., and *BSG*, 7e série, tome 5 (1884), pp. 317–26.

28/*Tagbuch*, I, pp. 123–40.

29/*Ar. Des.*, pp. 160–1, and *N. Negd*, p. 1.

30/*GJ*, 62 (1923), pp. 241–59.

31/Shortly before our arrival, Mr. Dale Garrison of Tapline, in company with some members of Aramco's Domestic Marketing Department, had completed a six-day journey from Turaif to Jidda via al-Jawf, Taymā', and Medina.

FIGURE 13 Rock drawings near Sakākah

FIGURE 14 F. S. Vidal sitting on the trunk of a petrified tree

1 Qaṣr Mārid

FIGURE 15 Al-Jawf

The most striking antiquity which al-Jawf has to offer is the great fortress called Qaṣr Mārid (Fig. 17 and colour plate 1). It is undoubtedly one of the most impressive structures to be seen in the whole of North Arabia.[32] The plan of the original structure has been obscured by later additions, but it appears to have been rectangular with four round corner towers. Atop the present wall are several conical towers whose lower parts are of stone and the upper parts of mud-brick. Towers of the same type are to be seen built into the walls surrounding the palm groves at Sakākah. An outer stone wall encloses the fortress. Both the outer wall and the towers suffered considerable damage when in 1853 Talāl ibn Rashīd of Ḥā'īl bombarded the fortress with two old cannons. Philby believed the structure to be mediaeval in date, but Guarmani[33] and Palgrave[34] were probably right in regarding at least the lower courses as ancient. We observed four inscriptions high up on the outer wall at the northwest corner of the fortress, two of which were certainly Islamic, but it was impossible to get near enough to photograph them. Whatever be the date of Qaṣr Mārid, its imposing size is a witness to the strategic importance of al-Jawf.[35] The area immediately north of the fortress is unoccupied and could be excavated.

32/L. Veccia Vaglieri ("Dūmat al-Djandal," *Enc. of Islam*, new ed.) mentions an ancient proverb in which Mārid is coupled with al-Ablaq, the great fortress of Taymā'. For sketches of Qaṣr Mārid, see Euting, *Tagbuch*, I, pp. 125–6. Shakespear's photograph is reproduced in Guarmani, *Northern Najd*, facing p. 102; two photographs by Philby are given in *GJ*, 62 (1923), facing p. 252.

33/*Northern Najd*, p. 102.

34/*Narrative* pp, 76–7.

35/For the sherds found at al-Jawf, see below, p. 174.

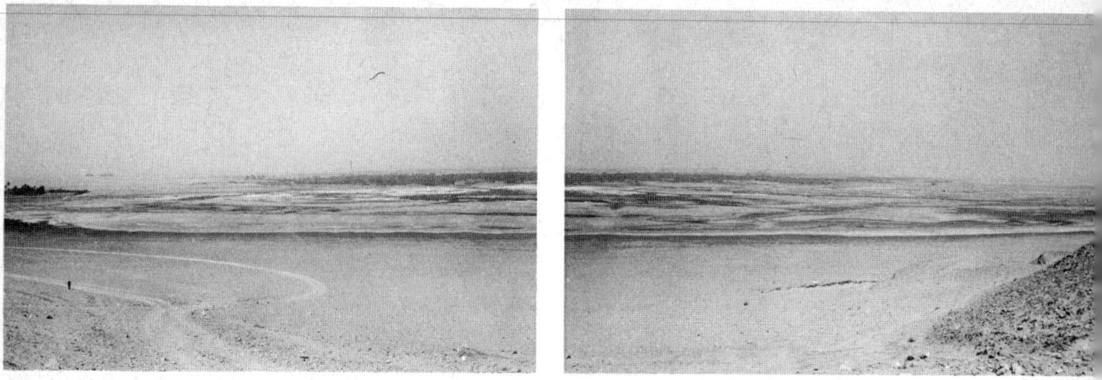

FIGURE 16 The oasis of al-Jawf

FIGURE 17 Qaṣr Mārid, the great fortress of al-Jawf

FIGURE 18 A spring at al-Jawf

Close to an ancient mosque said to have been built by the Caliph Omar (634–44 A.D.) is a stone minaret (see colour plate 2). It stands about fifty feet high, and has four windows, placed one above the other. The narrow street runs through thc base of the tower.

In response to our enquiries regarding the presence of any ancient inscriptions, we were shown a stone, bearing three lines of Nabataean writing, embedded in a street wall directly north of Qaṣr Mārid.[36] Other inscriptions were reported on a nearby ridge called Abū al-Jays. A search of the area turned up a few badly weathered Nabataean graffiti, five of which are given below (nos. 17–21). But there was one inscription which aroused our special interest – in spite of its badly weathered condition – for it was manifestly Minaean.[37] This is the first epigraphic evidence that has been found of the presence of South Arabian Minaeans at al-Jawf, although Arabian tradition remembered the presence there of an image of Wadd (the Minaean Moon-god).[38]

From our camp about two miles outside the oasis, we could see hundreds of camels going to and fro from the abundant springs of al-Jawf. They were said to be brought in from pasture for watering every five days. We ourselves took advantage of the bounteous springs to replenish our water supply (Fig. 18) and also purchased a fresh supply of petrol. With each of the Power-Wagons travelling through desert terrain consuming fuel at the rate of a gallon every five miles, we had to restock at every opportunity.

Between al-Jawf and Taymā', our next objective, there lies the most terrible desert in North Arabia, the Nafūd, a vast expanse of sand-dunes nearly two hundred miles from north to south and stretching a third of the way across the peninsula. It has been called Arabia's "Chinese Wall," for throughout the centuries it has served to protect her from invasion from the north. It can be crossed by camel, although the journey, particularly in the summer months, is hazardous and exhausting. To ordinary motor traffic it presents an insuperable obstacle and such traffic must take a roundabout route, skirting the northern and then the western edge of the dunes.

As one approaches from the north across a barren landscape strewn with flint and limestone chips, the dunes of the Nafūd loom up suddenly, rising to a height of twenty-five or thirty feet (Fig. 19). There is no zone of transition from one kind of desert to the other. We stopped to climb the dunes and gaze inward but there was nothing to be seen except a vast ocean of billows of sand as far as the eye could reach, its surface rippled into beautiful patterns by the action of the wind (Fig. 20). Farther south the sands of the Nafūd are said to be reddish in colour,

36/See below, Nabataean inscription no. 16, p. 144.
37/See below, Minaean inscription no. 1, p. 74.
38/See A. Grohmann, *Arabien* (Munich, 1963), p. 87, and Wallin in *JRGS*, 24 (1855), p. 157.

but here they were whitish, turning to soft yellow in the rays of the setting sun. We were surprised to see many *ghaḍa* bushes growing in the pure sand, particularly along the outer slopes of the dunes. The Nafūd is actually an important source of fuel, for the Bedouin gather the dead bushes and sell them in the towns and villages. *Ghaḍa* wood gives off a great deal of heat and burns for a surprisingly long time, as we ourselves found.[39]

About thirty-five miles west of al-Jawf we came to a fork in the road which was marked by a road sign. One track led north to the Wādī as-Sirḥān, the other, towards the left, in the direction of Taymā'. Six pilgrim buses were stopped beside the road, uncertain of which track to follow. All were in a hurry, trying to reach Mecca in time for the pilgrimage ceremonies. We were told that the pilgrims from Baghdad had been on the road for six days and that it would take them four more days to reach Mecca, *inshallāh*! We camped on the western edge of the Nafūd after a drive of about 150 miles. The night was cold and blustery with drifting sand, and two blankets on top of our sleeping-bags gave none too much protection.

The road from al-Jawf to Taymā' proved difficult. Long stretches of deep sand present a very real hazard and it would be impossible for an ordinary touring-car to negotiate them. Despite the sand this was the route being taken by the buses carrying pilgrims to Mecca. All the buses appeared to be crowded. Bags of drinking-water were suspended from the windows, and two long poles were lashed to the roof, to be used for prying the bus out of the sand should it become stuck. The buses are equipped with powerful motors and we observed only two stuck in the sand and abandoned. They were being guarded by local Bedouin until spare parts could be brought. The passengers had evidently found accommodation in more fortunate vehicles. One gains a new respect for Muslims when he sees the discomforts they endure in order to carry out the obligation of pilgrimage. Even in May the desert was becoming a furnace. What must it be like when the pilgrimage falls in mid-summer! Although Muslim pilgrims were once noted for their hostility to non-Muslims, the groups we passed waved to us in friendly fashion and we waved in return. We observed many camel skeletons, bleached and white, along the way and a few little mounds of sand with a cane stuck upright at one end where some poor *ḥājj* had succumbed to the rigours of the journey. In this desolate waste our attention was caught by a number of round white objects, resembling tennis-balls, lying on the ground (Fig. 21). They were the fruit of the colocynth plant (Ar. *ḥanẓal*).[40]

39/According to Musil (*Ar. Des.*, p. 110) "no other fuel furnishes so much heat as the *ghaza* and its coals will smoulder for over ten hours."

40/Called *shary* in eastern Arabia. It is a curbit (*Citrullus colocynthis* Schrad.) of the same genus as the watermelon. Poisonous if taken in quantity, it is extremely bitter, and the main source of the purgative colocynth, now no longer favoured because of its potency, but still exported from North Africa, and still carried in the pharmacopoeia (F. S. Vidal).

FIGURE 19 The edge of the great Nafūd desert

FIGURE 20 A look into the Nafūd

FIGURE 21 Colocynth growing in the desert between al-Jawf and Taymā'

We reached Taymā' on the afternoon of May 6 after a journey of 286 miles from al-Jawf. We drove directly to the site of the ancient city, which is about a mile south of the modern oasis, and there established our camp. The two Muḥammads were dispatched immediately into town to inform the Amīr, 'Abdallāh ash-Shunayfī, of our arrival and to give Muḥammad ibn Fahad a chance to see his father, who was a merchant there.

It was impossible to arrive at Taymā' without thinking of the lonely figure of Charles Doughty braving the hostile city nearly ninety years ago.[41] Twenty-nine years earlier (1848) the Finnish scholar Wallin had arrived, the first European that we know of to see this Arabian town. Wallin had approached it from the Red Sea via Tabūk. In 1864 Guarmani arrived, coming down from the north, probably across the Nafūd. Neither of these explorers left a description of the oasis. It was Doughty who first gave the Western world some idea of both the modern town and the ancient ruins. Doughty was followed in 1880 by Huber.[42] Four years later Huber paid a second visit to Taymā', this time accompanied by Euting.[43] A. Douglas Carruthers[44] and the French Dominican Fathers Jaussen and Savignac[45] made hasty visits to it in 1909. The latter two met with a hostile reception and were unable to stay long enough to examine the town. Philby does not seem to have visited it until 1951. He subsequently gave a lengthy description of it in his *Land of Midian*, pp. 72–103.[46] Probably some of the American oilmen have been there too, but they have published no account of their visits. None of the travellers mentioned appears to have approached it by the route we followed, a route which seems to date only from the introduction of modern motor traffic.

Our camp lay at the base of a high knoll on the summit of which were the ruins of a stone tower (Fig. 23). According to Doughty and Philby this tower is associated in local tradition with an ancient worthy named Badr ibn Jawhar about whom unfortunately nothing is known. On the sides of the knoll we picked up numerous sherds.[47] They showed little resemblance to the types found in Palestine and Syria, indicating that this was a distinct cultural area.

From the top of the knoll we had a good view of the oasis, a great cluster of green palms in a completely arid landscape (Fig. 22). Between us and the oasis

41/For Doughty's first visit, in the spring of 1877, see his *Travels*, I, pp. 284–300; for his second visit, in the autumn, see pp. 517–65.

42/"Voyage dans l'Arabie Centrale Hamâd, Šammar, Qaçîm, Hadjaz" (*BSG*, 7ᵉ série, tome 5 [1884], pp. 511–14).

43/*Tagbuch*, II, pp. 146–63, 198–207.

44/*Arabian Adventure* (London, 1935), pp. 84–114.

45/*Mission*, II, pp. 109–65. Musil was near Taymā' but does not seem to have entered it. See the map in his *N. Neǧd*, frontispiece.

46/The antiquities collected by Philby at Taymā' and other places are now with the Department of Antiquities at ar-Riyāḍ.

47/See pp. 175–6 and Figs. 84:2–4, 7–8 and 85.

lay the site of the ancient city, an uneven surface covered with sand, with some slabs of stone lying about. It was hard to believe that here once stood one of the most famous cities of North Arabia. It is impossible to tell without excavation how far back in time the history of Taymā' extends, but the presence of an abundant supply of water is guarantee that its origins are remote.[48]

North from our camp a sloping rampart extended for about half a mile. The camp itself was set in the corner of a depression formed by four similar ramparts (Figs. 24, 25), the one to the west appearing to be the main north-south wall of the ancient city. This "wall" appears as a great ridge of sand forty to fifty feet high. It consists of more than sand, however, for on top of the ridge a stone wall, two metres wide, lies exposed (Fig. 26). Because so much sand has drifted against the lower parts of the wall, it is impossible to tell without excavation how far down it extends. Doughty[49] estimated the wall of ancient Taymā' to have been three miles in circumference. Jaussen and Savignac[50] would reduce this to three kilometres or less. The difference in their estimates is doubtless due to the fact that it is difficult to tell whether some of the ridges are mere sand-dunes or walls covered with sand. We ourselves measured with the car what appeared to be the south wall of the city and found it alone to be three miles in length. We have since seen an aerial photograph of the site which suggests that the walls were much more extensive than previously thought. John Dayton, managing director of the British firm which is rebuilding the Ḥijāz Railway, visited Taymā' either shortly before or shortly after our visit and later photographed it from the air.[51] He speaks of the walls as running on for miles. Only archaeological investigation will enable the size of the ancient city to be determined with certainty. Philby[52] was of the opinion that the walls were designed to protect Taymā' from flash floods rather than from human enemies, but a section of stone wall at the south-east corner of the site is clearly defensive in character (Fig. 27).

Amīr 'Abdallāh ash-Shunayfī (Fig. 30), who was governor of Taymā' at the time of Philby's visit also, received us cordially and granted us permission to examine the antiquities of the area and to photograph and copy any ancient inscriptions. After the customary coffee-tea-coffee, a servant came in carrying what appeared to be a miniature incense altar on which sandalwood (*al-'ūd*) was burning (Fig. 31). He held it in front of the Amīr, who opened the folds of his garment and with this hand wafted the scented smoke into them. Then each of us was given the same treatment. This is an Arabian custom which we had not

48/See JS, *Mission*, II, pp. 143ff.
49/*Travels*, I, p. 287.
50/*Mission*, II, p. 151.
51/"Teyma, Arabian Seat of the Last King of Babylon" (*ILN*, Aug. 19, 1967, pp. 26–7).
52/*Midian*, p. 83. For floods at Taymā', see Dougherty, *Sealand*, p. 162, n. 507.

FIGURE 22 Looking north to Taymā' from the knoll above our camp

FIGURE 23 The knoll above our camp at Taymā', with remains of ancient tower

FIGURE 24 Ridge of sand possibly marking the line of a wall, ancient Taymā'

FIGURE 25 A gateway of ancient Taymā'

FIGURE 26 Wall running along top of ridge of sand, ancient Taymā'

FIGURE 27 A section of the wall of ancient Taymā'

FIGURE 28 Al-Haddāj, the famous well of Taymā'

FIGURE 29 An armful of *utrunj*, Taymā'

2 Tower beside mosque attributed to the Caliph Omar (634–44 A.D.), al-Jawf

FIGURE 30 The Amīr of Taymā', ʿAbdallāh ash-Shunayfī (fourth from the right), W. L. Reed, and F. S. Vidal (on the right) with members of the Amīr's household

previously encountered, and is intended as a mark of special honour to the guest. We were very appreciative of this courtesy extended to us by the Amīr.[53]

We departed to see the famous well al-Haddāj[54] (Fig. 28), which furnishes the life-blood of modern Taymā', as it doubtless did of ancient Taymā'. A great many pilgrims were gathered about the well, washing and refreshing themselves after the hot and rigorous ordeal they had been through. The well itself is a great, open pit about fifty feet in diameter and forty feet deep, the sides of which are cased with stone slabs. Until ten years ago the water was raised by numerous draw-wheels operated by camels, but now seven diesel-powered pumps have been installed, three of which were working at the time of our visit. The water is pumped to the palm groves which extend out from the well on all sides. Shortly after Doughty left Taymā' in 1877, a portion of the stone curbing of the well collapsed, leading to the discovery that one of the stones bore an ancient inscription. Although Doughty heard of the discovery, he does not seem to have seen the inscription when he returned to the city later the same year.[55] When Huber arrived three years later he saw an inscription embedded in the wall of a house

53/The custom is generally found only in the wealthier or more prominent households, but also in the poorer households on festive occasions (F. S. Vidal). See Euting, *Tagbuch*, I, p. 62; H. R. P. Dickson, *The Arab of the Desert* (London, 1949), pp. 197–200; and Ph. Lippens, *Expédition en Arabie Centrale* (Paris, 1956), p. 17.

54/Grohmann (*Arabien*, p. 42) gives the name with initial Ḥ but Doughty and Euting use *H*. See Dayton's photo of the well in *ILN*, Aug. 19, 1967, p. 27, Pl. 4.

55/See *Travels*, I, p. 532.

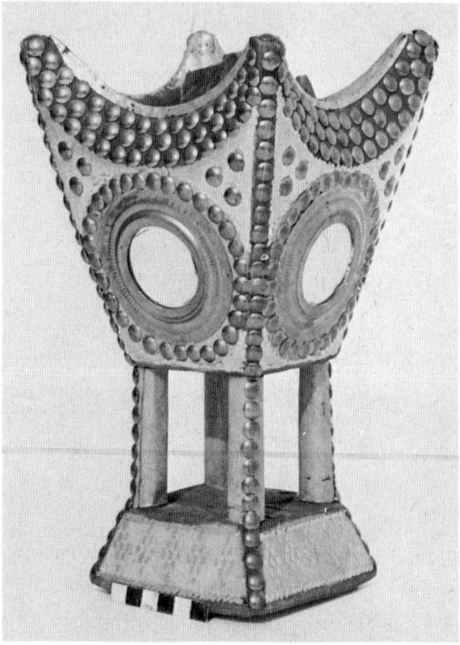

FIGURE 31 A censer (*mibkharah*)

in the western suburb called al-Gharb ("the West"). This was the Aramaic inscription which has become known as the Taymā' Stone.[56] Philby is probably right in believing that it is not the inscription that was found among the collapsed curbing of the Haddāj well.[57] The present whereabouts of the well-inscription is unknown.

Near the western edge of the oasis are the ruins of an ancient fort called Qaṣr Zallūm[58] (Figs. 32, 33). This is believed, rightly or wrongly, to be the famous Qaṣr al-Ablaq associated in tradition with a Jew named Samaw'al.[59] On its walls we found the inscription "in that strange Tayma character" which Doughty reproduces in his *Travels*.[60] It is now even less legible than it was in his day.

Amīr ʿAbdallāh had invited us for lunch, so after inspecting the Haddāj well, we returned to his residence. The sumptuous meal was held out under the palms, a delightful setting. The Amīr informed us that the present population of Taymā' is about three thousand. In 1951 he told Philby that the settled population of

56/Grohmann (*Arabien*, p. 43) suggests that the Taymā' Stone came from a temple of Ṣalm on the summit of Jabal Ghunaym, but this seems unlikely; see n. 69 below.

57/*Midian*, p. 82.

58/The correct form of the name is probably *Ẓalūm*, meaning "tyrant, oppressor."

59/For him, see JS, *Mission*, II, pp. 146–7, and the article "Al-Samaw'al" in the *Enc. of Islam*, 1st ed.

60/I, p. 296.

the oasis was about one thousand. Either his present estimate includes the Bedouin in the vicinity or else the population has greatly increased in the last few years. It is probable that the completion of the asphalt highway, which is being constructed from Medina northward and which at the time of our visit had reached within three miles of Taymā', will bring added prosperity and a still greater increase in population.

After lunch we were taken to see one of the palm groves nearby and obtained some idea of the marvellous fertility and luxuriance of this Arabian Garden of Eden. Under the lofty date-palms smaller trees and vines were growing. We were particularly impressed by a large yellow citrus fruit called *utrunj*, an armful of which was presented to us by the owner of the grove (Fig. 29). Although they contained little juice, our ever-thirsty palates found them most refreshing.

At a spot called by Huber Ghār al-Ḥamām, about two miles northeast of Taymā', we recorded a number of Thamudic graffiti (nos. 57–71) and some drawings of wild goats (*Capra nubiana* Cuvier) and horned cattle (Fig. 35). It is perhaps worth remarking that the cows are not of the humped variety so common in the East.

Since we had expressed a desire to see the ancient inscriptions found by Philby in 1951 on Jabal Ghunaym, the Amīr sent the man who had acted as Philby's guide to conduct us there. From Taymā' Jabal Ghunaym appears as a dark headland eight or ten miles to the southeast.[61] On the way there we drove over some fearfully rough ground to examine the intervening ridges but found no inscriptions.

The thousand-foot climb up the mountain was made without great difficulty since there was a well-defined pathway leading to the summit. The oasis of Taymā' was plainly visible to the north (Fig. 34), while down below the line of the new asphalt highway could be seen. Musil[62] speaks of an ancient burial-ground in front of Ghunaym but this we failed to see.

The rocks on the summit were covered with inscriptions. We already knew from studying Philby's copies, published by van den Branden,[63] that these inscriptions were among the earliest, if not the earliest, yet found in North Arabia. In view of their importance we endeavoured to obtain as good a photographic record as possible and also made hand-copies of many, although this latter operation was rendered difficult by a strong wind. Many of the inscriptions mention a god Ṣalm who, as we know from the Taymā' Stone, was worshipped at Taymā' in the sixth century B.C. This is one of several reasons for believing that the Jabal Ghunaym inscriptions date from that period. Six of the inscriptions refer to a war against Dedan and one to a war against Massā', who is reckoned in Genesis 25:14 among the sons of Ishmael. More interesting still, there are three

61/Grohmann (*Arabien*, p. 65) incorrectly places Jabal Ghunaym northeast of Taymā'.
62/*Ar. Des.*, pp. 105–6.
63/*TTP*, II, pp. 19–27.

FIGURE 32 Qaṣr Zallūm, ancient Taymā' (Vidal photograph)

FIGURE 33 Qaṣr Zallūm (Vidal photograph)

references to the NBYT who are almost certainly to be identified with the Arabian people called *Nebaioth* in the Old Testament and *Nabaiati* in Assyrian inscriptions. According to the tradition preserved in Genesis 25:13 (= I Chron. 1:29), a tradition which must surely be of Arabian origin, Nebaioth was the first-born of Ishmael. In other words, the Nebaioth were regarded as the most ancient of the North Arabian peoples. It was gratifying that on our first expedition into Sa'udi Arabia we should make contact, if only indirectly, with the earliest known inhabitants of the northern part of the peninsula. This was the first time that a reference to the Nebaioth has been found on Arabian soil.[64]

Having completed the recording of the inscriptions, we turned over a slab of rock lying on the summit in case it might have an inscription on its under side and were startled to discover that it bore a drawing of a strange-looking female figure seated on a chair or throne (Fig. 38). No facial features are depicted; instead the blank facial area is divided by lines into four lobes. One might be tempted to think that it is the back of the head that is depicted were it not for the fact that the body is shown as seen from the front, the breasts being clearly visible. This suggests that the face is represented as veiled.

According to S. A. Cook[65] "the veil is the symbol of Ishtar," but there seems to be no evidence to support this assertion.[66] However, we know from the Taymā' Stone that the goddess Asherah was worshipped at Taymā' in the sixth century B.C., and it is possible that the goddess depicted in the drawing is to be identified with her.[67] One wonders for how many centuries she has been lying on her face on the summit of Jabal Ghunaym. Nothing similar has yet been found elsewhere in Arabia, and in view of the fierce hostility of Islam to the ancient paganism it is unlikely that many such figures have survived.[68]

As we started to descend the mountain our attention was caught by some drawings of heads engraved on the east side of the summit. Two of the heads are oval in form and seem to be of comparatively recent origin for the lines of the engraving are light in colour, but there are at least three heads which appear to be ancient (Figs. 36, 37). These are triangular in outline. From the corners of the triangles two horns curve upward and inward. Between the horns of the head at the lower left is a six- (or seven-)rayed star with a crescent moon above. The central head, with close-set eyes, bears only a star. The head on the right is bearded, and the nose-line projects upward to meet a rectangle enclosing a star.

There can be no doubt that these three bucrania are representations of ancient

64/For the inscriptions referring to Nebaioth, see below, pp. 99–101.

65/*The Religion of Ancient Palestine in the Light of Archaeology* (Oxford, 1930), p. 128.

66/The veiled Ishtar supposedly found at Tell Halaf lacks verification. See R. de Vaux, "Sur le voile des femmes dans l'orient ancien" (*RB*, 44 [1935], pp. 397–412).

67/For the cult of Asherah in the Near East, see W. L. Reed, *The Asherah in the Old Testament* (Fort Worth, Texas, 1949).

68/For a further discussion of the drawing, see pp. 167–71.

FIGURE 34 Looking north towards Taymā' from the summit of Jabal Ghunaym
Power-Wagons at lower left

FIGURE 35 Petroglyphs at Ghār al-Ḥamām, northeast of Taymā'

FIGURE 36 Ancient Arabian gods, Jabal Ghunaym

FIGURE 37 Head of ancient Arabian deity, Jabal Ghunaym

FIGURE 38 An ancient Arabian goddess, Jabal Ghunaym

Arabian gods. Philby, who was the first Westerner to see them, believed that they all represent Ṣalm.[69] Since many of the inscriptions found on the summit invoke Ṣalm, it is probable that the bearded head at least represents him. The beardless heads might represent goddesses, but A. F. L. Beeston has drawn our attention to an engraved gem which shows a three-faced head surmounted by bull's horns. The central face is beardless, those at the sides bearded, the three faces representing the moon's phases. Engraved around the heads is the legend *T̲WRM* ("Bull"), a well-known name of the Moon-god.[70]

Philby locates the drawings on the northern flank of the mountain, whereas our notes locate them on the east side. The broad platform which he mentions as being in front of the drawings and which he thinks was the site of a sacrificial altar is actually a rather narrow ledge. However, he was undoubtedly correct in the belief that the summit of Jabal Ghunaym was an ancient Arabian high-place. The presence of these representations of a god (or gods), the slab bearing the figure of a goddess, numerous inscriptions invoking the god Ṣalm, and the traces of a well-defined pathway leading to the top of the mountain suggest that there was an open-air sanctuary on this summit.[71] No doubt the worship of the gods was normally carried on in the sanctuaries within Taymā' itself, but on certain festival occasions there may have been pilgrimages to this sacred spot. It is perhaps worth recording that no Islamic Arabic inscriptions were observed on the mountain.[72]

Our guide reported that there were many inscriptions on the summit of Jabal as-Samrā', the flat-topped mountain directly north of Ghunaym, but we were able to find only one Taymanite graffito (no. 45).

Up to this time we had entertained some hope of going on south as far as Jabal Mukattab near Medina where Philby had heard there were many inscriptions, although he himself had never been able to visit the place.[73] We decided, however, that insufficient time remained for us to venture so far south and that it would be wiser to devote such time as we still had to an examination of the important sites of Madā'in Ṣāliḥ, al-'Ulā, and the Wādī as-Sirḥān. We therefore prepared

69/*Midian*, p. 88.

70/See *JRAS*, 1952, pp. 22–3 and Pl. 3. Van den Branden divides the Arabian bucrania into four types: (i) those bearing the half-circle, the symbol of the lunar divinity; (ii) those bearing the star with rays, the symbol of the solar divinity; (iii) those bearing both of these symbols, "ce qui pourrait indiquer soit le caractère général de la divinité astrale représentée, soit celui du dieu-fils"; (iv) those bearing no astral symbol. He thinks the bucranium came to be used in North Arabia as a symbol for any god (*HT*, pp. 66–8, and *TTP*, II, pp. xxiv–xxv).

71/Grohmann (*Arabien*, pp. 43, 65) attributes to Philby the belief that there was a temple on Jabal Ghunaym, but Philby (*Midian*, p. 88) speaks only of a "high place" and clearly has an open-air sanctuary in mind.

72/Philby (*Midian*, p. 88) also noticed their absence.

73/*Midian*, p. 11.

FIGURE 39 Curious rock formation between Taymā' and Madā'in Ṣāliḥ (Vidal photograph)

FIGURE 40 The plain of Madā'in Ṣāliḥ (Jabal al-Ḥuwārah in the background)

FIGURE 41 Nabataean tombs in the side of Qaṣr al-Bint

FIGURE 42 The derelict Hijaz Railway, between Madā'in Ṣāliḥ and al-'Ulā (Vidal photograph)

to head for Madā'in Ṣāliḥ. Since our guide, Sārī, was unfamiliar with the road thither, the Amīr arranged for us to hire the services of a local guide. Before leaving we presented the Amīr with a bag of sherds which we had collected and also the sandstone slab engraved with the figure of the goddess. He kindly returned them to us in order that we might take them along for further study.

A short distance south of the oasis Reed observed three graves which had been opened by road-construction machinery. They were cut in the shale rock and were covered with flat stones. Any bones or pottery which they may have contained had been removed. These graves are not oriented toward the east or toward Mecca but toward Jabal Ghunaym, so are presumably ancient.

Picking up the asphalt highway south of Taymā', we revelled in its comfort for forty-seven miles, then turned off on to a desert track which leads in a generally southwesterly direction to Madā'in Ṣāliḥ. This track lay south of that taken by Jaussen and Savignac. For most of the way the country was flat, with only a few *ṭalḥah* trees (*Acacia seyal* Del.) to relieve the monotony; then came a region of red sandstone peaks resembling those of Petra. We halted for the night in a beautiful canyon at the foot of a three-hundred-foot cliff.

About twenty miles from Madā'in Ṣāliḥ is a great, sandstone rock, towering about one hundred and twenty-five feet above the plain (Fig. 39). Around its base, as well as on other rocks in the vicinity, we found a number of petroglyphs, one Thamudic inscription (no. 72), and several Nabataean (nos. 22–38), some of them so badly weathered as to be illegible.

Coming to the edge of a wide expanse of lower ground we saw in the distance the trees and vegetation which mark the site of Madā'in Ṣāliḥ. We were approaching what had once been one of the great caravan centres of North Arabia. Here the Nabataeans, who had their chief centre at Petra in southern Transjordan, took over and controlled the caravans coming up from South Arabia on their way to Egypt and Syria with loads of frankincense and myrrh and the exotic products of East Africa and India. The Nabataeans called their southern outpost Ḥegrā; later Arabs called it al-Ḥijr or Madā'in Ṣāliḥ.[74] On our right was a great loaf-shaped rock known as Qaṣr al-Bint in whose sides are hewn the facades of many Nabataean tombs similar to those at Petra (Fig. 41).[75] To the south, on the far side of the plain, was the great rock mass of Jabal al-Ḥuwārah (Fig. 40); to the west were the cliffs of Ḥarrat al-'Uwayriḍ.[76] Proceeding on, we came to a small cultivated area and then crossed the derelict Ḥijāz Railway (Fig. 42).[77] The station buildings of Madā'in Ṣāliḥ are still standing, though in a sad state

74/See Musil, *N. Ḥeǵâz*, appendix x: al-Ḥegr, pp. 299–301, and Grohmann, *Arabien*, pp. 44–5.

75/See Doughty, *Doc. épig.*, Pl. xxxiii; *Travels*, i, p. 109.

76/See Doughty, *Doc. épig.*, Pl. xxxii.

77/The railway suffered severely at the hands of Lawrence and the Arabs during the first world war. It was last used in 1921, to transport the Hashimite family to 'Ammān.

of disrepair; a few railway cars stand forlornly on the tracks, and a locomotive is still in the shop. In places the wind has blown the sand from beneath the tracks so that they hang suspended in the air.[78] The Amīr of Madā'in Ṣāliḥ resides on the second floor of the former station; we called on him to pay our respects, and then continued southward for fifteen miles to the oasis of al-'Ulā to see Amīr Aḥmad as-Sudayrī who is over the whole area, including Madā'in Ṣāliḥ. The Amīr was absent in Beirut and we were received by his young brother Musā'ad. In the late afternoon he took us to see the Amīr's garden, which was a delightful spot with date-palms, orange and lemon trees, and patches of melons, sweet peppers, onions, and alfalfa. The alfalfa grows so luxuriantly that it is cut every two weeks. An engine-driven pump keeps the plantation liberally supplied with water. There are many springs at al-'Ulā, an assurance that the oasis was inhabited in very early times.

We camped for the night in a bay in the sandstone cliffs about a mile east of al-'Ulā. Some difficulty which had arisen over the taking of photographs was cleared up by an overnight wire to Medina, and we were thenceforth allowed to move about freely and take whatever pictures we wished. We were also provided with an armed escort. The guide whom we had brought with us from Taymā' was now paid off and sent home via Medina.

The first European to visit al-'Ulā and its environs was Charles Doughty, in 1876–7. He was followed in 1880 by Huber, who paid a second visit to the site, this time accompanied by Euting, in 1884. Then in 1907, 1909, and 1910 Jaussen and Savignac carried out a very careful examination of the area and demonstrated that the field of ruins called el-Ḫereibeh (*al-Khuraybah*, "the little ruin") at the northeastern edge of the oasis marks the site of ancient Dedan (see colour plate 3A).[79] Biblical references[80] suggest that Dedan was one of the most important oases of North Arabia. It was natural, therefore, that on the morning of the 11th we hastened thither, pausing on the way only long enough to photograph some rocks covered with Islamic Arabic inscriptions.

The ruins of ancient Dedan are extensive, covering an area approximately 500 metres from north to south by 100 metres from east to west. The *tell* itself is low, being only from four to seven metres high. The site suffered severely from the construction of the Ḥijāz Railway, which cut through the western edge of the ruins, and even more from the 'mining' activities of the villagers of al-'Ulā in search of ready-cut building-stone. How much of the ancient city remains is doubtful. We picked up sherds, which differed from those found at Taymā',[81] one

78/The railway is in process of being rebuilt. See Daniel Da Cruz, "Pilgrim's Road," in *Aramco World*, Sept.–Oct. 1965, pp. 25–33.

79/See Doughty, *Travels*, I, pp. 139–66; Huber in *BSG*, 7e série, tome 5 (1884), pp. 517–23; Euting, *Tagbuch*, II, pp. 218–46; JS, *Mission*, II, pp. 29–77 and Atlas, Pls. VI–XXXVI.

80/See Gen. 10:7 (= I Chron. 1:9), 25:3; Isa. 21:13; Jer. 25:23, 49:8; Ezek. 25:13, 27:20, 38:13.

81/See pp. 176–8 and Fig. 84:1, 2–4, 9.

3A Al-Khuraybah, the site of ancient Dedan, with the oasis of al-ʿUlā beyond

3B A Nabataean tomb adorned with sphinxes, Madā'in Ṣāliḥ

broken copper coin, pieces of slag, and fragments of alabaster. There were a great many blue, or blue-green, stones lying about which appear to have been used for hammering or rubbing since they were worn on one side. One red sandstone block, not *in situ*, bore the diagonal dressing characteristic of Nabataean masonry.[82] Another block, half buried in the sand, bore a Lihyanite inscription (Pl. 25),[83] a reminder that following the downfall of the kingdom of Dedan a tribe known as Liḥyān seized control of the oasis. The Lihyanites have left a considerable number of inscriptions at Dedan, some fifty of which are monumental in character. The names of at least eight of their kings are known, so the kingdom must have lasted for a century and a half or more. Their chief god was Dhū-Ghābat, but many other gods and goddesses, including Allāh, Allāt, Manāt, and al-ʿUzzā, are mentioned in the inscriptions. In fact, these texts are the best witnesses we possess to the character of ancient North Arabian paganism.

During, and possibly prior to, the Lihyanite period a colony of Minaean merchants resided at Dedan, as is attested by the presence there of over two hundred Minaean inscriptions as well as by tombs carved in the face of the cliffs bordering the valley (Fig. 43).[84] Two of the tombs are protected by crude representations of lions. One of these is shown in Fig. 44.[85]

The most striking antiquity on the site of ancient Dedan is a large stone cylinder, over twelve feet in diameter and seven feet deep, with walls over eleven inches thick (Fig. 48).[86] According to local tradition it is the pail into which the pre-Islamic prophet Ṣāliḥ milked his camel. This camel, of a huge size, was brought forth by God from the rock in response to the plea of Ṣāliḥ who had been challenged by the Thamudic inhabitants of the area to perform a miracle as proof of his prophetic credentials. The camel yielded so much milk that it sufficed for them all, but when it drank, every three days, its thirst was such that it dried up all of their wells. So they hamstrung it and killed it. However, a calf came forth from its womb unharmed and then vanished into the great rock, now called Jabal al-Ḥuwārah (see Fig. 40), which stands on the southern side of the plain of Madā'in Ṣāliḥ. Three days later God sent a fearful wind and earthquake and the Thamūd were destroyed.[87] The presence of three steps inside the "pail" suggests that it was a reservoir for holding water. If so, it must have been filled by pouring water into it or else the ground around it was once level with the top of the tank,

82/For illustrations of Nabataean dressing at Petra, see *QDAP*, VII (1938), Pls. XVII:3, XLIX:2, and LXVIII:2.

83/See below, "Dedanite and Lihyanite Inscriptions," no. 9, p. 125.

84/See Doughty, *Travels*, I, p. 159, and JS, *Mission*, II, Atlas, Pls. III:1, XXI:2, XXIII:1–3, XXIV:1, 2, XXX:2.

85/See JS, *Mission*, II, Atlas, Pls. [illegible]:1, [illegible], [illegible], and Grohmann's discussion of the figures in *Arabien*, pp. 74–5.

86/See Doughty, *Travels*, I, pp. 139, 158; Euting, *Tagbuch*, II, pp. 239–40; and JS, *Mission*, II, pp. 56–7, and Atlas, Pl. XXVIII:1.

87/See Doughty, *Travels*, I, p. 96.

FIGURE 43 Minaean tombs in the cliffs at al-ʿUla
(Vidal photograph)

FIGURE 44 Minaean tomb at al-Khuraybah guarded by lions
(Aramco photograph, Saʿid al-Ghamidi)

FIGURE 45 Tombs at al-Khuraybah

FIGURE 46 Tomb at al-Khuraybah with Dedanite inscription

FIGURE 47 Tomb at al-Khuraybah with Dedanite inscription

allowing for gravity flow. Jaussen and Savignac found evidence that the reservoir stood in the centre of an open court along two sides of which ran arcades containing statues set on pedestals bearing dedicatory inscriptions.[88] Eventual excavation of this important site should yield a great deal of information regarding the early history of North Arabia.

We established our camp at the foot of the ridge immediately east of the ruins of Dedan. After exploring the tombs in this area (see Figs. 45–47, 49) we climbed the ridge behind them, finding a few inscriptions[89] on the way up. From the summit one could see a belt of green palms extending for four or five miles between the red sandstone cliffs (Fig. 50). Al-ʿUlā is undoubtedly the most strikingly beautiful oasis in all North Arabia. South of where we stood was another peak which intrigued us because the sides of the summit had been deliberately scarped to make access impossible except by a stairway, a few steps of which were visible near the summit (Fig. 51). To the right could be seen a high stone causeway linking this peak with another peak (Fig. 52) to which access was had, we were told, by a stairway leading up from the plain below. A large section of the causeway has fallen, making it impossible now to reach the scarped peak. One wonders if it is the site of an ancient high-place. An aerial photograph would probably reveal the true character of this mysterious summit.[90]

North of the peak on which we had been standing was a maze of walls of small, undressed stones, suggesting that the heights were once fortified. It was difficult, however, to see any plan in their arrangement.

On May 12 we drove back to Madā'in Ṣāliḥ to see the wonderful array of Nabataean tombs to be found in that area. Their existence was first made known to the Western world by Charles Doughty. Having heard rumours, while at Maʿān in southern Transjordan, of the presence of wonderful monuments and ancient inscriptions at Madā'in Ṣāliḥ, he attached himself to the pilgrim caravan of 1876, and accompanied it as far as that place. He spent some time there copying the inscriptions and studying the tombs before undertaking what turned out to be a two-year period of wandering in *Arabia Deserta*.

In Islamic tradition Madā'in Ṣāliḥ is usually referred to as al-Ḥijr, this being the Arabic form of the Nabataean-Aramaic name Ḥegrā. This tradition betrays no knowledge of the presence of the Nabataeans at al-Ḥijr; the town is associated only with the Thamūd, one of the vanished peoples of Arabia. God is said to have sent the Thamūd a prophet named Ṣāliḥ to turn them from the error of polytheism but they refused to heed him and as a result were destroyed. The empty tombs at al-Ḥijr were believed to be the former dwellings of the Thamūd.[91]

88/See JS, *Mission*, II, pp. 56–7, and Grohmann, *Arabien*, pp. 65–6, 76–8.
89/See below, "Dedanite and Lihyanite Inscriptions," nos. 1–5, pp. 122–3.
90/JS make no reference to this peak.
91/See Qur'ān 15:80–84.

FIGURE 48 W. L. Reed standing beside reservoir of ancient temple at Dedan

FIGURE 49 Cist-graves at al-Khuraybah

FIGURE 50 The oasis of al-ʿUlā

FIGURE 51 Peak with scarped sides behind al-Khuraybah

FIGURE 52 Stone causeway, left centre, leading to peak with scarped sides

According to Arab tradition there were once seven settlements in this area, whence it came to be known as Madā'in Ṣāliḥ, meaning "the cities of (the prophet) Ṣāliḥ." Of these, only one survives, and it has taken the name which formerly denoted the whole area.

The identity of the prophet of al-Ḥijr is a mystery. The fact that the tradition about him knows nothing of the Nabataeans suggests that his activity came after the collapse of Nabataean power. His name, Ṣāliḥ, means "virtuous, pious." This raises the possibility that it is a religious substitute for his actual name. In the Qur'ān he is depicted as an advocate of monotheism and a warner of judgment to come. The latter feature may indicate that he was a Christian or, at least, had come under Christian influence. R. B. Sergeant[92] has drawn attention to traditions that Hūd, the other great pre-Islamic prophet of Arabia, had a son, or grandson, with a Jewish name, Danyāl or Dhāniyāl (i.e. Daniel). It is possible, therefore, that Hūd was an early Jewish preacher of monotheism in South Arabia where Judaism had gained some foothold in the sixth century A.D.

After once again calling on the Amīr of Madā'in Ṣāliḥ, we drove southeastward about a mile and a half to inspect the tombs at Qaṣr al-Bint.[93] In the sides of this great white sandstone dome no less than twenty-three large tombs have been hollowed out. The most striking feature of the tombs is their facades, carved in the solid rock. These are of two main types, which may be called for the sake of convenience "A" and "B."[94] In type A the upper part of the facade is decorated with one or more rows of little step-pyramids in low relief, each having five steps to a side (Fig. 56).[95] Above and below them runs a line of moulding. Below the lower moulding is a framed, or recessed, panel, bearing an inscription which gives the name of the deceased and the year of his death. Some tombs have two rows of step-pyramids. The front of these tombs is otherwise unadorned except for the moulding around the entrance. The entrances seem to have been provided with wooden doors which could be locked. Bits of stucco still adhering to some of the tombs suggest that the facades were once covered entirely with plaster.

Facades of the B type are much more elaborate in character and reflect Graeco-Roman influence. This is sufficient to stamp the style as a later development than type A, but a comparison of the dated tombs at Ḥegrā shows that type A continued to be favoured by some Nabataeans even after the development of type B. In type B the moulding around the entrance is itself framed by two pilasters crowned by capitals of a distinctively Nabataean type (Fig. 53).[96] The architrave is unadorned but the frieze above it is embellished with alternating triglyphs and rosettes. The triangular pediment is sometimes bare (see Fig. 58), sometimes filled with figures. For example, the pediment shown in Fig. 55 is filled with a mask and two snakes.[97] Above the peak of the pediment there usually stands the figure of an eagle,[98] with a panel for an inscription just above it. Above each outer angle of the pediment stands an urn.[99] Thus a great deal of

92/"Hūd and Other Pre-Islamic Prophets of Hadramaut" (*Muséon*, 67 [1954], pp. 121–79; see especially pp. 166–71).

93/See Doughty, *Doc. épig.*, Pls. XXXIV–XLVI.

94/This is admittedly an overly simplified classification but it is sufficient for the present purpose. For Puchstein's classification, see Grohmann, *Arabien*, pp. 59–63.

95/See also JS, *Mission*, II, Atlas, Pls. XLVI:1, XLVII:2, 4, XLVIII:2, and XLIX:2.

96/For the different types of Nabataean capitals, see Grohmann, *Arabien*, pp. 62–3.

97/For the significance of the mask in Nabataean religion, see Nelson Glueck, *Deities and Dolphins* (New York and Toronto, 1965), pp. 242–3, 353–6, and Index; for the significance of the snake, pp. 479–93.

98/For the significance of the eagle, see Glueck, pp. 471–9.

99/For the connection of the urn with the cult of the dead, see Grohmann, *Arabien*, pp. 64 and 187.

FIGURE 53 A Nabataean tomb at Madā'in Ṣāliḥ with facade of later type
(Vidal photograph)

FIGURE 54 A Nabataean tomb at Madā'in Ṣāliḥ

FIGURE 55 Tomb pediment adorned with mask and two snakes; Madā'in Ṣāliḥ

FIGURE 56 A Nabataean tomb at Madā'in Ṣāliḥ with facade of early type

FIGURE 57 Nabataean tombs at Madā'in Ṣāliḥ (Aramco photograph, Sa'id al-Ghamidi)

FIGURE 58 A Nabataean tomb with plain pediment at Madā'in Ṣāliḥ (Vidal photograph)

care was lavished on the adornment of the entrances in facades of type B. The outer extremities of the facade are given the form of pilasters, these being much taller than those framing the doorway. The upper part of the facade is divided from the lower by a projecting ledge and is sculptured to represent a double staircase each with five steps, starting from the centre and ascending to the outer corners (see Figs. 54, 57, and colour plate 4A). It is difficult to resist the impression that the staircase had symbolic significance, being intended to suggest the ascent of the soul of the deceased to the celestial regions, and so served as a sort of "Jacob's ladder," a link between earth and heaven.[99a]

The interiors of the tombs exhibit great variety of arrangement, so much so that it is doubtful if any two are exactly the same. In some the chamber inside the door has a rectangular excavation in the rock floor for holding the coffin, or there are slots carved in the walls where several bodies could be placed and sealed up (see colour plate 4B).[100] In others there are alcoves leading off the entrance chamber where the bodies were stored (Fig. 59). Some of these alcoves have burial pits sunk in the floor. Many of the tombs are not completely finished and seem not to have been used for burials as intended. Some pieces of wood were found in a tomb near the west end of Qaṣr al-Bint, but there was no immediate way of knowing whether they were ancient or modern.

From Qaṣr al-Bint we proceeded about a quarter of a mile northeast to the irregular sandstone mass called Jabal Ithlib where Jaussen and Savignac found the religious centre of ancient Ḥegrā. At the northwest corner of the *jabal* is a huge room, about forty feet square and twenty-five feet high, which has been hollowed out of the solid rock.[101] It is known today as the Dīwān or Majlis as-Sulṭān, "the Sultan's council chamber" (Fig. 60). The front is completely open, but at either side the rock has been carved to give the impression of pilasters. Jaussen and Savignac believed that if the sand were cleared from the interior a triclinium arrangement might be revealed.[102] If so, it would be without parallel elsewhere at Ḥegrā. The absence of triclinia (dining-halls with rock couches carved in the floor on three sides where feasts for the dead were celebrated) is one of the things which distinguishes Ḥegrā from Petra. Since the Dīwān does not seem to have been designed as a tomb, it is natural to assume that it was used as a sanctuary. In support of this assumption is the presence of a crude image of some divinity carved in the rock in front of the entrance.[103]

99a/According to T. H. Gaster (art. "Angel" in *IDB*, I, 130) miniature ladders were often placed in Egyptian and Roman graves in order to facilitate the ascent of the soul to heaven.

100/See Doughty, *Travels*, I, Pl. II.

101/See Doughty, *Travels*, I, p. 118, and *Doc. épig.*, Pl. XLIV; JS, *Mission*, I, pp. 118, 405–10; Grohmann, *Arabien*, pp. 66–7.

102/For a large triclinium at Petra, see *QDAP*, VII (1938), Pl. LVIII:2.

103/See JS, *Mission*, I, pp. 410–13. For a similar carving, representing the goddess Allāt, at Jabal Ramm, see *RB*, 43 (1934), p. 584, and Grohmann, *Arabien*, pp. 78–9.

FIGURE 59 A Nabataean tomb with alcoves off the entrance chamber, Madā'in Ṣāliḥ

To the right of the Dīwān there begins a narrow defile (Fig. 61), which recalls the Sīq at Petra, the walls of which contain many so-called "Dushara niches" similar to those to be seen at Petra. In each of these niches are one, two, or three upright stones (betyls) which are not free-standing but carved out of the living rock (Figs. 62–64; see also Fig. 65). Since the chief god of the Nabataeans was Dūsharā (Greek Dusares), it is likely that one of the stones represents him. In that case the second and third stones would doubtless represent consorts, possibly Manōtu (Ar. Manāt) and Allāt.

The defile opens into a space where on the right one sees the beautiful arched niche, adorned with lamps, shown in Fig. 66, but containing no betyls. The rocks of this area, as well as the walls of the defile, contain a number of Nabataean inscriptions and some Thamudic (nos. 73–7). About thirty feet above the ground there is a man-made water-channel designed to bring in water from a well to the north of Jabal Ithlib and to catch the winter rains. At the top of the peak on the side of which this channel is hewn is a small room about ten feet in diameter. It may have served as a look-out post. There was no trace of a "high-place" in the vicinity, nor has any such yet been found in the whole Madā'in Ṣāliḥ area. This suggests that open-air sanctuaries like the great high-places at Petra date back to pre-Nabataean, i.e. Edomite, times.

Leaving Qaṣr al-Bint, we explored the region near the railway tracks in the hope of finding the site of ancient Ḥegrā. In the vicinity of a mushroom-shaped rock standing by itself (Fig. 67) there was some Nabataean ware of the thin,

4A A Nabataean tomb at Madā'in Ṣāliḥ

4B Burial slots in the wall of a Nabataean tomb, Madā'in Ṣāliḥ

FIGURE 60 Majlis as-Sulṭān

FIGURE 61 The defile beyond Majlis as-Sulṭān (Vidal photograph)

FIGURE 62 A Nabataean shrine
(Vidal photograph)

FIGURE 63 A Nabataean shrine with single betyl (Vidal photograph)

FIGURE 64 A Nabataean shrine with three betyls

FIGURE 65 Betyl at entrance to a tomb, Qaṣr al-Bint

FIGURE 66 Niche adorned with lamps

"egg-shell" type, both painted and unpainted, as well as some sherds of mediaeval Arab pottery[104] but there was no clear evidence of a *tell*, only a slight elevation of the *wādī* at this point. The remains in the Madā'in Ṣāliḥ area are so few that were it not for the number of tombs in the area, one would be inclined to doubt that a town ever stood there. Probably the majority of the houses were of sun-dried brick and have long since merged with the earth out of which they were formed. It must be remembered that according to Diodorus (xix.94–7) the Nabataeans had a law against building houses; hence Ḥegrā may have been largely a tent-city. Nonetheless one would expect to see more sherds lying about. They must lie buried beneath the sand.[105]

To the south of the spot where we found the sherds there is another group of seventeen tombs. To the west, across the railway, Jaussen and Savignac counted a group of twenty-eight more. One of these, belonging to type A, is notable in that the space between the two rows of step-pyramids is embellished with a mask and two rosettes (Fig. 69). Sand has drifted in front of the tomb and now reaches to the top of the entrance. On one of the tombs the customary urns have been replaced by the figures of two winged sphinxes (Fig. 68 and colour plate 3B).[106] Furthermore, the customary eagle is missing, although the pedestal on which it usually stands is present.

Following our inspection of this area we drove back eastward and skirted the edge of Jabal Ithlib, finding in the process the rather fine petroglyph shown in Fig. 70. Its light colour and the fact that it is not mentioned by Jaussen and Savignac indicate that it is a modern creation.

On May 13 we turned northward along the Darb al-Ḥajj, with Tabūk as our first objective. The road runs more or less parallel to the Ḥijāz Railway, which we crossed and recrossed several times. The stations of Abū Ṭāqah, Maṭāliʿ, and Dār al-Ḥamrā' are still standing but look very forlorn and deserted in the empty

104/See below, pp. 178–9 and Fig. 81. Doughty (*Travels*, I, pp. 112–13) reports seeing pot-sherds and broken glass some distance to the west of Qaṣr al-Bint.

105/Some of the inhabitants of Madā'in Ṣāliḥ, who have been trying recently to revive the old wells, have had to dig down six to eight feet before reaching then anciet well collar. This suggests that the floor of the entire plain may be at least that much higher than the old floor (F. S. Vidal).

106/See JS, *Mission*, II, Atlas, Pl. LI:2–3. As a result of the interest aroused in Madā'in Ṣāliḥ by our expedition, a number of persons have since visited the site. Among them were Thomas C. Barger, President of Aramco; Fred Davies, former Chairman of the Aramco Board; and a number of Aramco employees; also Parker T. Hart and Sir Colin Crowe, the American and British ambassadors respectively to Saʿudi Arabia. See Barger's "Notes on the Nabataeans," and the series of wonderful colour photographs taken by B. H. Moody, in *Aramco World* (special issue, "Arabia the Beautiful," Sept.–Oct. 1965). See also Lady Peter Crowe's report in *JRCAS*, July–Oct. 1964, pp. 291–300, and the report in the *New York Times*, [illegible], 19[illegible], p. XX [illegible].

The Saʿudi Arabian Department of Antiquities has since carried out a careful examination of the area and reports finding the site of the ancient city, together with part of its wall (communication from Mr. ʿĀdil ʿAyyāsh).

FIGURE 67 Possible site of ancient Ḥegrā

wilderness. At Khasham Ṣanaʿ the road shifted east of the railway and we did not see it again until Tabūk was reached.

The following morning high, picturesque dunes (Fig. 71) were encountered, and it was necessary to circle them to the east. We reached Tabūk (Fig. 72) about ten o'clock and found the city in a festive mood for this was the day of the "sacrificial feast" (*ʿīd al-aḍḥā*) which marks the culmination of the pilgrimage rites at Mecca. On this day the pilgrims sacrifice in the valley of Mina near Mecca, and Muslims everywhere follow their example. We went directly to the residence of the Amīr, Musāʿad as-Sudayrī, but were informed that he was absent in Germany. However, his nephew Aḥmad, a young man about eighteen years old, received us hospitably and invited us to dine with him that evening and share in the general festivities. The Amīr's guest-house was placed at our disposal and two men were detailed to attend to our needs.

The population of Tabūk is said to number about thirty thousand. There are four schools: primary, secondary, and industrial, and one for girls. The town has an airfield, and planes of the Saʿudi National Airline call there every day in the week except one.[107] A considerable volume of traffic passes through the town,

107/Sakākah also has an air service.

FIGURE 68 Close-up of sphinxes shown in colour plate 4A

FIGURE 69 Tomb facade embellished with a mask and two rosettes

especially at the pilgrimage season. On the year of our visit, we were told, 280 bus-loads of pilgrims had passed through. Once the asphalt road from Medina reaches Tabūk, and the Ḥijāz Railway is rebuilt, the volume of traffic should greatly increase.

Numerous inscriptions and monuments were said to be present at al-Qurayyah, thirty miles to the northwest. These are probably the ones recorded by Moritz.[108] The antiquities and inscriptions in the Tabūk area were recorded by Jaussen and Savignac,[109] Musil,[110] and Philby.[111] We decided, therefore, not to linger in Tabūk and on the morrow directed our course northeastward towards the Wādī as-Sirḥān.

The Wādī as-Sirḥān is a region which many Near Eastern scholars have wished to see since it was one of the most travelled highways between Syria and North Arabia.[112] We hoped to find there many ancient inscriptions left by the passing caravaneers. The terrain traversed on the way thither was sandy desert, copiously sprinkled with rocky debris, and with a surface sufficiently hard to make rapid progress possible. The road skirted the edge of the sandstone peaks of Jibāl aṭ-Ṭubayq which lie along the southeastern corner of Jordan. At one point we observed a drilling rig off to the left, evidence of the continued search for water, but there was no sign of life around it. After a drive of 190 miles we camped for the night.

The following morning, May 16, we entered the Wadī as-Sirḥān ("the valley of the wolf") (Fig. 73). It is not a *wādī* as ordinarily conceived but a shallow depression thirty to forty miles wide, running in a southeasterly direction from Bosra in Syria to al-Jawf in North Arabia, a distance of over 300 miles. It thus receives the drainage of a considerable area and, although the rainfall is rather light, it serves to feed a number of wells located along its length. The presence of these wells has made the *wādī* the favourite route for caravans plying between Syria and North Arabia. It must not be imagined, however, that the Wādī as-Sirḥān is a ribbon of green vegetation. For the most part it is just as barren as the bordering deserts. But there are two points where some semblance of fertility is found, and at these there exists a group of oasis-villages. The first group is located southeast of ʿAmmān and not far from the Jordan–Saʿudi Arabian border. According to the governor of the area there are about twenty settlements in this group, some of them being Bedouin camps. The best-known villages are

108/See his "Ausflüge in der Arabia Petraea" in *Mélanges de la Faculté orientale de Beyrouth*, III, 1908, pp. 407–10; also Grohmann, *Arabien*, pp. 37, 39–41.

109/*Mission*, I, pp. 57–70.

110/*N. Ḥeǧâz*, pp. 161–70.

111/*Midian*, chap. 6. For the inscriptions copied by Philby in this area, see van den Branden, *TTP*, II, pp. 64–142.

112/Palgrave passed through the *wādī*, as did Guarmani and Philby.

FIGURE 70 Rock drawing, Jabal Ithlib (composite photograph)

FIGURE 71 Dunes near Tabūk

FIGURE 72 Tabūk

FIGURE 73 Entering the Wādī as-Sirḥān

FIGURE 74 Foundations of a Nabataean sanctuary at Ithrā

FIGURE 75 Qaṣr as-Saʿīdī, Kāf

FIGURE 76 Jabal as-Saʿīdī with the oasis of Kāf at its base

an-Nabk, Kāf, Ithrā, Manwā, al-Qarqar (Karkar),[113] Ghaṭṭī, al-Ḥadīthah, and al-ʿIsāwiyah. They go by the collective name of Qurayyāt al-Milḥ ("the salt villages") because of the occurrence of considerable salt deposits in the area.[114] The other group of settlements is found in the Jawf region: al-Jawf, Sakākah, aṭ-Ṭuwayr, Qārah, and Muwaysin. Our visit to some of these has already been described. The region between these two groups of settlements, an interval of over 200 miles, is empty wilderness.

Not long after entering the Wādī as-Sirḥān we came to the village of al-ʿIsāwiyah (230 miles from Tabūk), the most southerly village of the Qurayyāt al-Milḥ group. After stopping briefly to drink coffee with the local dignitary, we pushed on to an-Nabk (Fig. 77), where the governor of the Qurayyāt al-Milḥ area, Amīr ʿAbdallāh ibn ʿAbd al-ʿAzīz as-Sudayrī (Fig. 79), resided[115]. When the Amīr was passing through Jerusalem in 1958 he had assured us that he would welcome a visit by scholars interested in the antiquities of his area. He now received us most cordially and displayed keen interest in the aims of the expedition.

He drove us in his own car to see the oasis of Kāf (Musil's Chaf), then six miles farther on to Manwā,[116] and finally to Ithrā (Guarmani's Etera), the second largest settlement of the Qurayyāt. Ithrā is a picturesque oasis, lying between a rocky ridge to the east and glistening salt flats to the west and south. The *qaṣr* is constructed of blocks of basalt and bears a Kufic inscription above the main entrance.[117] Embedded in one of the walls is a stone bearing a carving of a mustached face.

A short distance east of the village is a spot called Rās al-ʿĀnīyah where there is a large quinine (*kīnā*) tree. Near it the foundation courses of an ancient structure, twenty by eighteen metres, lie exposed (Fig. 74). The stones are of

113/The name appears on one Arabic road-sign as al-Qarqar, on another as al-Karkar. According to Dr. Vidal, the correct form is al-Qarqar. It is probably to be identified with Qarqor of Judges 8:10 where Gideon inflicted a defeat on Zebaḥ and Ṣalmunna, the kings of Midian.

114/Near Ithrā we observed a large number of shallow, rectangular pits dug in the plain where the subsurface salty water was being exposed to the sun and evaporated. The salt thus recovered was raked up in little heaps. A considerable amount of salt used to be exported to Syria, one camel-load of salt being exchanged in Damascus for one camel-load of grain. Today only enough is produced to meet local needs. The economic ties connecting the Wādī as-Sirḥān with Syria are further illustrated by Guarmani's statement that in his day many of the people from this area used to go to the Hauran every year at harvest time to reap and glean for the Druzes. Thus the *wādī* serves as the natural channel of communication between North Arabia and Syria. The pottery and inscriptions which we found in the upper parts of the *wādī* provide evidence of the close cultural relations between these two areas at an earlier period. Kāf is only 100 miles from ʿAmmān.

115/ʿAbdallāh as-Sudayrī is no longer Amīr of Qurayyāt al-Milḥ. In December 1964 he was appointed Deputy Minister of the Interior for Municipalities.

116/For a photograph of Manwā, see Philby in *GJ*, 62 (1923), facing p. 251.

117/This is reproduced in Euting, *Tagbuch*, I, p. 59.

basalt, and a number of them are dressed. The upper courses of the walls were probably of mud-brick and have long since disintegrated. Philby reports seeing at Ithrā "the remnants of a large building constructed of basalt blocks, some of which had inscriptions and figures in low relief."[118] He does not seem to have copied or photographed them, which is unfortunate since neither inscriptions nor reliefs are now visible. However, in walking over the site, the men accompanying us picked up two limestone slabs bearing Thamudic inscriptions.[119] The floor-plan of the structure – an outer rectangular wall enclosing a rectangular chamber – is similar to that of the Nabataean temple at Khirbat at-Tannūr in Jordan which Reed helped Nelson Glueck excavate in 1937.[120] This suggests that it may have been a Nabataean sanctuary. A number of Nabataean sherds of the beautiful, painted, "egg-shell" ware were picked up on the site, and some lamp fragments of Nabataean and "Herodian" types.[121] Also found was the bottom of a limestone cup (similar to ones found at Dhībān in Jordan and at Herodian Jericho and Roman al-Jīb, and dating from the Nabataean-Roman period, first century B.C. to first century A.D.); and a broken cultic (?) vessel, embellished with incised lines and engraved with a Thamudic inscription.[122] There were a few fragments of ostrich eggs, and one coin which was too badly eroded to be attributed but which was not unlike Nabataean coins in size. The archaeological evidence suggests that the Nabataean sanctuary was taken over by the "Thamūd" after the collapse of Nabataean power.[123]

On the south side of the oasis we were shown a stone which had been unearthed a few days prior to our visit. It bore three lines of Nabataean writing[124] and was reported to have come from a small room, now almost buried in the sand. Later, while we were being served tea in the village, the people brought in several other limestone slabs bearing Thamudic inscriptions. These, they said, had been found at the same site as the others mentioned above. It is obvious that this site should be kept in mind for excavation.

In the morning we returned to Kāf in order to have a closer look at the oasis. Kāf has been visited by several Europeans,[125] and Guarmani fled there when he

118/*GJ*, 62 (1923), pp. 248–9.

119/Our notes fail to distinguish these two inscriptions from the others brought to us later by the villagers (see Thamudic inscriptions nos. 78–92, pp. 133–5).

120/For the temple at Khirbat at-Tannūr, see Nelson Glueck, *Deities and Dolphins*.

121/See below, pp. 181–4.

122/See below, Thamudic inscription no. 91 and Pls. 8 and 17.

123/For a Thamudic sanctuary at Ghwāfa (Rawāfa) in Midian and dating from 166–9 A.D., see Musil, *N. Ḥeǧâz*, pp. 185–9, 258, 291; Philby, *Midian*, p. 156; Henri Seyrig, *Antiquités syriennes*, v (Paris, 1958), pp. 170–1 (= *Syria*, 34 [1957], pp. 259–61); Caskel, *LL*, p. 43; and Grohmann, *Arabien*, pp. 42, 49, 71.

124/See below, Nabataean inscription no. 130, p. 161.

125/For Huber's visit, see *BSG*, 7e série, tome 5 (1884), pp. 306–12. An aerial photograph of Kāf is reproduced in *GJ*, 62 (1923), between pp. 244–5.

FIGURE 77 An-Nabk

FIGURE 78 View of al-Qarqar from the top of 'Umm ʿAyyāsh

FIGURE 79 Amīr ʿAbdallāh as-Sudayrī, governor of Qurayyāt al-Milḥ, seated in centre

and his companions were attacked by Ruwālah raiders. The oasis lies about ten miles northwest of an-Nabk at the southern foot of a great basaltic rampart known as Jabal as-Sa'īdī, being hemmed in between this rampart and some salt marshes (Fig. 76). The oasis appears to be fighting a losing battle against the salt. Amīr 'Abdallāh informed us that twenty-five years ago his father founded an-Nabk because he felt that Kāf had no prospect for growth;[126] furthermore, it was plagued with malaria. Many of the inhabitants of Kāf moved to the new town but some of the older people refused to do so. According to the Egyptian doctor at an-Nabk the malaria situation has improved in recent years.

Since there appeared to be no antiquities above ground in Kāf itself, we decided to climb Jabal as-Sa'īdī in the hope of finding inscriptions. A ramplike road leads by a series of sharp turns up the face of the mountain. The flat summit, which covers an area of about five hundred square metres, is crowned by a fortress called Qaṣr as-Sa'īdī (Fig. 75).[127] According to tales heard by Guarmani the name derives from a wealthy Egyptian pilgrim from Port Said who constructed the fort in gratitude for a safe journey to Mecca.

Near the centre of the summit are the foundations of a rectangular building, about eleven metres long and six metres wide. The presence of some Nabataean sherds and the fact that the structure is oriented towards the east suggest that it was a Nabataean temple originally, but doubtless it served later as a mosque. Our search for inscriptions proved unrewarding, except for an Islamic inscription found in the gateway.

At the foot of the mountain, but on a shelf of higher ground than the oasis, stands the deserted but imposing fortress-residence built in the 1920s by Nūrī ibn Sha'lān, paramount sheikh of the Ruwālah tribe.

From Kāf we drove on to Ithrā,[128] seven miles to the southeast, to search for further antiquities. A villager conducted us to a spot a few miles away where there were two exceptionally fine rock-drawings of mountain goats (*wa'l*), then to some rocks not far south of Ithrā where there were a few Thamudic inscriptions.[129] A journey four miles farther on yielded one more inscription.[130]

We returned to the Amīr's garden at al-'Ayn for lunch. There under the palms a great feast was spread, and a large number of guests from an-Nabk and the surrounding villages were assembled. After the meal the Amīr presided at a

126/This explains why an-Nabk does not appear on Major Holt's map of the Wādī as-Sirḥān in *GJ*, 62 (1923), facing p. 270.

127/Philby was not allowed to visit the fort when he visited Kāf in 1923 (*GJ*, 62 [1923], p. 245). For a ground-plan of the fort, see Euting, *Tagbuch*, I, p. 72.

128/See Lady Anne Blunt, *Voyage en Arabie* (Paris, 1882); Huber, *Journal*, p. 24; Euting, *Tagbuch*, I, pp. 47–112; Philby in *GJ*, 62 (1923), pp. 248–9.

129/See below, Thamudic inscriptions nos. 93–97, p. 136.

130/See below, Thamudic inscription no. 98, p. 136.

FIGURE 80 Drawing of a ghoul (?) in old burial-ground in the *ḥarrah* beyond Ithrā

meeting held to discuss the establishment of a co-operative. In spite of his obvious enthusiasm for the project, objections were raised by the village representatives who wanted to be certain that the benefits would be shared equally by all the settlements.[131]

Following this, the Amīr drove us out eastward for fifteen miles into the *ḥarrah,* a black volcanic area covered with basalt boulders. At a spot called Fayḍat al-Qurayniyah we were astonished to see a large field of wheat. Two gazelles bounded out of it as we approached. Climbing a ridge to the west, we were shown an ancient burial-ground. On one of the stones was a drawing of a wild-looking female figure (Fig. 80), probably a ghoul (Ar. *ghūl*). Other stones bore three Thamudic inscriptions.[132]

The following day we drove to al-Ḥadīthah on the west side of the Wādī as-Sirḥān, about eighteen miles from an-Nabk. Al-Ḥadīthah serves as the Saʿudi

131/According to Dr. Vidal the co-operative was subsequently formed and has been operating quite successfully.

132/See below, Thamudic inscriptions nos. 99–101, p. 136.

customs post on the road leading to ʿAmmān in Jordan. The corresponding Jordanian customs post is said to be about twenty miles north. The local Amīr, a former colonel in the Saʿudi army, personally escorted us to see his garden, where he had cleaned out an old well and in the process found a few sherds. They were similar to Late Byzantine and Early Arab sherds found at Dhībān in Jordan, and are further evidence of the close cultural connections of Arabia with Jordan in times past.

About half a mile south of al-Ḥadīthah are the remains of an ancient irrigation channel, constructed of basalt stones and mud-plaster. Sherds picked up near the channel had the green glaze characteristic of the mediaeval Arab period. The ruins of a *qaṣr* are to be seen about two miles south of the village, but it was impossible to determine from the remains its size or plan. On a slight elevation not far away was an ancient cemetery where twelve graves were counted. The few sherds in the area seemed to be Late Byzantine or Early Arab.

We drove back across the Wādī as-Sirḥān to Kāf and from there went to see a large rock called Umm ʿAyyāsh ("the mother of sustenance") which, according to local tradition, had been an object of worship in pre-Islamic times. It is of conglomerate, about ninety feet high, and stands solitary in the plain a short distance east of al-Qarqar. A climb to the top disclosed no altar or inscription or any other evidence which would suggest the one-time existence of a cult at this spot.

We were hospitably entertained by the villagers of al-Qarqar (Fig. 78), who brought two inscribed stones for our inspection. One was Thamudic,[133] the other Palmyrene.[134] These stones, together with those from al-Qarqar and the sherds picked up at various places in the *wādī*, were left with Amīr ʿAbdallāh, who was planning to establish a small museum at an-Nabk.

We left an-Nabk at noon on the 19th, carrying with us pleasant memories of the cordial hospitality which had been extended to us by the Amīr and grateful to him for all the pains he had taken to show us the antiquities of his area. The road back to Turaif, our starting-point, led past Kāf and ʿIthrā and out into the stony *ḥarrah*. Emerging from the *ḥarrah* we came upon hard-packed sand across which we sped quickly, covering the one hundred miles to Turaif in less than three hours.

The expedition had covered some 1800 miles, had visited most of the important ancient sites of North Arabia, and had obtained an extensive photographic record of each. In spite of the hurried nature of the expedition we succeeded in finding and recording over three hundred ancient inscriptions. Some, the Tay-

133/See below, Thamudic inscription no. 102, p. 137.
134/See below, "Inscription palmyrénienne," p. 161.

manite, are among the earliest yet discovered in North Arabia, carrying us back in all probability to the sixth century B.C. A few Minaean and Lihyanite texts were found, as well as a considerable number of hitherto unknown Thamudic graffiti, also one hundred and thirty Nabataean, one Palmyrene, and one Proto-Arabic. Even where the texts had been recorded by earlier explorers, it was found that new interpretations were frequently necessary in the light of our growing knowledge of the ancient Arabian scripts. A few are of unusual interest because of the light shed on the religion of the pre-Islamic Arabs. We are aware, of course, that some of the interpretations we have proposed may require revision. The texts at least provide scholars with new source material which, when fully interpreted, will contribute to the reconstruction of the ancient history of North Arabia.

The number of inscriptions found did not come up to our expectations. There were two reasons for this: first, vast areas of North Arabia are devoid of rocks which might have served as writing material and, secondly, even in areas where rocks are to be found, the stone is friable sandstone and many of the inscriptions which they once bore are so weathered as to be no longer legible. Doubtless the basaltic *ḥarrahs* to the west and south of the area traversed contain numerous graffiti in a good state of preservation, as does the Jordanian *ḥarrah*, but the penetration of *ḥarrah*-territory presents obstacles of an unusually formidable kind. It is doubtful of such regions can ever be explored adequately except by the Arabs themselves. One grim fact constantly impressed upon us was that if the Sa'udi government wishes to recover the history of its people it must act promptly to salvage the inscriptions which still remain.

The sherds collected at various sites and which are presented below in chapter IV.2 fall into two main classes: (a) those from the Wādī as-Sirḥān which exhibit close connections with the pottery of the Transjordanian and Palestinian regions to the north, and (b) those from Taymā' and Dedan which are of hitherto unknown types and belong to a different, distinctively Arabian cultural milieu. Whether they have a relationship to the pottery of South Arabia remains for future determination. At any rate, the inscriptional evidence makes it abundantly clear that ancient Arabia did not dwell in cultural isolation. Possessing a distinctive culture of its own, that culture shows many evidences of having been interpenetrated by influences from the outside. The important role which Arabia played in the economic life of the ancient world brought it into close and constant contact with its neighbours.

During the periods when the caravan trade flourished, we may be sure that the oases of North Arabia supported a much larger population than they do today when they are no longer on one of the principal arteries of the world's trade. Yet these caravan cities have left no large *tells* such as one sees in other parts of the

Near East. The *tell* at ancient Dedan is no higher than that which marked the site of Ezion-geber, Solomon's seaport on the Gulf of ʿAqabah. At Madāʾin Ṣāliḥ (ancient Ḥegrā) we had difficulty finding any slight elevation which might have marked the site of the ancient city. Even at Taymāʾ, where great walls largely buried in sand are an impressive feature of the landscape, there remains nothing which can be called a *tell.* The reason for this absence of *tells* is probably that most of the buildings were of mud-brick which has crumbled into dust and been carried into the desert by the winds. Even where the constructions were of stone, the stones have been carried off and used in later rebuilding. We can only hope that there are some places where the drifting sand covered up objects of historical interest before they fell a prey to human vandals. It may be recalled that Jaussen and Savignac found a great many inscribed stones embedded in the walls of the houses of modern al-ʿUla. There can be little doubt that the site of ancient Dedan would yield much of interest to the archaeologist and historian, as would the site of ancient Taymāʾ. There is also a spot in al-Jawf, as noted above,[135] that would repay investigation.

Our hope is that the expedition which we carried out will open the way for archaeological research in Saʿudi Arabia. It noted some of the places where excavation should and could be undertaken, and learned the most feasible ways of getting at them. It also gained experience of the supply problems which an archaeological expedition would encounter. It is to be hoped that before many years have passed, an expedition undertaken in co-operation with scholars at Riyadh University will be possible.

A final note. It is not without interest to recall that our expedition marked the two hundredth anniversary of the first European scholarly expedition to Arabia, that of Carsten Niebuhr and his companions in 1762.[136]

135/See p. 17.

136/For a fascinating account of this expedition, see Thorkild Hansen, *Arabia Felix* (London, 1964).

II The Arabian Inscriptions

F.V.WINNETT

1 Introduction

The Old Arabian script was used in North Arabia from at least the end of the eighth century B.C.[1] to at least the fourth century A.D. During this long period the original form of the script underwent many modifications, and regional varieties of it developed. The inscriptions which we recorded in 1962 reflect only partially the complexity of this development. The earliest texts found by the expedition are those from Jabal Ghunaym near Taymā'. These have been labelled "Taymanite" since the type of script employed is found only in the Taymā' area.[2] Reasons are given below for dating them not later than the sixth century B.C. Three texts found at Sakākah in the Jawf area are written in a closely related, but not identical, script[3] and must be of approximately the same age. The script employed in some of the inscriptions from al-ʿUlā (Dedan) is also similar to Taymanite and may be equally early since it is inherently probable that if the art of writing was known at Taymā' in the sixth century B.C., it was also known at Dedan at the same time.

The later inscriptions are usually lumped together under the rubric "Thamudic." They still defy satisfactory classification. In my *Study of the Lihyanite and Thamudic Inscriptions*, published in 1937, I divided them into five types, labelled A, B, C, D, E, although I recognized that such a classification was neither complete nor entirely satisfactory.[4] It failed to account for all of the evidence in that many inscriptions either do not fall into any of the five classes proposed or exhibit characteristics of more than one group. Furthermore, no attempt was

1/See A. van den Branden, *Les Inscriptions dédanites* (Beyrouth, 1962), pp. 29–46. See below, p. 90.

2/For "Taymanite" as the gentilic form of "Taymā'," see Huber, *Journal*, p. 325 ("Un habitant de Teima s'appelle Teimâny"); Doughty, *Travels*, Index: "Teymâny, a man of Teyma," and Nab. TYMNY', "de Teima" (J. Cantineau, *Le Nabatéen*, II [Paris, 1932], p. 156). Cf. also Julius Lewy in *HUCA*, 19 (1945–6), p. 443, n. 179.

3/See below, "Inscriptions from the Jawf area" nos. 21–23 (pp. 60–1) and Pls. 1 and 3.

4/For criticisms of my classification, see G. Ryckmans in *Muséon*, 50 (1937), pp. 328–9; H. Grimme in *OLZ*, 41 (1958), cols. 350–2; R. Savignac in *RB*, 46 (1937), pp. 568–81; and E. Littmann, *TS*.

made to explain the relationship of the five scripts to one another. Van den Branden attempted to supply this deficiency by suggesting that we should think in terms of a single, primitive Thamudic script which tended to become more and more cursive.[5] He believes that about the first century A.D. it spread from the Taymā' area, where it originated, to Madā'in Ṣāliḥ in the Ḥijāz and to Jabal Serrā' in Najd, then in the third century A.D. spread over all North Arabia. The process of evolution was, however, not uniform in any area since some texts retained primitive alongside more evolved forms. In two areas, Taymā'-Dedan and Tabūk, the tendency to cursive affected certain letters more than elsewhere, resulting in the development of distinctive scripts in these areas.

Neat and attractive as van den Branden's theory is, it may be doubted if Thamudic research has yet reached the point where any convincing picture of the development of writing in North Arabia can be drawn.[6] In the present work the Thamudic texts are classified into three groups: Najdi (my former "Thamudic B"), Hijazi ("Thamudic C and D"), and Tabuki ("Thamudic E").[7]

The inscriptions given below are grouped according to the place where they were found, and each place has been provided with a historical introduction in the hope that their significance will thereby be more apparent.[8]

Little would be gained by attempting to give a complete list of all the signs occurring in early Arabian inscriptions since the value of some is still undetermined. It has seemed best, therefore, to restrict the Table of Scripts (Pl. 1) to the signs which occur in the texts here published. For the sake of convenience many of the signs are shown in one position only, but it should be remembered that they may revolve around the points of the compass.

5/*Les Inscriptions thamoudéennes* (Louvain, 1950).

6/For an incisive criticism of van den Branden's theory, see J. Ryckmans, "Aspects nouveaux du problème thamoudéen" (*Studia Islamica*, 5 [1956], pp. 5–17) and van den Branden's reply, "L'Unité de l'alphabet thamoudéen" (*Studia Islamica*, 6 [1957], pp. 5–27).

7/"Thamudic A" has been renamed "Taymanite."

8/The numbering used for Huber's texts is that employed by van den Branden in *Les Inscriptions thamoudéenes*.

2 Inscriptions from the Jawf Area

A/HISTORICAL BACKGROUND

The name al-Jawf, meaning "the cavity" or "basin," properly denotes the whole lower region of the Wādī as-Sirḥān. This regional name has, however, come to be applied to one of the oases in the basin, the one which was known to the ancient Assyrians as Adummatu and to the Hebrews as Dumah. The Assyrian records show that in the seventh century B.C. it was the principal Arab settlement in upper North Arabia for it was against it that Sennacherib struck when he attempted to bring the Arabs into submission. The oasis appears to have lain within the territory of the great Bedouin tribe of Qedar, for the king of Qedar appears in an inscription of Ashurbanipal in close association with the high preistess of Adummatu.[1]

The most interesting fact about Adummatu to be gleaned from the Assyrian records is that it was the seat of a series of North Arabian queens. Although the brief notices of Queens Zabibe, Samsi, and Iati'e do not definitely associate them with Adummatu, being content to call them "queens of Arabia," Queens Te'elḫunu and Tabua/Tarbua are so associated, making it probable that the other three resided there also.[2] Furthermore, the fact that Queen Te'elḫunu is called the priestess of the goddess Dilbat (i.e. Ishtar), who was worshipped

1/See *ANET*, p. 301. Although Ḫaza'il is called "king of the Arabs" rather than "king of Qedar," there is little doubt that he could have been so called since his son Iauta' is referred to as "king of Qedar" (see Luckenbill, *AR*, no. 869). For Sennacherib's attack on Adummatu, see *ANET*, p. 291; Luckenbill, *AR*, no. 518a; and T. Rosmarin, "Aribi und Arabien in den babylonisch-assyrischen Quellen" (*JSOR*, 16 [1932], pp. 29–37).

2/Julius Lewy (*HUCA*, 19 [1945–6], p. 421, n. 88) speaks of the queens mentioned in the Assyrian sources as "rulers of various Arab towns." For a discussion of them, see N. Abbot, "Pre-Islamic Arab Queens" (*AJSL*, 58 [1941], pp. 1–22). Zabibe appears in the annals of Tiglath-pileser III (744–27 B.C.), Samsi in the annals of Tiglath-pileser and Sargon II (721–05 B.C.), Iati'e in those of Sennacherib (704–681 B.C.), Te'elhunu in those of Ashurbanipal but she was a contemporary of Sennacherib, and Tabua/Tarbua in the annals of Esarhaddon and Ashurbanipal (668–33 B.C.).

locally under the name of ʿAtarsamain, suggests that all these queens were high-priestesses of this goddess. They seem to have exercised more than religious powers, however, for both Tiglath-pileser III (744–27 B.C.) and Sargon II (721–05), in referring to the tribute received from foreign rulers, put Queen Samsi on a par with Pir'u of Musru ("Pharaoh of Egypt") and It'amar the Sabaean. The exalted position held by these North Arabian queens can only be accounted for by the assumption that the cult of Ishtar-ʿAtarsamain enjoyed tremendous prestige and popularity in North Arabia at that time.[3] There can be no doubt that an important sanctuary of ʿAtarsamain once existed in Adummatu/al-Jawf. Esarhaddon (680–69 B.C.), in an attempt to win the goodwill of the Arabs, had a star of reddish gold, decorated with precious stones, made for the shrine.[4] The star was no doubt a symbol of the goddess herself.

Although the chief deity of Adummatu, and possibly of North Arabia generally, at that time was the goddess ʿAtarsamain, five other divinities appear in the list of Arab gods carried off from the oasis by Sennacherib (704–681 B.C.), viz., Dai, Nuhai, Ruldaiu, Abirillu, and Atarquruma. They doubtless had shrines of their own in the oasis, possibly within the temple complex of ʿAtarsamain. The inscriptions from North Arabia attest the persistence of the worship of some of these gods after the Assyrian period: how long after is as yet uncertain.[5]

Adummatu must have suffered severely in the attempts of the Assyrians to subdue the tribes of North Arabia. It may also have suffered again when Nebuchadrezzar, king of Babylon, smote Qedar and the kingdoms of Ḥaṣor (cf. Jer. 49:28–33 and possibly Isa. 21:13–17). But the blow was not mortal, as the Hebrew prophets expected it would be, for Qedar, and doubtless Adummatu as well, continued to flourish (cf. Isa. 42:11, 60:7). If the town of [*A*]*dummu* beseiged by Nabonidus' forces in his third year (*ca.* 552 B.C.)[6] is Adummatu,[7] it must have suffered once more. Whether the identification be correct or not, there can be no doubt that Adummatu was situated within the North Arabian territory occupied by Nabonidus.

Following the collapse of the Chaldaean empire in 539 B.C., Adummatu may have been occupied by Persian forces, although there is no reference to this in historical sources. Xenophon (*Cyropaedia*, vii.4.16) states that Cyrus subjugated

3/See *ANET*, p. 299. I. Rabinowitz (*JNES*, 15 [1956], p. 8) says that the expression "the confederation of (the worshippers of) Atarsamain" was used as a generic designation of the northern Arabs.

4/See *ANET*, p. 301.

5/See below, Thamudic inscriptions nos. 3, 21–23, 25 and the notes on them.

6/See *ANET*, p. 305.

7/W. F. Albright (*JRAS*, 1925, pp. 293–4) favours the identification. Sidney Smith (*Isaiah Chapters XL–LV* [Schweich Lectures, 1940; London, 1944], p. 37) thinks that some place in Edom is meant, but this seems less probable. See Dougherty, *Sealand*, p. 71, n. 225.

the Arabs before he attacked Babylon. Herodotus (iii.97), on the other hand, claims that "the Arabs were never reduced to the subjection of Persia," but sent to Cyrus an annual gift of 1000 talents of incense. Certainly many Arab chiefs do seem to have felt it wise to court the favour of the new master of the Near East. An inscription of Cyrus states that "all the kings of the West land living in tents brought their heavy tributes and kissed my feet in Babylon" (*ANET*, p. 316). There is no suggestion in all this of the establishment of Persian garrisons in Arabia. The reference to a *fḥt* ("satrap" or "governor") in an inscription (JS 349 lih.) at Dedan may indicate the presence of a Persian "resident" there, but the inscription is capable of other interpretations.[8]

Our discovery of a Minaean inscription in the neighbourhood of al-Jawf shows that the Minaean traders established in Dedan had relations with the oasis. By the first century A.D. it was in Nabataean hands as a Nabataean inscription from al-Jawf, dating from 44 A.D., testifies.[9] A three-line Nabataean inscription pointed out to us in one of the streets of al-Jawf, and a few Nabataean graffiti from nearby Jabal Abū al-Jays, also attest a period of Nabataean occupation.[10]

No Thamudic inscriptions were found at al-Jawf, nor is there any epigraphic evidence of the Assyrian or Chaldaean periods of occupation. The reason for this is not far to seek. There is no rocky outcrop in the oasis which might have served as writing material and attracted the engraving of inscriptions. The ancient history of Adummatu/al-Jawf can only be recovered by excavation.

At Sakākah, on the other hand, where there are rocky outcrops and ridges, twelve Thamudic inscriptions were found,[11] as well as one Nabataean[12] and a few Islamic Arabic, also one in a script which seems to be intermediate between Nabataean and Arabic.[13] Of the Thamudic texts found at Sakākah, nos. 21–23 are written in a script which closely resembles Taymanite[14] and which is presumably of much the same date. These three inscriptions are the earliest yet found in the whole Jawf area and may be accepted as evidence of the type of script which was used in ancient Adummatu. Numbers 3–5 and 25–27, found a few miles from Sakākah, are in the Najdi form of Thamudic. The remainder are in the Hijazi and Tabuki forms of Thamudic. The only other inscriptions (apart from Nabataean) found so far in the Jawf area are twenty Thamudic graffiti, of Hijazi type, found by Huber and Euting at aṭ-Ṭuwayr, about seven kilometres south of Sakākah, and published by van den Branden (*IT*, pp. 41–51). They contribute little to our knowledge of the ancient history of the area.

8/See pp. 115–7 and Dougherty, *Nab. and Bel.*, chap. xii: The Conquest of Arabia by Cyrus.
9/See J. Starcky, "Une inscription nabatéenne provenant du Djôf" (*RB*, 64 [1957], pp. 196–115).
10/See below, Inscriptions nabatéennes nos. 16, 17–21, pp. 144–6.
11/See below, nos. 12–23, pp. 77–81.
12/See below, no. 15, p. 144.
13/See p. 11 and Fig. 8.
14/See pp. 80–1 and the Table of Scripts, Pl. 1.

B/MINAEAN INSCRIPTIONS

Jabal Abū al-Jays, near al-Jawf[15] (*no. 1*)

1 Phot(ograph) W 4:13 and copy. Pl. 2.

m(ʿ)*ḏ bn mrḍ*(ʿ) …	*Muʿadh b. MRḌ*(ʿ) …
… *s bn m* …	… *S b. M* …

The form of the *ḏ*-sign indicates that the inscription is Minaean. The *ḏ* seems to have only one cross-bar, as sometimes in Minaean graffiti (cf. JS 52, 68, 79, 82, etc.). The location of the inscription – on a ledge of rock projecting into space – made it impossible to ascertain the exact form of some of the letters. The n. pr. MʿḎ occurs in *EDAr.* LXXI (min.). Five Minaean inscriptions have been found at Jabal Ramm, about twenty-five miles east of ʿAqaba,[16] but this is the first Minaean inscription to be found in the region of al-Jawf. G. Ryckmans has recently published fifty Minaean graffiti found by Philby and Bogue in the northern Ḥijāz.[17] Some of these had already been recorded by Doughty and by Jaussen and Savignac.

C/THAMUDIC INSCRIPTIONS

(*i*) *Al-Qalʿah*[18] (*nos. 1–11*)

1 Copy. H (Hijazi Thamudic). ↑ Pl. 3.

wʾn ks[*ṭ*] …	*And I am Kās*[*iṭ*] …

The name is probably to be restored as Kāsiṭ (common in Saf.; cf. *RNP*, I, 115, etc.) or as Kāsib (cf. JS 435 tham.).

2 Phot. R 101:27A and copy. H. ↓ Pl. 3.

ʿw bn rš	*ʿUwa b. Rashaʾ*
wdd fḥbb	*loves the mouth of Ḥabīb.*

For ʿW, see Littmann, Voc. – RŠ, cf. Ar. *rašaʾ*, "young gazelle." – *wdd f*: Jamme (*TS*, pp. 12, 45–6) rightly questions the interpretations of this expression which have been previously proposed ("grüsste" by Littmann, "salut à" by van den Branden, "love to" by myself) since the preposition *f* never has the meaning "to," in Classical Arabic at least. He would translate by "Love [is] in," but this sounds equally improbable. The presence of the *f* might possibly be explained

15/See p. 19.
16/See *RB*, 43 (1934), pp. 578–9 and 590–1.
17/"Inscriptions sud-arabes. Vingt-deuxième série" (*Muséon*, 78 [1965], pp. 215–28).
18/See p. 7 and Fig. 3.

by the fact that *wdd* means "to desire, wish for" as well as "to love," and that in Arabic the prep. *fī* is used after verbs signifying desire (cf. Wright, *Ar. Gram.*, II, p. 155D). I would suggest, however, that *f* = *fā*, accus. of *fam*, "mouth," and that *wdd f* be rendered "he loves the mouth of," i.e. "is fond of." Bedouin men are accustomed to greet one another with kisses on the cheeks and on the mouth.

3–7 Phot. R 101:12A–15A and copy. The rock bears several drawings of animals, men, and tribal marks (*wusūm*). Pls. 3 and 10.

3 N (Najdi Thamudic). ← Pls. 3 and 10.
hr(ḍ)w hb l'ff mḍ w'r
O Ruḍā, give to 'FF pain and disgrace.

hb, Impv. of *whb*, "to give"; cf. Hu. 74, 313, 763. – The n. pr. 'FF is new. For the 'alif-sign, see JS 325 tham. – *mḍ*, cf. Ar. *maḍḍ*, "pain, anguish." – *'r*, cf. Ar. *'ār*, "shame, disgrace." – It is generally assumed that RḌW was a goddess, the principal basis for this being the drawing of a female figure which accompanies the Safaitic inscription, *CIS*, v, 4351. But several deities are mentioned in the inscription and it is by no means certain that the female figure represents RḌW.[19] Drawings of a naked female with arms upraised, holding her hair, appear also in *CIS*, v, 286, 1259, 3146, Littmann, *Saf. Insc.*, nos. 142–3 and 403–4. But, as Miss Höfner[20] says, "Die zu den Zeichnungen gehörigen Texte geben keine sicheren Anhaltspunkte, welche Gottheit gemeint sein könnte, ja, ob die Gestalt überhaupt eine Gottheit sein soll." The drawings may be merely an expression of male interest in the female figure.

The fact that at Palmyra the gods Azizu and Arṣu represented the morning and evening star respectively[21] favours the view that in Thamudic RḌW was a god and represented the evening star.[22] The Safaitic Arabs worshipped the god under two aspects, RḌW and RḌY, possibly the evening and morning stars respectively.[23] Littmann (*TS*, pp. 106–7) suggested that RḌW may have been

19/Van den Branden (*HT*, p. 113) asserts that the verb associated with Ruḍā is always in the feminine form, indicating that Ruḍā is feminine. The only example he adduces is *CIS*, v, 5011: *'wdt rḍw* but *'wdt* may be the noun *'uwādah*, "return," rather than a verb, the inscription meaning "(Grant) a (safe) return, Ruḍā" (from a raid or journey about to be undertaken). In the majority of instances the verb associated with RḌW is *s'd*, *'wr*, or *flt*, all being imperatives. But since Safaitic writing does not differentiate between masc. and fem. sing. imperatives, it is impossible to determine the gender of RḌW from the verb used with it.

20/In Haussig, *WM*, I, pp. 463–4.

21/See Sourdel, *Cultes*, pp. 74–5, and Starcky, *Palmyr.*, *Nab. et Arabes*, pp. 212, 225–6.

22/See the Safaitic text, *CIS*, v, 1077, which invokes RḌW and is engraved around the figure of a star.

23/As further evidence that RḌW is feminine, vdB (*HT*, p. 112, n. 430) refers to *CIS*, v, Pl. XCVI, where Dunand 1339a (= *CIS*, v 286) is accompanied by the figure of a woman, but the divine name in this case is RḌY.

masculine and RḌY feminine. A similar pair of deities appears in Lihyanite, han-'Aktab (masc.) and ha-Kutbay (fem.).[24]

G. Ryckmans (*RNP*, I, 32), followed by van den Branden (*IT*, p. 13), regards the form of the name RḌW as evidence that it was of Nabataean origin, but he (or she) appears in Najdi Thamudic texts which seem to antedate the Nabataean period. J. Ryckmans[25] and Borger[26] even find a reference to her in the list of Arabian gods carried off from Adummatu by Sennacherib (704–681 B.C.)[27] where they think the name *Ruldaiu* is a corruption of Ruḍā. Whatever his (or her) origin may have been, RḌW became one of the most popular deities in North Arabia. It should be observed, however, that he (or she) appears only in three early texts from Sakākah (see nos. 21–23 below), in Thamudic texts of the Najdi type, and in Safaitic; there is no mention of him (or her) in other types of Thamudic or in South Arabic. In no. 23 below, RḌW is mentioned in association with NHY and ʿTRSM, the latter being another name for the evening star.

4 N. ← Pls. 3 and 10.

lʿkbl — *By ʿAkabʾil.*

The name is new, but ʿKBT occurs in JS 175 tham. and ʿKBN in JS 378 and 579 tham.

5 N. ← Pls. 3 and 10.

. . ldd lmʿ — *Ludād polished* (?).

There may be one or two letters before *ldd*, making the interpretation uncertain. The n. pr. LDD occurs in Sab. (cf. *RNP*, II, 79) and Saf. (DM 482 which *CIS*, V, 482 emends to L(')DD). – *lmʿ*, cf. Ar. *lamaʿa*, "to shine, sparkle," II: "to polish, burnish."

6 H. ← Pls. 3 and 10.

zn nsr — *This is Nasr.*

For NSR, cf. *RNP*, I, 41; II, 95; and *HTIJ*, no. 121.

7 H. ← Pls. 3 and 10.

ṯry — *Thuray.*

This name occurs several times in Saf. (cf. *RNP*, I, 217; II, 134).

24/See J. Strugnell, "The Nabataean Goddess 'Al-Kutba' and Her Sanctuaries" (*BASOR*, no. 156 [1959], pp. 29–36); W. F. Albright, "Some Notes on the Nabataean Goddess 'Al-Kutba' and Related Matters" (*ibid.*, pp. 37–8); J. T. Milik and J. Teixidor, "New Evidence on the North-Arabic Diety Aktab-Kutba' " (*ibid.*, no. 163 [1961], pp. 22–25).

25/"Aspects nouveaux du problème thamoudéen" (*Studia Islamica*, 5 [1956], p. 5, n. 2).

26/*Orientalia*, 26 (1957), p. 10. See also S. Moscati, *An Introduction to the Comparative Grammar of the Semitic Languages* (Wiesbaden, 1964), p. 28.

27/See *ANET*, p. 291. If Ryckmans and Borger are correct, RḌW should be vocalized as Ruḍā, as Albright (in the *Haupt Anniversary Volume* [Baltimore, 1926], p. 147, n. 4) suggested.

8–11 Phot. R 101:18A, 19A, 23A, 24A and copies. Nabataean inscriptions nos. 1–5 are above the Thamudic.

8 H. ↓ Pls. 3 and 10.

wdd frḫm *He loves the mouth of Rakhīm.*

For *wdd f*, see no. 2. – RḪM (cf. Ar. *raḫīm*, "soft, gentle") is new but RḪMN and RḪMT occur in *CIS*, v, 1223 and 1812.

9 T (Tabuki Thamudic). ↓ To the left of no. 8. Pls. 3 and 10.

l'nmr bn ʿfr *By 'Anmar b. ʿIfr.*

For 'NMR, see J. Ryckmans in *BOr*, 17 (1960), p. 203b. – ʿFR is found in Saf. (L 1104); ʿFRW in Tham. (*HTIJ*, no. 137).

10 To the left of no. 8. Pls. 3 and 10.

kfngny ?? *?*
lrnfbbtr . . . . ?? *?*

I am unable to offer any certain reading or interpretation of this text.

11 T. Circular direction, beginning at the lower right. Below no. 10. Pls. 3 and 10.

lyʿly bn rš ḏ'l ḥṣd wwṯm ʿl hn' wʿr ṯdy

By Yaʿlay b. Rasha' of the tribe of Ḥaṣad. And he mourned for Hānī' and smote (the) breast.

RŠ, see no. 1. – The tribe of ḤṢD is mentioned here for the first time. – The expression *wṯm ʿl* occurs in *HTIJ*, no. 494, where Harding renders it by "he was sad on account of." The use of *waṯama* in Cl. Ar. with the meaning "pound, paw the ground, wound" (Hava) suggests that in Tham. it meant "to give vent to grief in a frenzied manner." – *ṯdy* (Ar. *ṯady*) usually denotes the female breast, and *ṯundu'ah* (or *ṯunduwah*) the male breast, but *ṯady* is sometimes used for the latter (see Lane, p. 333). – *ʿr*, cf. Ar. *ʿarā*, "to smite."

(*ii*) *Sakākah* (*nos. 12–23*)

12–18 On the summit of a ridge west of the stepped well.[28]

12 Phot. R 2:15 and copy. T. Written in an S-direction, beginning at the upper left. Nabataean inscription no. 15 is to the left; see p. 12. Pls. 3 and 11.

lydʿ bn whb wtšwq l'bh

By Yadaʿ b. Wahb. And he longed for his father.

For other occurrences of *tšwq* in Tham., see vdB, *IT*, p. 518.

13 Phot. W 2:12 and copy. T. → To the right of no. 12. Pls. 3 and 11.

ḏkrt'lt kll s(ṯ)rt *May 'Allāt remember every wish!*

28/See p. 11.

For *ḏkrt'lt* (elsewhere without 'alif), see my *Study*, pp. 6 and 42, and vdB, *IT*, p. 512. G. Ryckmans (*RNP*, I, 3; *Religions*, p. 15; and commentary on *CIS*, V, 8) vocalizes the name as *'Ilat* or *Lāt*, but Greek transcriptions of such names as WHBLT, SʿD'LT, ʿBDLT, and TYMLT (see *RNP*, I, pp. 225, 240, 241, and 252) show that in Syria the name of the goddess was sometimes pronounced *'Allāt* (probably under the influence of Syr. *'allāhᵉtā*, "the goddess"), sometimes as *'Ilat*, the latter being the original Arabian form. The form *'Allāt* is usually regarded as a contraction of *al-'ilāhat*, "the goddess." An objection to this theory is that in pre-Islamic times the definite article throughout the greater part of Central and North Arabia was *h*, not *'l*. However, *'l* does occur sporadically and in such a manner as to suggest that it may have been prevalent in the region later controlled by the Nabataeans. It may have been from an Arab of this region that Herodotus (III, 3) got the form *'Alilat*. Under Syrian influence this was later modified to *'Allāt*. In the present work I have chosen to retain this familiar form.

The identity of 'Allāt/'Ilat has been a matter of debate. G. Ryckmans (*Religions*, p. 15), Dussaud, (*Pénétration*, p. 46), and Starcky (*Palmyr., Nab. et Arabes*, p. 212) would identify her with the planet Venus. Van den Branden (*HT*, pp. 91–2) agrees with Grimme and Nielsen in identifying her with the sun. In my article, "The Daughters of Allah" (*The Moslem World*, 30 [1940], pp. 12–15), I suggested an identification with the moon. However, if she was the feminine counterpart of the primitive Semitic god, 'Il, as Nielsen suggested, it is unlikely that she was identified originally with any celestial luminary. Since the supreme god is usually a sky-god to begin with, 'Ilat will originally have been a sky-goddess, a view which receives support from Herodotus' identification of her with Urania (I, 131). Later she seems to have been regarded as the great Mother-goddess (see Grohmann, *Arabien*, p. 82). For a summary of the available evidence and the varying interpretations of it, see M. Höfner in Haussig, *WM*, I, pp. 422–4 and 473–4.

sṭrt: the second sign has four lateral strokes in the hand-copy, thus resembling Lih. *ṭ*. The last sign is not visible on the photograph; cf. Ar. *suṭrah*, "wish, desire."

14 Phot. W 2:12 and copy. T. → Below no. 13. Pls. 3 and 11.

ḏkr'lh slm — *May 'Allāh remember Sālim.*

This is the only occurrence of *ḏkr'lh*. For references to 'Allāh in Thamudic, see vdB, *IT*, pp. 11, 520; for references in Safaitic, see *WSIJ*, no. 279. See also my article, "Allah before Islam" (*The Moslem World*, 28 [1938], pp. 239–48; Sourdel, *Cultes*, pp. 87–8; Grohmann, *Arabien*, pp. 87–8; Starcky, *Palmyr., Nab. et Arabes*, pp. 203–5; vdB, *HT*, pp. 89–90, and M. Höfner in Haussig, *WM*, I, pp. 420–2.

15 Phot. W 2:15 and copy. H. → To the left of no. 12. Pls. 3 and 11.

l'g' bn (d)yrt bn ḥmlt

By 'Aga' b. Dayrat b. Ḥāmilat.

'G' occurs in Hu. 423, 733, 747. – For DYRT, see *WSIJ*, nos. 244, 251. – For ḤMLT, see *RNP*, I, 94.

16 Phot. W 2:12 and copy. T. ← Below no. 14. On the edge of the rock bearing nos. 13–15. Pls. 3 and 11.

(l)my . . . . . w'frn bn sy

(By) MY . . . . . and 'FRN b. Siyy.

'FRN is new but 'FR occurs in no. 9. – For SY, cf. *WSIJ*, nos. 9, 785. VdB (*IT*, p 538) wrongly gives it as occurring in Hu. 623.

17 Phot. W 2:12 and copy. T. → Immediately below no. 16. Pls. 3 and 11.

lslm bn snh wnṯl bmṯġr

By Sālim b. Sanih. And he emptied (his quiver) in the gate (?).

The n. pr. SNH is new; cf. Ar. *sanih*, "aged." – *nṯl*, cf. Ar. *naṯala*, "to empty (a quiver), cleanse (a well), take off (a coat of mail)" (Hava). – *mṯġr*, cf. Ar. *ṯuġrah*, "gap, opening, breach," and Heb. *ša'ar*, "gate."

18 Phot. W 2:17 and copy. T. Somewhat circular direction, beginning at the lower left. Below no. 15. Pl. 3.

. . . 'b ḏ'l bdn wtšwq lqsy

. . . 'B of the tribe of Badan. And he longed for Qasī.

Two Saf. inscriptions (*WSIJ*, nos. 87 and 237) are by members of the tribe of Badan. The Safaitic script seems to be merely a northerly extension of the Tabuki Thamudic script in which this inscription is written. – For QSY, see *CIS*, v, 172, etc.

19–20

19 Phot. W 2:18 and copy. T. Spiral direction, beginning at the left with the middle line. Pls. 3 and 11.

ġwṯ bn (z)dl tšwq 'l z'm b[n] (t)'m t(l).ywš . . . t wrt 'lḫldt fwrṭt

Ghuwayth b. Zayd'il. He longed for Za'm b. Ta'm ...

I am unable to offer a satisfactory interpretation of this inscription. The last word is probably *wrṭt* (Ar. *warṭah*, "difficult situation, trouble," Wehr). For the two different forms of *w* in the same inscription, see no. 48a and vdB, *IT*, p. 26. – *ḫldt* could be either a n. pr. (cf. *CIS*, v, 1344, 2417, L 138), a substantive (Ar. *khiladah*, "earrings, bracelets," Salmoné), or a verb (Ar. *ḫalada*, "to be everlasting, remain forever").

20 Phot. W 2:20 and copy. T. ⇆ Pl. 3.

lslm b[n] ... *By Sālim b. ...*
... bn (')t . . . *. . . T b. ...*

For the form of the *m*, see nos. 14 and 17.

21–23 Three inscriptions in the Jawfian script.[29]

21 Phot. W 2:24, 25 and copy. ← Pls. 3 and 12.

hrḍw s'lt klb bz

O Ruḍā, the petition of Kalb is here.

s'lt, cf. Ar. *su'lah*, "petition, request." – *bz*, cf. JS 517 (in the Taymā' script) *bḏh* in JS 279 lih., and Heb. *bāzeh* (see vdB, *IT*, p. 36). In this and the two following inscriptions the *h* is tailless, as frequently in Taymanite.

22 Phot. W 2:24, 25 and copy. Jawfian script. ← Below no. 21. Pls. 3 and 12.

hrḍw wdd 'wṣ 'wḏ 'h

O Ruḍā, love (from) 'Uwayṣ. (Grant) protection. He is plague-stricken.

For 'WṢ, cf. 'BD'WṢ in JS 272 lih. – *'wḏ* could be either Impv. II, *'awwiḏ*, "protect," or the subst. *'awaḏ*, "place of refuge, protection." – *'h*, cf. Ar. *'āha*, *'īha*, "to be plague-stricken," *'āhah*, "disease."

23 Phot. W 2:22 and copy. Jawfian script. ← To the right of nos. 21 and 22. Pls. 3 and 12.

hrḍw wnhy w'trsm s'dn 'l wddy

O Ruḍā and Nuhai and 'Attarsam, help me in the matter of my love.

A word-divider is employed between the divine names. – *s'dn* (Ar. *sā'idni*, "help me") occurs frequently in Tham. (see vdB, *IT*, p. 516). – Hu. 736 is very similar: *hrḍw s'(d)n 'l wddy*. The last word recurs in JS 276 tham. where it appears to be a n. pr. since it is preceded by *nm*. It is improbable that it is such in the present inscription or in Hu. 736 since it is highly unlikely that inscriptions for help against an individual named WDDY would be engraved at two widely separated spots, one at Sakākah, the other in the Jabal Misma' region southeast of Taymā'. *wddy* is, therefore, to be explained from Ar. *wadād*, *widād*, *wudād*, "love." – The god NHY is frequently invoked in Thamudic inscriptions of the Najdi type (see vdB, *IT*, p. 536, and *HT*, pp. 104–6; also M. Höfner in Haussig, *WM*, I, pp. 456–7). He also appears in three Safaitic inscriptions: *CIS*, v, 3879, L 317, 1067 (see Littmann, *TS*, pp. 141–2). A *Nu-ḫa-a-a* appears in the list of Arabian gods

29/See p. 69.

carried off from Adummatu by Sennacherib of Assyria (704–681 B.C.).[30] Since the *ḫ* in the name could represent various Arabic laryngeals,[31] it is probable that the reference is to NHY, to be vocalized, therefore, as *Nuhai* (cf. Ar. *nuh^{an}*, "intelligence, mind"). NHY may have been a name of the Sun-god; cf. Hu. 327: *bnhy (š)msʿly nm yhṯ(ʿ)*, "By Nuhai, exalted Sun! By Yahthiʿ." VdB (*IT*, p. 157) translates "Par Nahy. Šamsʿalay à Yahṯiʿ," but a n. pr. Šamsʿalay is not met with elsewhere.

ʿTRSM is a contraction of ʿṮTRSMN,[32] " ʿAthtar of the heavens," ʿAthtar being the South Arabian form of Ishtar but conceived as masculine. In Assyrian the name of this Arabian divinity appears, rather oddly, in an Aramaic form, *Atarsamain* (cf. *ANET*, pp. 291 and 299; also Luckenbill, *AR*, II, no. 869). Whether the final *-sm* in the Arabic spelling of the name is to be vocalized as *-sam* and regarded as a contraction of Aram. *samain* or to be read as Ar. *samāʾ*, "heavens," is uncertain since it is not yet clear how the ending *-āʾ* was represented in ancient Arabian writing. The gender of ʿTRSM is also uncertain. Since ʿAthtar was a god in South Arabia, it is possible that among the northern Arabs who employed the Najdi type of Thamudic script and who alone invoke ʿTRSM in their inscriptions, he retained the same gender.[33] It seems more likely, however, that ʿTRSM was a goddess, as she certainly was in the oasis of Adummatu (cf. *ANET*, p. 301).[34]

(iii) Al-Madarah, south of Qārah[35] *(no. 24)*

24 Phot. W 3:8 and copy. → On a sloping pillar of rock. Pls. 4 and 13.

bddlld ?

For a somewhat similar inscription, *ddlldd*, see JS 10, 155 and Ph. 247e. Van den Branden (*IT*, p. 427, and *TTP*, II, pp. xxix–xxx) has suggested that the inscription is to be read in two different directions: *ddl* ←→ *ldd*, "A Dâd." The suggestion is ingenious and may be correct, although it does not seem to solve the problem presented by the inscription before us. See also *ddʿldd* (JS 697).

30/See *ANET*, p. 291.

31/See W. F. Albright in *BASOR*, no. 66 (1937), p. 31, and R. Borger, "Assyriologische und altarabistiche Miszellen" (*Orientalia*, 26 [1957], pp. 8–11). For the representation of *h* by *ḫ* in Neo-Assyrian, see W. von Soden, *Grundriss der akkadischen Grammatik* (Rome, 1952), 24a, 25a.

32/Van den Branden (*IT*, p. 13) regards JS 137 as providing an exception to the rule that the name is always contracted, but on p. 329 he correctly reads ʿTRSM. The next element which he reads as *wdd* is really *fhwdd* (hence: "O ʿAttarsam and O Wadd").

33/Van den Branden (*HT*, pp. 109–10) regards ʿTRSM as masculine. See also M. Höfner in Haussig, *WM*, I, pp. 427–8.

34/For her priestesses, see pp. 71–2.

35/See p. 12.

(*iv*) *5 km southwest of Sakākah, on the road to al-Jawf*[36] (*nos. 25–48*)

25 Phot. R 102:8 and copy. N. ⇆ Pls. 4 and 13.

hrḍw bk 'lr(h)w — *O Ruḍā, through thee (comes) tranquillity.*

wdd 'ty bn nṯ nb — *Love from 'Atay b. Nathth. He is thirsty (?).*

L. 2 is in a smaller hand. The definite article *'l* occurs in no. 19 also. – *rhw*, cf. Ar. *rahw*, "tranquillity, calm." – 'TY is found in Saf. (cf. *RNP*, I, 172, and *CIS*, v, 100). – *NṮ* occurs in Saf. (*CIS*, v, 1357, 1419, etc.). – *nb* may be a dialectical form of *lāba*, "to thirst."

26 Phot. R 102:8 and copy. N. ← Below no. 25. Pls. 4 and 13.

nm 'gg — *By 'Aggāg.*

The inscription is accompanied by a very good drawing of a lion.[37] There may be some connection between the drawing and the fact that the n. pr. 'Aggāg is derived from a root meaning "to roar." Apart from no. 27, the only other occurrence of the name is in JS 486: *nm 'gg hrhwy*, "By 'Aggāg the Edessene" (?) (cf. ar-Ruhā', the Ar. name of the city of Urfa, Gr. Edessa). – *nm* is the Najdi equivalent of Taymanite *lm*[38] (see my *Study*, pp. 24, 28–9; Littmann, *TS*, p. 33; and vdB, *IT*, pp. 41 and 515). The use of the prep. *l* before 'GG in no. 27 might seem to support the view of Jamme (*TS*, p. 44) that *nm* is not a prep. but a verb (either *namma*, "to calumniate, slander," or *nāma*, "to sleep") or, in some instances, a n. pr. Against this is the fact that in the inscriptions the verb seldom comes first, although a few cases do occur; e.g., see nos. 60 and 63.

27 Phot. W 3:18 and copy. N. ← Pls. 4 and 13.

l'gg — *By 'Aggāg.*

The inscription is accompanied by a very good drawing of a mountain goat (*wa'l*). – Here the author employs the preposition *l* rather than *nm* as in no. 26. Some Najdi Thamudic inscriptions are introduced by *nm*, others by *l* (see my *Study*, p. 29).

28 H. Copy. ← Pl. 4.

... (*w*)*d ḥrg* — *... Love (?) from ḤRG.*

VdB (*IT*, p. 427) reads ḤRG in JS 181 tham.

29 Phot. W 3:15 and copy. H. → Pls. 4 and 13.

wdd (r)w(ḥ) — *Love from Rawāḥ (?).*

The rock bears drawings of animals and of a bulky figure wearing a fringed skirt or mantle.

36/See p. 13.

37/See p. 13.

38/For *lm*, see below, Taymanite inscription no. 2.

30 Phot. R 102:12. T. → Pls. 4 and 14.

lslm bn ʿbd — *By Sālim b. ʿAbd.*

31 Phot. R 102:12. T. ← Below no. 30. Pls. 4 and 14.

lʾmt bn mlk — *By ʾAmat b. Mālik.*

For other occurrences of ʾMT in Tham., see vdB, *IT*, p. 520.

32 Phot. R 102:12. T. ← Below no. 31. Pls. 4 and 14.

lwʿd — *By Wāʿid.*

WʿD occurs in Saf. (cf. *RNP*, I, 80). To the left of the inscription is the drawing of an insect (beetle?) attacking a rectangular-shaped object.

33 Copy. T. The lower and middle lines read l. to r., the top line r. to l. It begins with the lower line. Pl. 4.

wdd fwʿd wtšwq lzd

He loves the mouth of Wāʿid, and he longs for Zayd.

For the seven parallel lines accompanying the inscription, see M. Höfner in Haussig, *WM*, I, p. 444.

34a Copy. H. → Begins with lower line. Pl. 4.

sqmdd — *And this is Badan.*

wzn bdn — *He is lovesick.*

sqmdd occurs in Hu. 441, 772, and JS 561. Albright (*BASOR*, no. 66 [1937], p. 31) suggested that it was a proper name composed of the *safel* of *qwm* + *Dād*, meaning "Dād (= Adād) has raised." G. Ryckmans (*Notes épig.*, p. 330) objected to equating *dd* with *Adād* on the ground that *dd* never has that meaning in South Arabian names. Littmann (*TS*, p. 49, no. 36) regards the form either as a n. pr. Saqīmdad or as a verb meaning "he is suffering from worms" (cf. Ar. *dūd*, "worms"). Van den Branden renders it by "Dâd est malade." Although DD does occur as a n. pr. in Sab., Tham., and Saf. (cf. *RNP*, I, 65; II, 44), it seems unlikely that an individual named Dād was the only one who advertised the fact that he was sick. Since so many of the inscriptions have an erotic character, the interpretation which I proposed in my *Study*, p. 23, and defended in my *Notes*, p. 305, still seems the most probable. In Semitic the root *dd* expresses the idea of "love"; cf. Ak. *dād*, "love, loved one," Heb. *dôdîm*, "love," *dûdāʾîm*, "mandrake, love-apple," Syr. *dād*, "friend, loved one." It seems unlikely that the lowest line is by the same hand as the other two lines since the *n* has a different form.

34b Copy. H. → Pl. 4.

ʾn rḥl — *I am Raḥḥāl (?).*

RḤL occurs in Saf. (*CIS*, V, 3519).

35 Copy. H. → Pl. 4.

ḫbbt *Khubaybat.*

ḪBBT occurs elsewhere in Tham. (cf. *HTIJ*, nos. 50, 324, 440).

36 Phot. R 102:17 and copy. H. ↓ Pls. 4 and 12.

wdd fḫrm *He loves the mouth of Khuraym.*
w'n kny *And I am KNY.*

ḪRM occurs frequently in Tham. (see *HTIJ*, pp. 22 and 52), also in Lih. (JS 46) and in Saf. (cf. *RNP*, I, 106). – KNY is new.

37 Phot. R 102:17 and copy. H. ↓ To the right of no. 36. Pls. 4 and 12.

...frš ... *... FRŠ ...*

The name is new; cf. Ar. *firāš*, "blanket." The inscription is accompanied by the drawing of a hand and forearm, with the letter *w* beside it (see no. 56 and JS 50 and 610 tham.). JS (*Mission*, I, p. 122) suggest that the representation of a hand, often found with inscriptions, was designed to ward off evil.[39] See also Haussig, *WM*, p. 443, and Wehr: *ḫumaisah* (p. 262).

38 Phot. R 102:17 and copy. H. ↓ To the right of no. 37. Pls. 4 and 12.

wlʿbš *And by ʿBŠ.*

The name is new; cf. Saf. and Nab. ʿBŠT.

39a Phot. R 102:16 and copy. T. ↓↑↓ Pls. 5 and 14.

lʿlqmt wtšwq 'l . . r ftšwq 'l ḫff

By ʿAlqamat. And he longed for . . R and he longed for Khufāf.

ʿLQMT: cf. the name of the famous Jāhilīyya poet ʿAlqamah b. ʿAbadah and Ar. *ʿalqamah*, "bitterness." – ŠKR occurs in SAr. and Lih. (cf. *RNP*, I, 209). – ḪFF does not appear elsewhere in the inscriptions but is found in later Arabic in the forms Khufāf and Khafīf (cf. *RNP*, I, 105).

39b *... d'l* *... D'L.*

39c Illegible. Above are four circles.

40 Phot. R 102:16 and copy. T. ↑↓ Pls. 5 and 14.

lẓʿn wtšwq 'l ḥgy

By Ẓāʿin. And he longed for Ḥaggay.

This inscription shows the form of *ẓ* in the Tabuki type of Thamudic. ẒʿN is common in Saf. (cf. *RNP*, I, 110; II, 67; and *WSIJ*, p. 177). ḤGY is found in Minaean (cf. *RNP*, I, 88) and in Saf. (L 615 and *CIS*, V, 2831). The latter text is by Ḥaggay b. Ẓā(ʿ)in.

39/See also M. Höfner in Haussig, *WM*, I, p. 443, no. 12.

41 Copy. T. → Pl. 4.

lʿbr bn ḫld wglṭ

By ʿAbr b. Khālid. And he shaved (his head).

ʿBR is new. – *glṭ*, cf. Ar. *galaṭa*, "to shave (the head)." Since the root *wlṭ* does not occur, the sign composed of two concentric circles must here have the value *g* as in JS 96 and 207 tham., but in no. 19 above it has the value *w*.

42 Copy. T. → Pl. 4.

lgrm bn ġr (w)mrṭ

By Garm b. Ghayr. And he plucked out (his) hair.

For GRM, cf. *RNP*, I, 63. – ĠR (Ghayr) is common in Saf. – *mrṭ*, cf. Ar. *maraṭa*, "to pluck out hair."

43 Phot. R 102:18. H. ↓ Pls. 5 and 14.

(a) *r' bmwg*
(b) *r' bn mwg* *R' b. Mawwāg.*

(b) seems to be a correction of (a). In (a) the *n* of *bn* was omitted. In (b) *r* has the form of a straight line. It is unlikely that (b) is to be read *l'bn mwg* since I know of only one instance (in an unpublished text) where "son" is expressed by *'bn*. – The name R' is new. – MWG may occur in Hu. I.R. 22 (see vdB, *IT*, p. 117); cf. Ar. *mawwāg*, "agitated, rolling."

44 Phot. R 102:18 H. ↓ Pls. 5 and 14.

kd qf šwr

KD followed (the tracks of) Shawir.

KD occurs in Saf. (WH 1481, etc., unpublished). – *qf*, cf. Ar. *qafā*, "to follow." – For ŠWR, cf. *RNP*, I, 207.

45 Phot. R 102:19. T. → Pls. 5 and 14.

lškyt hbkrtn

The two young she-camels are by Shakīyat.

The name is new; cf. Ar. *shakīya*, "complaint." A drawing of two camels accompanies the inscription.

46 Phot. R 102:20. T. ↑↓ Pls. 5 and 15.

lʿ(ṣ) bn mrwḏ srṭ *Laʿ(iṣ) b. MRWḎ drew (them).*

The inscription is accompanied by several drawings. – LʿṢ occurs in Saf. (cf. *RNP*, I, 133, II, 00). Possibly the name should read as L'T (cf. *RNP*, I, 302). – MRWḎ is new; cf. Ar. *rāḏa*, "to ramble about." – *srṭ*, cf. Syr. *sᵉraṭ*, "to scratch, write, draw," and Ar. *saṭara*, "to write, record, draw up, compose."

47 Phot. R 102:21. T. ← Pls. 5 and 15.

lzd bn mlk *By Zayd b. Mālik.*

48a Phot. R 102:22. T. ↓↓↓ Pls. 5 and 15.

(i) *lʿmrt ḏlʾ* (*h*)*g*

(ii) *lʿmr*(*t*)

(iii) *lʿmrt ḏʾhl gf*(*f*) (*wš*)*wq*

By ʿAmirat of the tribe of Gaf(*īf*). (*And*) *he was filled with longing.*

These texts seem to represent three different attempts by the author to engrave an inscription. The first was marred by the misspelling of *ʾhl*; the second was abandoned after making one stroke of the *t*; the third was carried to completion. – *ḏʾhl* occurs here for the first time in Tham.; Saf. employs *ḏʾl*. – For GFF, cf. *RNP*, I, 63. For the g-sign, see no. 85. (*wš*)*wq*: For the omission of the cross-bar of *w*, see no. 19 and Dedanite and Lihyanite inscription no. 8. *šwq* seems to be the passive of *šāqa*, II.

48b *zbn* *Zaban.*

ZBN occurs in Saf.; cf. *CIS*, v, 165, etc.

(*v*) *7 km southwest of Sakākah, on the road to al-Jawf*[40] (*nos. 49–56*)

49–53 Phot. W 3:23.

49 + 50 H. ↓ To the right in the photograph. Pls. 6 and 16.

ḥslt wdd fgl *ḤSLT loves the mouth of Gall.*

ḤSLT is new, although ḤSL occurs in Saf. (cf. *RNP*, I, 96). Possibly ḤBLT (Ḥablat) should be read (cf. JS 28 tham.). – GL: the form of the *g* is unusual; cf. no. 47. GL occurs in Saf. (cf. WH 806, 1489, etc., unpublished).

51 Copy. H. ↓ Pls. 6 and 16.

srrt (*bn*) *qḥf w*(*ʾs*)*f*

SRRT b. QḤF. And he was sad (*?*).

SRRT is new; cf. Ar. *sarīrah*, "secret, inner self," and the n. pr. Surūr. – QḤF is also new; cf. Ar. *qāḥif*, "rapid, impetuous." – *ʾsf*, cf. Ar. *ʾasifa*, "to be sad."

52 Copy. H. ↓ Pls. 6 and 16.

lšwql (*bn*) *mʿ* . . . *By Shawqʾil* (*b.*) *Mʿ* . . .

ŠWQL may occur in JS 477 tham.

53a Copy. H. ↓ Pls. 6 and 16.

lbsrq b(*n*) *.lm* . . . *By Bi-Sirq*(*?*) *b. .LM* . . .

BSRQ occurs in Hu. 171 (see vdB, *IT*, p. 103).

40/See p. 13.

53b Copy. The inscription is illegible except for the first two letters: *yš*.

54 Phot. W 3:20. H. ↓ Pl. 5.

wdd fyšb — *He loves the mouth of Yashibb.*

YŠB occurs as the name of an ethnic group in Sab. (cf. *RNP*, I, 205 = 401). Cf. also *TTP*, I, p. 30. Possibly ʿŠB (which is found in Saf., e.g. *CIS*, V, 310) should be read.

55 Phot. R 102:23. T. Circular, beginning at the top left. Pls. 6 and 15.

lrqm bn ḥmz wrʿy

By RQM b. ḤMZ. And he shepherded (the flock).

RQM is new; cf. Ar. *raqim*, "misfortune, calamity." – ḤMZ is also new, but ḤMZN occurs in Saf. and Tham.

56 Phot. R 102:24. H. ↓ Pls. 6 and 16.

zn lḥy mḥb ... — *This is Luḥayy, the lover of ...*

For the pattern of the inscription, see JS 185, 204, 606, etc. For the significance of the hand on either side of *mḥb*, see no. 37.

3 Inscriptions from the Taymā' Area

A/HISTORICAL BACKGROUND

The presence at Taymā' of the great well called al-Haddāj[1] makes it highly probable that human occupation of the oasis dates back to a very remote period. The earliest literary reference to Taymā' is found in an inscription of the Assyrian king, Tiglath-pileser III (747–27 B.C.), who claims to have received tribute from it as well as from several other Arabian oases.[2] The Hebrews knew of its existence, but the five biblical references to Taymā' (Gen. 25:15 = I Chron. 1:30; Isa. 21:14; Jer 23:23; Job 6:19) do not seem to carry us back beyond the sixth century B.C. In spite of the paucity of references to it in the records of surrounding nations, Taymā' must always have been an important station on the caravan routes leading from South and Central Arabia to al-Jawf and thence along the Wādī as-Sirḥān to Syria.[3] Here caravans could rest and restock with provisions and water before commencing the next stage of their long journey. However, it was not until the sixth century that Taymā' attained to a more important role. About the year 552 B.C. Nabonidus, king of Babylonia (555–39 B.C.), father of the Belshazzar mentioned in the Book of Daniel, took up residence in Taymā' and spent ten of the sixteen years of his reign there.[4] His motive in doing so has long been the subject of scholarly speculation.[5] It now appears from an inscription of Nabonidus found in 1956 at Ḥarrān in Turkey[6] that it had something to do

1/See above, p. 27.

2/See *ANET*, pp. 283–4.

3/For the position of Taymā' on the ancient trade routes, and for information on the oasis collected by previous scholars, see JS, *Mission*, II, p. 144, n. 3; Musil, *Ar. Des.*, appendices V and VI; and R. P. Dougherty, "Nabonidus in Arabia" (*JAOS*, 42 [1922], pp. 305–16), *Nab. and Bel.*, pp. 138–42, "A Babylonian City in Arabia" (*AJA*, 34 [1930], pp. 296–312), "Tema's Place in the Egypto-Babylonian World of the Sixth Century B.C." (*Mizraim*, I [1933], pp. 140–3).

4/See above, p. 91.

5/See Dougherty, *Nab. and Bel.*, chap. xi: Conjectural Reasons for Nabonidus' Stay at Tema; and Julius Lewy in *HUCA*, 19 (1945–6), pp. 434–89.

6/See C. J. Gadd, "The Harran Inscriptions of Nabonidus" (*Anatolian Studies*, 8 [1958], pp. 35–92).

with the king's plans to rebuild the great temple of the Moon-god Sin at Ḥarrān. The Babylonian priests stirred up Nabonidus' subjects to violent opposition to the project, and so serious did the situation become that the king withdrew from Babylonia entirely, leaving his son Belshazzar in charge, and retired to the oasis of Taymā' in North Arabia, some five hundred miles to the southwest. According to the so-called "Verse Account of Nabonidus,"[7] the prince (*malku*) of Taymā' was slain in battle. Nabonidus took up his residence in Taymā', "the forces of Akkad [were also stationed] there." "He made the town beautiful, built (there) [his palace], like the palace in (Babylon)." Somewhere beneath the sands which now cover the site of ancient Taymā' the palace of Nabonidus lies buried. An excavation of the site should uncover important historical monuments.

Practically no ancient inscriptions are in evidence at either ancient or modern Taymā'. Apart from the illegible Aramaic inscription referred to above,[8] we found only two.[9] It is possible, of course, that inscribed stones are embedded in some of the houses of modern Taymā', such as Jaussen and Savignac found in the houses of modern al-ʿUlā, but we heard no reports of any. However, on the summit of Jabal Ghunaym about fourteen kilometres south of Taymā' we found forty-five inscriptions which have proved to be of exceptional interest.[10] Many of these had already been copied by Philby in the course of his visit to Taymā' in 1951.[11] Philby gave his copies to van den Branden, who published them in 1956.[12] Unfortunately the copies were far from accurate, with the result that van den Branden was unable to offer a satisfactory interpretation of them. The photographs and hand-copies which we were able to obtain in 1962 have made it possible to determine the reading of the inscriptions with a fair degree of accuracy, except in a few cases where weathering has rendered the texts largely illegible. Even with an assured reading the interpretation of the texts is difficult, and some of the translations proposed below must be regarded as tentative.

The inscriptions are among the earliest yet discovered in North Arabia, a fact which makes them of more than passing interest. About 125 graffiti employing the same script were found by Jaussen and Savignac at al-Khabu al-Gharbī and al-Khabu ash-Sharqī, six to nine miles southwest of Jabal Ghunaym.[13] Philby found others in various places in the Taymā' district.[14] Since this script occurs

7/*ANET*, p. 313; Sidney Smith, *Babylonian Historical Texts* (London, 1924), chap. III, pp. 27–97; and Dougherty, *Nab. and Bel.*, pp. 105–11.

8/P. 28.

9/See Taymanite inscriptions nos. 46 and 47, p. 108.

10/See pp. 29–31 and Fig. 34. John Dayton (*ILN*, Aug. 19, 1967, p. 27) gives several inscriptions which he found on the walls.

11/*Midian*, chap. 4.

12/*TTP*, II, pp. 19–27 and Pls. V–VI.

13/*Mission*, II, pp. 131–2, 156, and Atlas, Pl. LVIII.

14/See vdB, *TTP*, II, nos. 257a, 271ak, al, 276g, j, 277, 279–80.

only in the vicinity of Taymā', it must have been the type of writing employed in the oasis itself and may appropriately be labelled "Taymanite."[15]

Inscriptions in a closely related script have been found in Iraq. One of these (Burrows 1–2) can be dated on archaeological grounds to the seventh century B.C.[16] Another, an inscribed cylinder seal,[17] is dated by Albright on stylistic grounds to the late eighth or seventh century B.C.[18] Thus this type of writing must have been in use in North Arabia by the late eighth century B.C. at least. In my *Study* (p. 50), I dated the inscriptions in the Taymā' script (which I then called "Thamudic A") to the sixth or early fifth century B.C. The grounds for this dating were the occurrence in the inscriptions of Ṣalm-names,[19] and the evidence provided by the Taymā' Stone[20] that a god named Ṣalm of Hagam was introduced into Taymā' at that time. However, the Taymā' Stone also indicates that another Ṣalm, Ṣalm of Maḥram,[21] was already established in the town; hence the Ṣalm-names referred to may reflect the worship of this older Ṣalm. If so, the inscriptions may date from a period prior to the introduction of Ṣalm of Hagam. Palaeographically the Taymā' script seems to represent a somewhat later stage of development than the script employed in the Iraqi texts mentioned above.

The content of the Jabal Ghunaym texts may shed some light on their date. Four of them (nos. 20–23) refer to the "war of (i.e. against) Dedan," three (nos. 11, 13, 15) to the "war against Nabayāt," and one (no. 16) to the "war against Massā'." It may be that these were separate wars in which Taymā' was involved at various times, but since the inscriptions referring to them employ a uniform script and appear to constitute a homogeneous group, we seem justified in regarding the wars as having occurred at approximately the same period and as having been related in some way. It is unlikely that a caravan centre as isolated as

15/See p. 69.

16/See E. Burrows, "A New Kind of Old Arabic Writing from Ur" (*JRAS* [1927], pp. 795–806); G. R. Driver, *Semitic Writing* (Schweich Lectures, 1944; rev. ed., London, 1954), p. 124; W. F. Albright, "The Chaldaean Inscriptions in Proto-Arabic Script" (*BASOR*, no. 128 [1952], pp. 39–45), and B. Kienast in H. Lenzen, *Vorläufiger Bericht über die von dem Deutschen Archäologischen Institut unternommen Ausgrabungen in Uruk-Warka, Winter 1955–56* (Abhandlungen der Deutschen Orient-Gesellschaft, Nr. 3), pp. 43–4 and Tafel 46. For a further example of Old Arabian writing from Iraq, see R. D. Biggs, "A Chaldaean Inscription from Nippur" (*BASOR*, no. 179 [1965], pp. 36–38). See also vdB, *ID*, pp. 37–39.

17/See D. H. Müller, *Epigraphische Denkmäler aus Arabien* (Vienna, 1889), Pl. 5.

18/Albright in *BASOR*, no. 128 (1952), p. 42.

19/ṢMDʿ (JS 517, 519), ṢMR' (JS 504), ṢMRF' (JS 376), ṢMMLḤ (JS 455), ṢMNTN (JS 421), ṢMNʿM (JS 517, 540), ṢMŠKR (JS 520), ṢLM'NKD (JS 546), ṢLMNTNT (Hu. 668). It is to be noted that when used in name-formations ṢLM is usually contracted to SM (cf. Heb. *yiqqaḥ* < *yilqaḥ*).

20/*CIS*, II, 113. See also H. Donner and W. Röllig, *Kanaanäische und aramäische Inschriften*, II (Wiesbaden, 1964), nos. 228A and B, pp. 278–80.

21/Maḥram and Hagam (vocalizations conjectural) were doubtless the names of the sanctuaries in Taymā' where the cults of these gods were carried on.

Taymā', and so dependent for its prosperity on the maintenance of peace, would engage in military operations – against the Nabayāt to the east, the Massā' to the north, and Dedan to the southwest – unless the circumstances were very unusual. But a very unusual situation did develop at Taymā' in the middle of the sixth century B.C. when the oasis came under new management. The Neo-Babylonian king, Nabonidus, not only occupied the oasis with his army but settled down there and remained for ten years (*ca.* 552–42 B.C.). Nabonidus was not content to sit idle in Taymā', as we learn from an inscription which he left at Ḥarrān: "I hied myself afar from my city of Babylon (on) the road to Tema', Dadanu [Dedan], Padakku [Fadak], Ḫibra [Khaybar], Iadiḫu [Yadī'?], and as far south as Iatribu [Yathrib, mod. Medina]; ten years I went about amongst them (and) to my city of Babylon I went not in."[22] Although there is no suggestion that these movements of the king had a military character, it is unlikely that he was able to visit the oases, in the first instance at least, without a display of force.[23] The "war against Dedan," mentioned in the four inscriptions listed above, may thus refer to Nabonidus' initial visit to "Dadanu." Gadd suggests that this war is to be identified with the expedition of Nabonidus into Arabia, but he is inclined to place it before the king's arrival at Taymā'.[24] The discovery of references to wars against Nabayāt and Massā' as well makes it more probable that these wars were campaigns conducted by Nabonidus after he established himself in Taymā' and that the Arab inhabitants of Taymā' participated in them. The Ḥarrān inscription makes no explicit mention of an attack on the Nabayāt or Massā' but one (damaged) passage does refer to conflict with the "people of the land of the Arabs,"[25] and the two tribes may have been involved in these struggles.

If the wars mentioned in the Jabal Ghunaym inscriptions were indeed campaigns conducted by Nabonidus, the inscriptions can be dated *ca.* 552–42 B.C.

22/See C. J. Gadd, "The Harran Inscriptions of Nabonidus" (*Anatolian Studies*, 8 [1958], p. 59).

23/Gadd (pp. 86–7) believes that Nabonidus' Arabian army contained many Jews (conscripted no doubt from the exiles in Babylonia) and that garrisons of these were posted in the various oases which he occupied. He finds support for this belief in two passages in the Harran inscription H2, A and B: (1) "They kept guard for me, they accomplished my command in the seclusion of tracts far distant and roads secluded which I travelled" (col. 2, lines 8–10); (2) "In plenty and wealth and abundance my people in the distant tracts I spread abroad, and in prosperity I took the road to my own land" (col. 3, lines 15–17). These garrisons, he suggests, were the origin of the Jewish colonies which are found in Taymā', al-'Ulā (Dedan), Fadak, Khaybar, and Tabūk at the rise of Islam. The theory offers an attractive solution to a long-standing historical problem. For a discussion of the whole matter, see the important article by Izhak Ben-Zvi, "Les Origines de l'établissement des tribus d'Israël en Arabie" in *Muséon*, 74 (1961), pp. 143–90. See also C. C. Torrey in *JAOS*, 73 (1953), pp. 223–4.

24/"The Harran Inscriptions of Nabonidus," pp. 78 and 84. Van den Branden (*TTP*, II, p. xiv) had already suggested a connection between Ph. 266a and the campaign of Nabonidus. It is unwise, however, to base any conclusions on the supposed reference to the "spear of the king of Babylon" in Ph. 279aw since Philby's copy does not inspire confidence.

25/See Gadd in *Anatolian Studies*, 8, p. 59.

However, this identification, and consequently the date of the inscriptions, must remain conjectural until more definite information is forthcoming.

While the identification of the wars is uncertain, the ten-year residence of Nabonidus at Taymā' is a historical fact, one, moreover, which must have had a stimulating, even if ephemeral, effect on the cultural life of the town. Large numbers of foreigners must have resided in the oasis, and there must have been constant contacts with the outside world. The languages employed by the Babylonian officials were no doubt Babylonian and Aramaic, but the indigenous population would continue to speak and to write Arabic. The inscriptions on Jabal Ghunaym may be an expression of the intellectual stimulus experienced by the Arabs of Taymā' at this time, leading to a more extensive use of writing on their part.

Another monument, more certainly from the Babylonian period of Taymā' 's history, is the Taymā' Stone. A fifth century date for this monument has sometimes been advocated, but as Sidney Smith declared: "The difficulty about dating this stele later than the 6th century is the relief, which in no way resembles 5th century work. The choice between 550 and 500 is one of historical probability."[26] More recently Gadd[27] has drawn attention to the striking similarity of the representation of the god, Ṣalm of Hagam, in the relief sculptured on the left side of the Taymā' Stone to the representations of Nabonidus on the reliefs discovered in 1956 by D. S. Rice at Ḥarrān. Both wear the same kind of tall, pointed helmet with a flap at the back of the neck; both hold in their left hand a staff with encircling rings. The similarity between the two representations is so close as to make it highly probable that the Taymā' Stone comes from the same period as the Ḥarrān reliefs.

In the Ḥarrān reliefs the king's right hand is upraised in adoration of the Sun-god, the Moon-god, and Ishtar, who are represented by their emblems. On the Taymā' Stone Ṣalm also has his right hand outstretched,[28] and Gadd interprets the gesture as one of adoration of the winged disc depicted hovering above him. However, in this case the arm is stretched out straight rather than upraised towards the divine emblem. The gesture seems intended rather to suggest Ṣalm's acceptance of the offering of the priest (shown in the lower panel of the relief in the act of sacrificing) and the bestowal of blessing upon him. Nevertheless it is evident that Ṣalm of Hagam is regarded as standing on a somewhat lower plane than the god represented by the winged disc. Gadd (p. 42) thinks that the winged disc is here a symbol of the older Ṣalm, Ṣalm of Maḥram, "who might thus be

26/*Isaiah Chapters XL–LV* (Schweich Lectures, 1940; London, 1944), p. 143. J. Cantineau, *Le Nabatéen*, I (Paris, 1931), p. 11, dates it "au moins l'époque perse, sinon l'époque néo-babylonienne."

27/In *Anatolian Studies*, 8, pp. 37ff.

28/See the excellent photograph of the relief in *Anatolian Studies*, 8, Pl. III; also in D. G. Hogarth, *The Penetration of Arabia* (London, 1904), facing p. 282.

the 'image' of a sun-god." There can be no doubt that the disc represents the Sun-god, but the frequent association of bucrania with inscriptions mentioning Ṣalm strongly suggests that Ṣalm of Maḥram was a Moon-god.[29] If Taymā' was a centre of Moon-worship, it would help to explain the attraction which the city had for Nabonidus.

The use of *ṣalm*, meaning "image, statue," as a divine name is found in Assyria where the statues of the gods and kings sometimes received worship under that name.[30] In view of this Assyrian practice, and in view of the fact that Ṣalm of Hagam and Nabonidus are depicted in much the same fashion, it is perhaps not overly hazardous to suggest that Ṣalm of Hagam was none other than the deified Nabonidus. There seems to be no evidence of a cult of Nabonidus in Babylonia itself, but in Arabia Nabonidus faced a special problem and he may well have instituted a cult of himself there in order to strengthen his position. It may be significant for the nature of the cult that the priest placed in charge was an Egyptian, as the name of his father, Peṭ-osiri, shows. An Egyptian priest might be expected to be particularly well-versed in the ritual befitting a deified monarch. The Babylonian name, Ṣalmšezib, which the priest bears, could have been assumed after his appointment to the new office.

The older Ṣalm, Ṣalm of Maḥram, seems to have been a Moon-god. Whether the application of this name to the Moon-god was due to Assyrian influence or was an independent development is not certain. The Ṣalm who appears in the proper names and whose head is engraved on the summit of Jabal Ghunaym must surely be this older Ṣalm. As for the cult of Ṣalm of Hagam, it may be taken for granted that it did not long survive Nabonidus' defeat and death at the hands of the Persian forces under Cyrus in 539 B.C.

B/TAYMANITE INSCRIPTIONS

(*i*) *Jabal Ghunaym*[31] (*nos. 1–44*)

1 Phot. R 103:27 and copy. (Ph. 266b, 1–3.) Lines 1 and 2 r. to l., line 3 l. to r. Pls. 18 and 21. VdB, *TTP*, II, p. 20.

bḥgg	*b. Ḥaggāg*
nm ḏ'b mn sm'l ṣl	*By Dhi'b. From SM'L Ṣal-*
m ltwy	*m has turned away.*

29/See pp. 100–4. For the association of the bull with the Moon-god in South Arabia, see *Handbuch der Altarabischen Altertumskunde*, I, ed. D. Nielsen (Copenhagen, 1927), pp. 214 and 211, and G. Ryckmans, *Religions*, p. 310. In Babylonia, see J. Lewy in *HUCA*, 19 (1945–6), pp. 450–89. See also Dougherty, *Nab. and Bel.*, p. 48, n. 166.

30/The references to Ṣalm in Assyrian inscriptions have been brought together by R. Frankena, *Tākultu* (Leiden, 1954), p. 112. See Gadd's comments in *Anatolian Studies*, 8, p. 42.

31/See p. 29.

bḥgg: Inscriptions in the Taymā' script always employ *b* for "son of" (as does Phoenician), never *bn* except in JS 512. Dhi'b was a son of Ḥaggāg as no. 5 shows. The position of *bḥgg* suggests that it was an afterthought. – For *nm*, see Thamudic inscription no. 26. – *ḏ'b*, Ar. *ḏi'b*, meaning "wolf," = Heb. *zĕ'ēb* (in Judges 8:25 the name of a Midianite chief captured and killed by Gideon). In Dedanite and Lihyanite the sign H , here rendered by *ḏ*, has the value *z* (as in Phoenician, Old Hebrew, and Moabite); to represent *ḏ* a diacritical stroke was added, thus Ħ . Taymanite, however, does not have separate signs for *z* and *ḏ*, the two sounds having apparently fallen together in that dialect. It is possible, therefore, that the sign H should always be transliterated by *z* in Taymanite. I have chosen to render it by *ḏ* because this yields a closer correspondence with known Arabic forms. For a discussion of the signs for *z* and *ḏ* in Thamudic, see the commentary on Thamudic inscription no. 57 below.[32] – Since invocations addressed to Ṣalm never employ the vocative *h*, as van den Branden has pointed out,[33] it is possible that *ṣlm* is here to be regarded as in the vocative. But in view of the inscription found at Taymā' by John Dayton and published by him in *ILN*, Aug. 19, 1967, pl. 3,[34] it seems more probable that *ṣlm* is to be taken as the subject of *ltwy*. For the latter word, cf. Ar. *lawā*, VIII, + *'an*, to "turn one's back on something" (Wehr, p. 885).[35]

VdB reads (on the basis of Philby's imperfect copy): (1) *bḥmm* (2) *lmhk bmn sm' nṣr* (3) *lt'*, "Bi-Ḥimmâm. Par Mahîk Bawmân. Samî' aide! Par Tay'."

The occurrence of the inscription in the Taymā' area and the fact that it invokes the principal god of Taymā' combine to suggest that Dhi'b was a citizen of Taymā'. Since there is no other oasis in the vicinity, the whole region being empty desert, it is probable that SM'L is not a place-name but the name of the tribe to which Dhi'b belonged. The theory that the oasis of Taymā' was inhabited by the tribe of SM'L receives some support from an Assyrian inscription of the time of Sennacherib (704–681 B.C.) which states that one of the gates of Nineveh was called "the Desert Gate" because through it came "the men of Sumu'il, the men of Tema" (^{amêl}*Su-mu-'i-il* ^{amêl}*Te-e-me*) bearing gifts to the Assyrian king.[36] R. Campbell Thompson translates "the men of Sumu'il and the men of Tema," although no conjunction appears in the original. If the phrases are in apposition, it suggests that Sumu'il was the name of the tribe to which the inhabitants of Taymā' belonged.[37] It is true that Sumu'il is spelled with an 'alif and SM'L with

32/See p. 108.

33/In *Syria*, 35 (1958), p. 112.

34/The inscription, which appears to be complete, reads as follows: *wmn sm'l ṣlm ltwy*.

35/Before the discovery of the Dayton inscription, Beeston suggested to me the rendering "Ṣalm has inclined (graciously)."

36/See R. C. Thompson and M. E. L. Mallowan, "The British Museum Excavations at Nineveh, 1931–32" (*AAA*, 20 [1933], p. 98).

37/In the first century A.D. Taymā' appears to have been occupied by the tribe of SLMW; see

an ʿayin but since the cuneiform script had no special symbol for ʿayin + vowel, Sumu'il may well be an Assyrian transcription of Ar. SMʿL. The latter is doubtless an abbreviated form of SMʿ'L (cf. ĠWRL, NʿML, Y'RŠL, YʿḎRL, and Y'WSL in JS 432, 450, 431, 530, 568, and 567, all in the Taymanite script). The form SMʿ'L is found in Saf. (*CIS*, v, 2177, 3349 and L 647).

In an inscription of Ashurbanipal (668–33 B.C.) Uate' (var. Iaute') (b. Ḫaza'il) is twice called "king of Sumu'il."[38] In another inscription[39] he is called "king of Qedar," Qedar being the tribe which dominated the oasis of Adummatu (mod. al-Jawf), 200 miles to the north of Taymā'. It would seem that Uate', and doubtless his father Ḫaza'il before him, controlled both Adummatu and Taymā'. This would explain why both are sometimes referred to by the more grandiloquent title, "king of the Arabs," or "king of Arabia."[40] In spite of their royal title they seem to have been Bedouin sheikhs without any settled abode.[41]

When a reference to Sumu'il was first discovered in Assyrian, Delitzsch suggested that there was some connection between this name and that of the biblical figure of Ishmael, the reputed ancestor of the northern Arabs. His suggestion subsequently received the endorsement of two other prominent Assyriologists, R. C. Thompson[42] and Julius Lewy.[43] The discovery in early Arabian inscriptions of two references to SMʿL, which may be the Arabic original of Assyrian Sumu'il, raises the problem once more. The tradition found in Genesis 25:12–18 (cf. also 16:10–12 and 17:18–21) that the northern Arabs were descended from Ishmael is not one that the Hebrews are likely to have invented; they must have derived it from the Arabs. A change from Ar. *Sumuʿ(')il* to Heb. *Yišmaʿ'ēl* implies, of course, that the Hebrews learned of this ancestral figure from an Arab group which tended to insert an *i*-vowel before an initial sibilant (a common occurrence in modern Arabic) so that *Sumuʿ(')il* became *Ismuʿ'il* and then *Ismaʿ'il.* However, in view of the occurrence of the name YSMʿ'L/YSMʿL in ancient North and South Arabic, the relationship of SMʿL to Heb. YŠMʿ'L must remain conjectural until more evidence bearing upon the identity of SMʿL has been discovered.

JS 1, 8, and 19 nab., also F. Altheim and R. Stiehl, *Die Araber in der alten Welt*, I (Berlin, 1964), p. 105, and W. W. Tarn in *JEA*, 15 (1929), p. 21.

38/See *ANET*, p. 300.

39/Luckenbill, *AR*, ii, no. 869.

40/Luckenbill, *AR*, ii, nos. 518a, 536, 551, 819–23, 940, 943, 946.

41/Jer. 49:28–33 seems to suggest that a place called Ḥāṣōr was their headquarters but probably Ḥāṣōr is Ar. *ḥaḍar*, "a civilized region with towns and villages and a settled population (as opposed to desert, steppe)" (Wehr, p. 184). Isa. 42:11 refers to the *ḥᵃṣērîm* of the Qedar (cf. Ar. *ḥaṣr*, "encirclement, enclosure").

42/See n. 36.

43/"The Late Assyro-Babylonian Cult of the Moon and Its Culmination at the Time of Nabonidus" (*HUCA*, 19 [1945–6], p. 432, n. 143).

2 Copy. (Ph. 266x.) ← Pl. 18. VdB, *TTP*, II, p. 23.

lm hb'l bʿgl mn smʿl ṣlm ltw

By Habb'il b. ʿIgl . From SMʿL Ṣalm has turned away.

For my interpretation of *lm* as an early form of the prep. *l*, see my *Study*, p. 24. Jamme (*TS*, p. 42) has recently proposed that it is the verb *lamma*, "to stop," but such a meaning is inappropriate in the present context. – The name HB'L is new; cf. HB in Saf. (*CIS*, v, 1287, etc.) and HBM in Jamme, *Pièces épig.*, no. 269. – For ʿIgl, see vdB's note, and *RNP*, I, 157. Other sons of ʿIgl are mentioned in nos. 3 and 26 and in Ph. 292k. – For SMʿL and for *ltw* (=*ltwy*), see no. 1. – VdB reads: *nmš b(w)'l bʿgl: mnsʿ*, "Namiš b. Wâ'il b. ʿIgl: Un vent du nord (souffle)!"

3 Phot. R 104:3A and copy. (Ph. 266ao.) ← Pls. 18 and 21. VdB, *TTP*, II, p. 26.

nṣr bʿgl hlk ḏn krfty hrkb

Naṣr b. ʿIgl has passed away. This is KRFTY, the (i.e. his) riding camel.

By a brother of the author of no. 2. A word-divider in the form of a point placed below the horizontal axis of the inscription is used after most words. – *hlk*, cf. Ar. *halaka*, "to perish, die." – *krfty* may be connected with the root from which SAr. *krf*, "cistern," is derived. A crude drawing of KRFTY accompanies the inscription. – VdB reads: *nṣr bʿglh lkḏ nkr fty hrkb*, "A aidé Baʿagilah en ce qui concerne le malheur de Fatiyy; le cavalier."

4 Phot. R 103:30 and copy. (Ph. 266ap.) → Pls. 18 and 21. VdB, *TTP*, II, p. 26.

lmt bšrṣ — *By Mawt b. ŠRṢ.*

Only a few Taymanite inscriptions are introduced by simple *l*. The n. pr. Mawt ("Death") recurs in Ph. 275z; see also *RNP*, I, 125; Littmann, *TS*, p. 73; and *HTIJ*, nos. 83 and 270. – The first sign of the second name seems to be a development of the old sign for s^3 (Beeston) or *ś*. Since a root *s^3rṣ* is unknown in Ar. and a root *šrṣ* does occur, it is probable that the s^3 sign came to be used in Taymanite as an alternative for the normal *š* sign (see also JS 454), as happened in Hijazi Thamudic (see Pl. 1). – VdB reads *šmt bḍrm*, "Šamit b. Ḍarim." – The *wasm* engraved both above and below the inscription is similar to, but not quite identical with, that which appears with JS 428, 559, and 560 (all in the Taymanite script). – The camel was manifestly drawn by the same hand as the camel in no. 3, making it probable that both inscriptions were written by the same person.

5 Phot. R 103:29 and copy. (Ph. 266 au, 1–5.) L. 3 from l. to r.; the other lines from r. to l. Pls. 18 and 21. VdB, *TTP*, II, p. 27, and Jamme, *TS*, pp. 37, 72, 74.

1	*ḏ'b bḥgg k'l šmt*	*Dhi'b b. Ḥaggāg purchased the black camel*
2	*'ṯt wndrt*	*of a woman and it died.*
3	*klʿ y'ḏnk*	*Kulāʿ exhorts thee,*

4 *ḏt hn'n* — *Dhāt-HN'N,*
5 *(b)gml 'yr* — *(to give) in exchange for the camel an ass.*

The word-divider (in the form of a point) is placed at the top of the line (contrast no. 4). It is used only after the first three words of l. 1 and the first word of l. 2. – For Dhi'b, see no. 1. Three of his sons are mentioned in nos. 8–13. – *k'l*, cf. Ar. *ka'ala*, "to buy or sell something in compensation of a debt" (Hava). The first letter may be *s*, but the diagonal slant of the upper stroke suggests that *k* was intended. – *šmt*, cf. Ar. *šāmah*, "mole, black camel." – *'ṯt*, "woman, wife," as in SAr. and Lih. – *ndrt*, cf. Ar. *nadara*, "to be rare, unique," also "to die" (cf. *Lisān al-'Arab*, Beirut ed. 1955–6/1374–6, vol. 22, p. 200). – *kl'*, cf. Ar. *kulā'*, "strength." The context calls for a proper name to serve as subject of the following verb. KL' does not appear elsewhere as a n. pr. but KL'N occurs in Tham. (JS 582), ḎKL'N and 'lht KL'N in *CIS*, IV, 541, 85 and 621, 2; cf. also DKL'N in *CIS*, IV, 539, 4. For the Himyarite prince Dhū'l-Kala', see Caussin de Perceval, *Essai sur l'histoire des Arabes avant l'Islamisme*, III (Paris, 1848), 292, 316, 392, etc. – *y'ḏnk* is probably the Imperf. of *'aḏana*, IV, "to notify, exhort," with the 2nd sing. pron. suffix. The suffix of the 2nd person is extremely rare in the inscriptions, only three other instances being known. Two of these occur in Jamme, *Pièces épig.*, no. 367; *b'ḏnk 'nby šymm 'bdk ...*, which Beeston (*Muséon*, 66 [1953], p. 178) translates: "In subjection to thee, O 'Anbay the Patron, (is) thy servant ..." (see also Beeston, *Desc. Gram.*, 37:1). For occurrences of *b'ḏn* without the suffix, see Jamme, *Doc. sud-arabe*, p. 304. See also no. 6 below – *ḏt hn'n* is probably the name of the woman referred to in l. 2 – *(b)gml*: the first letter has a slightly rounded form, raising the possibility that it is to be read as *f*. If it is *b*, it may be taken as the *b* of exchange. – *'yr*, cf. Ar. *'ayr* which, like Heb. *'ayir*, can denote the domestic as well as the wild ass. It would seem that the woman, Dhāt-HN'N, from whom Dhi'b bought the camel, was exhorted by Kulā', possibly the Amīr of Taymā', to give compensation for the dead animal in the form of an ass.

VdB reads: (1) *ḏ'b bw(l)s b'ḫrm* (2) *'t twb* (3) *sn ?ḏ'y 'lb* (4) *ḏt rf'* (5) *sgm lb'*, (1) "Ḏi'b b. Walas b. 'Aḫram. (2) Signe de Tawâb. (3) Sîn! ... a tracé (ceci). (4) Celle-ci (est) Rifâ'. (5) Sagm à Bâ'."

Jamme (*TS*, p. 72, n. 26) reads l. 1 as *ḏ'b kḥ sb 'tlm*, "Ḏi'b has outdone [and] transpierced 'Atlum." On p. 74, n. 32, he gives l. 2 as *n'ṯ twb*, "Tawwâb was far"; on p. 37, l. 3 as *bl'y 'ḏn nsn*, "Bal'ay has informed Nawsân," and l. 4 (reading from r. to l.) as *[l]'blḫd*, "him of the clan of Ḫalab'i[*l*]." On p. 74, n. 32, he reads l. 5 as *sgm lb(y)*, "Sâgim was satiated."

6 Copy. (Ph. 266n.) ⇇ Pl. 18. VdB, *TTP*, II, p. 22.

rm?kb — ?
. . n(b)ybd'?(l)dd 'ḏ(n)k — ?

VdB reads: (1) *ṣm w'b* (2) *ds ṣm't 'ḏnk*, (1) "Ṣimm et 'Ab. (2) Ṣâmi' at a foulé au pied ton autorité."

7 Phot. R 103:35 and copy. (Ph. 266m.) ⇆ Pls. 18 and 21. VdB, *TTP*, II, p. 21.

(a) *lṣd bḏ'b*	*By Ṣadd b. Dhi'b.*
(b) *fḥk bḥgg 'b*	*Faḥak b. Ḥaggāg ...*

The n. pr. ṢD occurs in Lih. and Saf. (cf. *RNP*, I, 181–2). – For Dhi'b, see no. 1. – FḤK recurs in nos. 8–11; it is found also in Saf. (*CIS*, v, 2484, 4688, 5277), a fact which is against vdB's interpretation of the form in Ph. 266ao(2) as "à Ḥakk." Both Dhi'b and Faḥak were sons of Ḥaggāg. – There may have been a letter (now obliterated) before *'b*; hence the significance of the end of the inscription is uncertain. – VdB reads: *ḥy(w) b'b* (b) *wmḥbk ḥg*, "Ḥayw b. 'Ab. (2) Et ton ami a fait le pélerinage." He thinks the inscription may be Lihyanite but the script is of the normal Taymanite type.

8 Phot. R 103:36 and copy. (Ph. 266u, v.) → Pls. 18 and 21. VdB, *TTP*, II, p. 23.

fḥk	*Faḥak.*

The name appears twice. – VdB reads *mḥb*, "Muḥibb," but see nos. 7, 9–11.

9 Phot. R 104:3A, 4A and copy. (Ph. 266ao, 2.) Top line r. to l., line 2 seemingly in a spiral direction, beginning at the r. Pls. 18 and 22. VdB, *TTP*, II, p. 26.

fḥk bḥgg (nṣr lṣl)m
wḥrḍ nml km. . . .(y lṣl)m msm(w)

Faḥak b. Ḥaggāg (gave assistance to Ṣal)m.
And he was sick with pimples, like ... to Ṣalm ...(?)

By the author of nos. 7b and 10. Part of the inscription has been obliterated, making it difficult to divine its meaning. – For *nṣr lṣlm*, see no. 11. – *ḥrḍ*, cf. Ar. *ḥaruḍa*, "to be constantly affected by disease so as to be at the point of death" (Lane), II: "to spur on, incite." – *nml*, cf. Ar. *nimāl*, "spots, pimples, slander" (Salmoné). – The last word may be *msm'* = ? – VdB reads: (1) *fḥk bḥmmn* (2) *wḥrml lkm (w)msm w . . .*, "A Ḥakk b. Ḥamâmân, et Ḥaram'il Lakkâm, et Musimm et ..."

10 Phot. R 104:9A, W 5:16–19 and copy. S-direction. Pls. 18 and 21.

fḥk bḥgg yyb

Faḥak b. Ḥaggāg is plague-stricken (?)

yyb is possibly for *yaiba'u*, an Imperf. form of *wabi'a*, "to be plague-stricken, poisoned." Above the inscription is the outline of a head, probably that of Ṣalm. For similar drawings, see nos. 25, 26, 37, and 44.

11 Phot. R 104:8a and copy. (Ph. 266ag.) ⇇ Pl. 19. VdB, *TTP*, II, p. 25.

fḥk bḥgg (n)ṣr lṣlm	*Faḥak b. Ḥaggāg gave assistance to Ṣalm*
bḍr nbyt	*in the war against Nabayāt.*

fḥk bḥgg: see no. 7b. – *nṣr lṣlm*: I was at first inclined to interpret this phrase as "was helped by Ṣalm," comparing the use of *l* to introduce the agent after a passive verb in Heb., but such a construction is unknown in Cl. Ar. Beeston (in a private communication) says: "If Ṣalm was indeed the deified king who conducted the wars, then the phrase could plausibly mean *he gave assistance to Ṣalm.* This type of phraseology occurs dozens of times in South Arabian texts where a chieftain records that he *assisted his lord so-and-so in the war.*" – *ḍr*, "war," occurs frequently in SAr. – Immediately above the inscription may be discerned the letters ... *ḍrd* ..., to be restored as ... [*b*]*ḍr d*[*dn*] ..., "in the war against Dedan ..." (see nos. 20–23). Another fragmentary inscription, *bḍr nbyt*, "in the war against NBYT," is not reproduced on the plates.

VdB reads: (1) ... *k bḥgg* (2) ... *bḍr*(*n*) *byt*, "(1) ... k b. Ḥaggâg ... (2) ... b. Ḍirrân a passé la nuit (ici)."

The NBYT, mentioned here and in nos. 13 and 15, occupy a position parallel to that of DDN (Dedan) in nos. 20–23, a fact which suggests that they were an entity of comparable importance and not some insignificant tribe. Since the Assyrian inscriptions mention a North Arabian people called *Nabaiati*,[44] and the Old Testament mentions a North Arabian *N*ᵉ*bāyôt* (Nebaioth),[45] there can be little doubt that the NBYT of the Jabal Ghunaym inscriptions are to be identified with them. The discovery of the Arabic spelling of Nebaioth administers the *coup de grâce* to the old theory that the Nebaioth were the same people as the Nabataeans (Ar. *Nabaṭ*, *'Anbaṭ*), for it is highly improbable that an original *Nabayat* (attested by the Assyrian transcription) would both lose the *y* and alter *t* to *ṭ*.[46]

Neither the Old Testament, the Assyrian records, nor the Jabal Ghunaym inscriptions tell us in what part of North Arabia the Nebaioth dwelt. However, by combining the references to them in Assyrian inscriptions with a knowledge of North Arabian topography, it is possible to fix their location with some degree of probability. An inscription of Ashurbanipal (668–33 B.C.) relates that when he attacked Uate' b. Ḫaza'il (lord of the oasis of Adummatu, mod. al-Jawf), Uate' fled to the land of Nabaiati, which is described as lying "at a great distance,"

44/See Oppenheim's translation of the annals of Ashurbanipal in *ANET*, pp. 298–300; also Harper Letter no. 260, on which see Albright, *Massa'*, pp. 4–6.

45/Gen. 25:13 (= I Chron. 1:29), 28:9, 36:3; Isa. 60:7.

46/The theory of an equation with the Nabataeans is rejected by J. A. Montgomery, *Arabia and the Bible* (Philadelphia, 1934), p. 31, n. 11, by Nelson Glueck, *Deities and Dolphins* (New York and Toronto, 1965), p. 4, and by Altheim and Stiehl, *Die Araber in der alten Welt*, I, p. 281, n. 108, but it is still accepted by Dussaud, *Pénétration*, p. 22.

and there sought refuge with its king Natnu.[47] In trying to get away from the Assyrians, Uate' might have fled west or southwest, but both Hebrew and Assyrian sources give us the names of the principal tribes in that direction[48] and the Nebaioth do not appear among them. He might have fled south along the western edge of the Nafūd – following much the same route that we took – but that would have brought him to Taymā', and the Nebaioth were not at Taymā', as the Jabal Ghunaym texts show. The most natural line of flight for him would be southeastward across the Nafūd. This vast region of sand-dunes would have interposed an effective barrier to any Assyrian pursuit. Once across the Nafūd, the first oasis of any size that Uate' would have come to would be Ḥā'il. Hence this is probably where the land of Nabaiati was located.[49]

The fact that Nebaioth is accorded the status of first-born of Ishmael in Hebrew tradition (Gen. 25:13), and doubtless in Arab tradition as well, must reflect a belief that they were the most ancient of the North Arabian peoples and that their territory was the motherland of the northern Arabs.[50]

12 Phot. R 104:12A and copy. Boustrophedon, beginning with the second sign at the upper right. Pls. 19 and 21.

y'ḏrl bḥ(g)	*Ya'dhir'il b. Ḥagg-*
g (ḥ)dd lṣlm	*āg was keen for Ṣalm.*

Y'ḎRL occurs in JS 568 (Taymanite script). – The letter before *dd* is not clear but is probably *ḥ*; cf. Ar. *ḥadda*, "to be sharp, keen." – The *m* of Ṣalm is written above the initial *l*. A bucranium, the symbol of Ṣalm, is engraved on the top of the stone bearing the inscription.

13 Phot. R 104:22A and copy. ⇄ Pls. 19 and 21.

y'ḏrl bḥgg [nṣr	*Ya'dhir'il b. Ḥaggāg [gave assistance*
lṣlm] bḏr nbyt	*to Ṣalm] in the war against Nabayāt.*

47/See *ANET*, p. 298.

48/See Gen. 25:1–4 and 36:1–43, also the annals of Sargon II (721–05 B.C.) in *ANET*, p. 298.

49/Albright (*Massa'*, p. 12) suggested, but without giving any supporting arguments, that the homeland of the Nebaioth was in the Ḥā'il area. The considerations advanced above tend to support his suggestion.

50/It is of interest to recall that the Edomites were closely related to the Nebaioth. According to Gen. 36:3 (late J) Esau's wife, the Ishmaelitess Basemath, was a sister of Nebaioth. Late J must have had a reference to Nebaioth at an earlier point in his narrative, explaining who he was, but this reference was omitted by P in favour of the Ishmaelite genealogy given in Gen. 25:1–17. P affirms that Basemath was a Hittite (Gen. 26:14) and that it was Esau's wife Maḥalath who was a sister of Nebaioth (Gen. 28:9). In any case, both writers agree that the Edomites were closely related to the Nebaioth. It seems then that the Edomites were of pure Arab stock and came originally from Najd. The tradition of their North Arabian origin was expressed by making Esau's wife an Ishmaelitess. Since Hebrew tradition made Esau a twin-brother of Jacob, it was precluded from making him himself an Ishmaelite.

See nos. 11 and 12. The sign to the right of the inscription is either a *wasm* or an attempt to draw the head of Ṣalm; see no. 25.

14 Copy. (Ph. 266t, 2.) → Pl. 19. VdB, *TTP*, II, pp. 23.

ṣmrf'	*Ṣamrafa'*
bḥgg nṣr lṣlm	*b. Ḥaggāg gave assistance to Ṣalm.*

ṢMRF' (= *Ṣalm-rafa'*, meaning "Ṣalm has healed") occurs in JS 376 (Taymanite script). Cf. RF' and YRF'L in JS 518 and 537 (both in Taymanite script). – VdB reads: (1) *s'd* (2) *bḥmmḥ(b)*, "Sa'ad. Muḥibb."

15 Phot. R 104:8A, 9A, W 5:16–19. (Ph. 266ac.) ← Pls. 19 and 21. VdB, *TTP*, II, p. 24.

nṣr lṣlm
'rm bfsḥ bḍr nbyt
'Arim b. Fasiḥ gave assistance to Ṣalm in the war against Nabayāt.

For 'RM, see *RNP*, I, 171, and Jamme, *Doc. sud-arabe*, p. 320. Owing to the limited space available, the author wrote the *m* lying face down. – FSḤ is new; cf. Ar. *fasīḥ*, "wide." – VdB reads: (1) *(n)ṣr l't* (2) *'rw bys ḥb ḍrn byt*, "Naṣr à 'Ayt. 'Arw b. Ya's aime Ḍirrân. Il a passé la nuit (ici)."

16 Copy. ← Pl. 19.

ṯr nṣr bḍ[r]	*Thawr helped in the war*
ms(')	*against Massā'.*

ṮR: see *RNP*, I, 215, and Jamme, *Doc. sud-arabe*, p. 311. There can be little doubt that MS' is to be identified with the Massā' listed in Gen. 25:14 as one of the sons of Ishmael. The fact that it is there mentioned after Dumah and before Ḥadad and Tema might suggest that its location should be sought somewhere between al-Jawf and Taymā'.

An inscription of Tiglath-pileser III from about 735 B.C. twice mentions a town called Mas'a (^{URU}*Ma-as-'a-a-a*), immediately after Taymā' in each instance.[51] Albright thinks the Massā' were Aramaeans because of the appearance of a Mash among the sons of Aram (Gen. 10:23) and would locate them somewhere in the Syrian desert southeast of Damascus.[52] The identification of Ishmaelite Massā' with Aramaean Mash is questionable; also the region southeast of Damascus does not contain any oasis which might have served as a location for the town of Mas'a. The fact that chapters 30 and 31 of the Hebrew Book of Proverbs are attributed to members of the tribe of Massā' suggests that the tribe was situated not too far from Palestine. It is not reckoned among the sons of

51/For this inscription, see Albright, *Massa'*, p. 3, n. 4.

52/Albright attempts to use Harper Letter no. 260 as a clue to the location of Massā' but the Massā' raiding party to which it refers may have been operating at some distance from its base.

Midian in Gen. 25:4 so cannot have been in the land of Midian southeast of ʿAqaba. Dr. Vidal has suggested that the area next to the northwestern tip of the Nafūd may have been the habitat of the Massāʾ. The rocky plateau is dotted with wells and has long been known as one of the peninsula's best gazelle-hunting areas. We ourselves saw a number of gazelles at the southern tip of the Wādī as-Sirḥān. An abundance of gazelles would indicate the presence of adequate grazing. A tribe established in this area would have the additional tactical advantage of being able to vanish into the neighbouring Nafūd if attacked by a too-powerful foe.[53]

17 Copy. ← Pl. 19.

ʿlʾl bʾsgr nṯr bd̮r . . . k . .

ʿAlayʾil b. ʾAsgar fell in the war against ...

ʿLʾL occurs in JS 378, 579, and 542 (probably) (all in the Taymanite script), in Lih. (JS 203, etc.), and in the form ʿLYʾL in Min. and Nab. – ʾSGR is new; cf. Ar. *ʾasgar*, "having bloodshot eyes" (Lane). – *nṯr*, cf. Ar. *naṯara*, "to fall (leaves)." In view of the frequent occurrence of *nṣr bd̮r* in these texts, the sign read as *ṯ* may be an aberrant form of *ṣ*, or the copy may be at fault.

18 Phot. R 104:14A, 15A, W 5:14 and copy. (Ph. 266ah.) ← Pls. 19 and 22. VdB, *TTP*, II, p. 25.

bʾsgr ʿlʾl — *b. ʾAsgar, ʿAlayʾil.*

The order of the names is noteworthy; cf. no. 17. VdB takes the two large signs to the right as part of the inscription and reads *tr?z bʾs gr ʿlʾl*, "... b. ʾAws ʿAlayʾil a commis une faute," but it is more probable that they are *wusūm*.

19 Phot. R 104:8A and copy. L. 1 is written upside down from l. to r., l. 2 from r. to l. Pl. 19.

ʿlʾ bʾ — *ʿAlayʾil*

bʾtw — *b. ʾAtw.*

This ʿAlayʾil is different from the one mentioned in nos. 17 and 18. – The author has written the letters *bʾ* twice. ʾTW, cf. Ar. *ʾatw*, "gift." It recurs in JS 495, 544, and 555 (all in Taymanite script). In my *Study*, p. 22, I incorrectly took the word as a substantive with the 3rd sing. pron. suffix.

20 Phot. R 103:33, 34, W 5:29 and copy. (Ph. 266a.) It begins at the lower right. Pls. 19 and 22. VdB, *TTP*, II, pp. 19–20.

bhšrkt nṣr bd̮r ddn yrh lṣlm

Bi-ha-Shirkat gave assistance in the war against Dedan, spying out for Ṣalm.

53/See the map, p. 2.

BHŠRKT (meaning "the son of the company") must be a n. pr.; otherwise the name of the author of the inscription is not mentioned, which would be very unusual. HŠKR occurs in Saf. (WH 223, etc., unpublished), raising the possibility that in HŠRKT we have a case of metathesis. – *ḍr*: possibly *ḍrr* ("wars") should be read as in no. 22. – *yrh*: the *h* has a tail as in nos. 2 and 3 whereas in *bhšrkt* it is tailless. Since neither Ar. *rāha* nor *rahā* has a meaning suitable to this context, *yrh* should probably be explained from Syr. *rᵉhā*, "to watch (from a hiding-place), spy out, be on the look out for." – VdB takes the inscription as beginning near the end of the upper line, after the word-divider, and reads *yrhl hlws bn šrkt nṣr bḍr ddn*, "Yarhil ha-Lawwâs b. Šuraykat a aidé dans la guerre de Dedan," but the presence of the letters *lm* outside the line framing the inscription shows that they mark its conclusion. The writer manifestly misjudged the amount of space required and had to write the last two letters outside the frame.

21 Phot. R 103:32. ⇄ Pls. 19 and 22.

... b	*... in*
ḍr ddn	*the war against Dedan.*

22 Phot. R 103:32. → Pls. 19 and 22.

... (*ṣ*)*lm bḍrr ddn*	... (*Ṣa*)*lm in the war against Dedan.*

23 Phot. R 103:32. ← Pls. 19 and 22.

... *bḍr ddn*	... *in the war against Dedan.*

24 Phot. R 103:32 and copy. (Ph. 266p, 4.) ← Pls. 19 and 22. VdB, *TTP*, II, p. 22.

... *rb'l brḥm b...*	... *Rabb'il b. Raḥīm b. ...*

RB'L: see *RNP*, I, 248; II, 122. – RḤM occurs in JS 552 (Taymanite). – VdB reads *ḥ*(*b*) *w'lḥm*(*m*), "Ḥubb et 'Ilḥamam."

25a Phot. R 103:31. (Ph. 266 o, part.) ← Pls. 20 and 22.

lmḥ	*Lāmiḥ* ?

LMḤ is new; cf. Ar. *lāmiḥ*, "brilliant, shining (star)." The inscription seems to be related to the drawing below, for the top of the head has been left open to allow for the insertion of the letters. The head itself bears an eight-rayed star, indicating its divine character. On either side, but on a lower plane, are two other heads, triangular in outline. The irregular spacing of the trio probably indicates that they do not form an intentional triad. For other drawings of heads of deities, see nos. 10, 26, 45 and Figs. 36 and 37. – Philby's copy of the inscription gives '*mt*; VdB does not deal with it. There is an inscription below the three heads but the reading is uncertain.

25b Phot. R 103:32. (Ph. 266p, 1.) ← Pls. 20 and 22. VdB, *TTP*, II, p. 22.

ṣlm *Ṣalm.*

VdB vocalizes the name as *Ṣalam.*

25c Phot. R 103:32. Pls. 20 and 22.

This inscription does not seem to be Taymanite.

26 Phot. R 103:31 and copy. (Ph. 266 o.) ← Pls. 20 and 22. VdB, *TTP*, II, p. 22.

ṣmkfr (b) ʿgl *Ṣamkaffar (b.) ʿIgl.*

ṢMKFR (= *Ṣalm-kaffar*, meaning "Ṣalm has pardoned") is new but KFR, KFR', and KFR'L occur in JS 497, 452, 503, and 521 (all Taymanite). – For ʿGL, see no. 2. To the right of the inscription is a drawing of a head marked with a crescent which suggests that it represents the Moon-god. A line encloses both drawing and inscription, showing that they are the work of the same hand. – VdB reads *'ms wrk ʿgl*, "Hier les chameaux ont été marqués."

27 Phot. R 103:31 and copy. (Ph. 266 at.) ← Pls. 19 and 22. VdB, *TTP*, II, p. 26.

lnḥ(l)t *By Naḥ(l)at.*

The fourth sign is probably *l*; it might be *r*. Cf. Ar. *naḥlah*, "bee," *naḥīl*, "skinny, gaunt," and *niḥr*, "skilled." Neither NḤLT nor NḤRT occurs elsewhere in the inscriptions. – VdB reads *lnrn*, "Par Nawrân."

28 Phot. R 104:6A and copy. (Ph. 266aa.) ← Pls. 19 and 22. VdB, *TTP*, II, p. 24.

nfs bḥmn *Nafis b. Ḥimmān.*

NFS, see *RNP*, I, 143. – ḤMN, see *RNP*, I, 95, and *HTIJ*, no. 480. – VdB reads *lfsd bḥmn*, "Par Fâsid b. Ḥimmân."

29 Phot. R 104:7A and W 5:21, 22 and copy. (Ph. 266z, 1–2). Pls. 20 and 22. VdB, *TTP*, II, pp. 23–4.

lm 'lnʿm b . . r q(l)sʿ *By 'Ilnaʿam b. ...*

'LNʿM is new. According to *RNP*, I, 237, it occurs in JS 1bis tham. but the reading is doubtful. VdB may be correct in taking the signs which I have read as *q(l)sʿ* as a separate inscription running from r. to l.: *ʿsl mw ...*, "ʿAssal ..." The next line he regards as divisible into two parts: (a) *l'ml*, "Par 'Amil"; (b) *(s)w'mʿl*, "Par ʿAmm'aws."

30 Phot. R 104:7A, W 5:22 and copy. (Ph. 266y, 1–2.) ⇆ Pls. 20 and 22. VdB, *TTP*, II, p. 23.

krkr b(t)l(ʿ) yṯ *Karkar b. (T)L(ʿ) was*
b lṣlm bḥdd *attacking for Ṣalm with fury (?).*

For names derived from *karkara*, "to repeat, laugh loudly," see Jamme, *Doc. sud-arabe*, p. 316. – TLʿ is new; cf. Ar. *talīʿ*, "tall." – *yṯb* may be the Imperf. of *waṯaba*, "to leap, rush, pounce," *waṯbah*, "attack, assault, aggression." – *ḥdd*, cf. Ar. *ḥiddah*, "vehemence, fury." – VdB reads *kr kr't ly(q)h ddḥsm bṣlm*, "Kâri' at a ramené des chamelles. Dâdḥasam b. Ṣalam."

31 Phot. R 104:7A, W 5:22 and copy. (Ph. 266ab.) Above no. 29. Below Ph. 266aa on vdB's Plate v. → Pl. 20. VdB, *TTP*, II, p. 24.

nṣr bḥdd	*Naṣr b. Ḥudād.*

ḤDD: see *RNP*, I, 88; II, 58; L 873; and *HTIJ*, p. 52. – VdB reads from r. to l. *ddḥt bṣn*, "Dâdḥatt b. Ṣann."

32 Phot. R 104:10A, W 5:1, 15 and copy. (Ph. 266ad, 1–2.) ⇄ Begins at the lower right. Pls. 20 and 22. VdB, *TTP*, II, pp. 24–5.

b . . . . .' nṣr lṣ[l]m nṣr hḏb

... gave assistance to Ṣalm swiftly.

Literally "gave assistance to Ṣalm with a swift assistance." Cf. Ar. *haḏib*, "swift." – VdB reads *'b ḏ'nṣlm ... 'rr...*, "'Ayb ḏû-'Awnṣalam ... 'Irâr ..."

33 Phot. R 104:10A, 11A, W 5:20 and copy. Begins at the upper right. ⇄ Pls. 20 and 23.

(a) *mntt nṣr bḍ(r)*	*MNTT assisted in the war*
ddn	*against Dedan.*
(b) *(bḍ)r ddn*	... *(in the wa)r against Dedan.*

MNTT, cf. MNTTM, the name of a SAr. district in *RÉS* 4176, 6.

34 Phot. R 104:13A, W 5:26, 27 and copy. (Ph. 266ai, 1–2.) → Pls. 20 and 23. VdB, *TTP*, II, p. 25; Jamme, *TS*, p. 75, n. 37.

l'(bw)	*By '(BW).*
(w)qṯb lṣlm	*And he has presented a gift to Ṣalm.*

The inscription is badly weathered. The meaning of *qṯb* may possibly be deduced from *maqṯab*, "gift" (Salmoné, p. 745). The inscription is on a horizontal surface, making it impossible to tell with certainty which line should be read first. VdB take the lines in the reverse order to that adopted here and reads: (1) *wqṯ bwlm* (2) *'bd b(t)*, "Par Qaṯṯ b. Walm. 'Abd a passé la nuit (ici)." His reading of the second part bears little resemblance to Philby's copy. Jamme reads the first part as *wqt rbw lm*, "Waqat has cared for Lamm," but the photograph does not support his reading.

35 Copy. (Ph. 266d, 1–3.) Begins at lower left. → Pl. 20. VdB, *TTP*, II, p. 20.

hkdl bmk'l nṣr lṣlm

Hawkad'il b. Makk'il gave assistance to Ṣalm.

HKDL occurs in JS 505 (Taymanite script). VdB, *IT*, p. 292, derives the name from Ar. *hkd*, "to press," but cf. Ar. *wakada*, iv, "to fix, fasten." – MK'L is new but MK occurs in Saf. (WH 259 and 1955, unpublished). – VdB, who reproduces the inscription upside down, reads: (1) *dhr* (2) *lbmkk bnṣr* (3) *l'lm*, "(1) Dahîr. (2) Par Bi-Mukâk b. Naṣr. (3) Par 'Allâm."

36 Phot. R 104:14A, W 5:14, 23 and copy. (Ph. 266ah, 2.) ← Pls. 19 and 22. VdB, *TTP*, ii, p. 25.

sqʿ bm(k)'l	*SQʿ b. Makk'il.*

By a brother of the author of no. 35. SQʿ is new; cf. Ar. *saqaʿa*, "to slap, clap." – VdB reads *(l)sqy bmkbl*, "Par Saqy b. Mukabbil."

37 Phot. R 103:38. (Ph. 266al, 1–3.) L. 2 from r. to l. Pls. 20 and 23. VdB, *TTP*, ii, pp. 25–6.

1	. . . *ṯbdnwd*	...
2	*bh mṣryt*	*lay with an Egyptian woman*
3	...	...
4	*wsm*	...

The four lines of writing are in a poor state of preservation. – *bh*, cf. Ar. *bāha*, "to lie with." – *mṣryt*, cf. Ar. *miṣriyyah*, "Egyptian woman." One might be tempted to translate "Muṣrite woman" and to revive the theory of an Arabian *Muṣri/Muṣru* were it not for the fact that evidence for the existence of such seems insubstantial. See the comments of J. Ryckmans on *RÉS* 3022 in *Scrinium Lovaniense* (Gembloux, 1961), p. 56, and H. Tadmor in *IEJ*, 11 (1961), p. 146.– The last sign in l. 2 has the form of the letter *h* but it is probably a *wasm*; see the *wasm* in no. 12. – VdB reads: (1) *ʿbd bt* (2) *ḏb mṣry* (3) *bws*, "(1) ʿAbd a passé la nuit (ici). (2) Ḏabb, un Egyptien. Wasm. (3) ... Bûs." – To the right of the inscription is a drawing of a head, triangular in outline. See nos. 13, 25, 26, and 45.

38 Phot. R 103:28 and copy. (Ph. 266f.) ⇆ Pls. 20 and 23. VdB, *TTP*, ii, p. 21.

bṣdqn	*Bi-Ṣidqān*
bdmt	*b. Dawmat.*

ṢDQN occurs in Sab. (*RÉS* 4648, Jamme 725, etc.), Qat. (Jamme 881E), and Hadr. (*RÉS* 5035); see also *RNP*, i, 182. – DMT occurs in Ph. 269 where vdB (*TTP*, ii, p. 30) regards it as a place-name. See also BDWMT (Bi-Dawmat) in JS 337. – VdB reads *bhddn bʿmt*, "Bi-ha-Dudan b. ʿAmmat."

39 Phot. R 103:37. (Ph. 266am.) ← Pl. 23. VdB, *TTP*, ii, p. 26.

hydʿ bʿšmt	*Haydaʿ b. ʿAshmat.*

HYDʿ is a hypocoristic of HYDʿ'L which occurs frequently in Sab. (cf. *RNP*, i, 231; ii, 49). G. Ryckmans is inclined to regard the *h* in the Sabaean occurrences as a divine symbol, but this is unnecessary. – ʿŠMT is new but ʿŠM occurs in

Sab., Tham., and Saf. (cf. *RNP*, I, 171; II, 111). – VdB reads *(h)ydy bʿšm* "Ha-Yadiyy b. ʿAšam."

40 Copy. → Pl. 20.

k'b — *Ka'b.*

K'B is new; cf. Ar. *ka'b*, "sorrow," *ka'ib*, "gloomy, morose." – The final stroke may be designed merely to mark the end of the inscription.

41 Copy. ← Pl. 20.

kfr'l — *Kaffar'il.*

See no. 26.

42 Phot. W 5:25. Begins at lower left. ⇆ Pls. 20 and 23.

.ḥm nṣr lṣlm

.ḤM gave assistance to Ṣalm.

43 Copy. (Ph. 266r, part.) ⇆ Pl. 20. VdB, *TTP*, II, p. 22.

lqbb. bb . . . — *By Qubāb? b. B . . .*

l'ns — *By 'Ins.*

QBB, cf. *RNP*, I, 313. Possibly the name should be restored as QBBN; see *RNP*, I, 365. – For 'NS, see *RNP*, I, 239. There is a point between the *l* and the n. pr. – VdB reads *bb snk*, "Bâb. SNK."

44 Phot. R 104:5A. (Ph. 266w.) ← Pls. 20 and 23. VdB, *TTP*, II, p. 23.

mltw — *Mulātū* (?).

MLTW, cf. MLT in JS 185 tham., *CIS*, v, 1086, etc. – VdB reads from l. to r. *wtl*, "Watal," but the direction in which the letters face suggests that the inscription is to be read from r. to l. – Near the inscription is a drawing of a head marked with a circle enclosing a cross (probably an astral symbol). The light patina of the engraving suggests that the drawing is a later imitation of the heads shown in Figs. 36 and 37. – The three treelike signs which also accompany the inscription are of a type found associated with several Taymanite inscriptions (see JS 423, 434, 504, and 528 tham.). Their exact significance is uncertain.[54]

(*ii*) *Jabal as-Samrā'*[55] (*no. 45*)

45 Copy. ← Pl. 20.

... ḥmd b(')w(l) — *... Ḥamd b. ('A)wā(l).*

HMD, cf. *RNP*, I, 93. – 'WL, cf. *RNP*, I, 284

54/See M. Höfner in Haussig, *WM*, I, p. 503.
55/See p. 34.

(iii) Taymā' (nos. 46, 47)

46 Copy. ← Pl. 20.

lṣbr 'k(h)(?) *By Ṣābir ...*

For Ṣābir, cf. Yāqūt, II, 518; for *Ṣubayr*, cf. Ibn Dor. 135, 16. HṢBR occurs in JS 292 lih.

47 Copy. ← Pl. 20.

khf ṣbr *The grave of Ṣābir.*

khf, cf. Ar. *kahf*, "cave." It is used in Lih. with the secondary meaning "tomb" (cf. JS 124, 130, 138).

C/THAMUDIC INSCRIPTIONS

Ghār al-Ḥamām[56] *(nos. 57–71)*

57 Copy. (Hu. 522 = Eut. 717 = Ph. 273b.) ↓ Pls. 6 and 15. VdB, *IT*, p. 258, *TTP*, II, p. 37, and *TTHE*, p. 134; Jamme, *TS*, pp. 14–15.

zn ḏ'(r) bn ḥyt *This is Dhu'(r) b. Ḥayyat.*

Ḏ'(R): the inscription reads Ḏ'B, but since neither the name nor the root appears elsewhere in Ar., it is probable that the author intended Ḏ'R (Ar. *Dhu'r*). – VdB and Jamme read *ḏn ḥgb bn ḥyt* but this involves attributing the value *ḥ* to two different signs. While it is true that different forms of the same sign appear occasionally in Thamudic inscriptions (see, for example, the two forms of *w* in JS 596), the slight curl in the shaft of the third sign of the present inscription recalls the curved or hooked shaft of the *ḏ*-sign in Tabuki Thamudic (see Pl. 1). It seems probable, therefore, that the sign should be given the value *ḏ* (so Littmann, *TS*, pp. 10–13). If this is correct, the initial sign of the inscription must be given the value *z*. This results in a demonstrative pronoun *zn* and gives to Thamudic what Grimme (*OLZ*, 41, 6 [1938], col. 351) calls "einen ganz vulgären Anstrich," but I can see no escape from it. Littmann tried to avoid this result by giving the first sign the value 'alif. 'Alif is sometimes represented by a sign which resembles *z*, but the cross-bar is much longer (see JS 749 tham. where the two signs appear in juxtaposition). It was pointed out above[57] that the Taymanite script did not have separate signs for *ḏ* and *z*, which suggests that the Taymanite dialect employed only one of these phonemes. The same is true of Najdi Thamudic. Dedanite and Lihyanite, however, developed a sign for *ḏ* by adding a vertical

56/I have retained the name which Huber gives for this spot. Philby calls it Ghīrān al-Bināt, Reed's journal gives it as al-Qārah, mine as al-Ghār. It is about two miles northeast of Taymā'.
57/See p. 94.

stroke to the cross-bar of the *z*-sign, thus H (*z*) Ħ (*ḏ*). The latter sign appears to have been the origin of the tailed *ḏ*-sign which appears in Hijazi and Tabuki Thamudic and in Safaitic (see JS, *Mission*, II, pp. 535ff.).

58 Phot. R 103:18 and copy. (Hu. 521 = Eut. 718 = Ph. 273a.) H ↓ Pls. 6 and 16. Winnett, *Study*, p. 40; Littmann, *TS*, p. 72; vdB, *IT*, pp. 257–8, and *TTP*, II, p. 37; Jamme, *TS*, p. 14.

zn mḥb ztrft — *This is the lover of Zāt-RFT.*

The letters are separated from each other by a point. The name ZTRFT is new and of uncertain meaning. Another possible translation is: "This is Muḥibb. This is RFT" (so vdB). Littmann reads *'n mḥb 't lft*, "Ich bin ein Liebender; du hast (mir) Unrecht getan," but see the comment in no. 57 on the sign which he takes as 'alif. The straight stroke to which he gives the value *l* is *r* in Hijazi Thamudic (see Pl. 1). Jamme reads *ḏn mḥb ḏtrft*, "Has perished Muḥibb, he of the clan of Turfat."

59–65 On a flat rock surface, making it difficult to tell in some cases which is the top side of the inscription and consequently the direction of reading.

59 Phot. R 103:21 and copy. (Hu. 517 = Eut. 709 + 710 = Ph. 272l.) H. ⇄ Begins at lower right. Pls. 6 and 16. VdB, *IT*, p. 256, *TTHE*, p. 134, and *TTP*, II, p. 36; Jamme, *TS*, p. 14.

yd' bn wgz fr'y

Yada' b. Wagz, and he shepherded (the flock).

References to shepherding are found elsewhere only in Tabuki Thamudic and in Safaitic. – For YD', see *RNP*, I, 111; II, 69. – WGZ, cf. Ibn Dor. 282, 12. For the *g*-sign, see JS 205 tham. The sign to the left of the *g* is too far removed to be an integral part of the inscription unless it serves to indicate the change in the direction of the inscription. – VdB reads both lines from l. to r.: *wrb 'dy ḏn bdy*, "Par Rabb (fils de) 'Adî. Celui-ci est Bâdiy." – Jamme reads *wnb 'dy ḏn bdy*, "'Adî was blamed [for] Badî has perished."

60 Phot. R 103:21 and copy. (Hu. 516 = Eut. 712 = Ph. 272k.) H. → Pls. 6 and 16. VdB, *IT*, p. 256, and *TTP*, II, p. 36; Jamme, *TS*, p. 33.

nḥt zmm drḥ — *ZMM* (*b.*) *DRḤ engraved* (*this*).

nḥt, cf. Ar. *naḥata*, "to cut, hew (stone)," used in JS 74 lih. of the carving of a statue. The chief objection to taking it as a verb here is that the subject usually precedes the verb, but see no. 63. – VdB reads from r. to l.: *ḥr dmm dt ḥn*, "Dimâm est retourné. Celui-ci est Ḥann." Jamme has rightly perceived that the direction of reading is from l. to r. He translates: "Nâḥit has blamed (*ḏmm*) Dâriḥ." This is more in conformity with the normal pattern of the inscriptions, but one would expect a more significant statement.

61 Phot. R 103:21 and copy. (Hu. 515 = Eut. 711 = Ph. 272j.) H. → Pls. 6 and 16. VdB, *IT*, p. 256, *TTHE*, p. 134, and *TTP*, II, p. 36.

w'ṭlmn *And 'Aṭlamān.*

'ṬLMN is new; cf. Ar. *ṭulmah*, "a small round cake of bread." For the *ṭ*-sign, see JS 205 and 206 tham. – VdB reads: *w'(n) ṭlmn*, "Et je suis Ṭalīmān."

62 Phot. R 103:22 and copy. (Hu. 514 = Eut. 708 = Ph. 272g.) H. → Pls. 6 and 16. VdB, *IT*, p. 256, *TTHE*, p. 133.

wz ḥdr myṯn ʿl d'

And this is Ḥādir, drowsy because of illness.

ḤDR, see Ibn Dor. 135, 2–4 for Ḥadir and Ḥudayr. – *myṯn*, cf. Ar. *wasina*, "to sleep," *mīsān*, "sleepy." – *d'*, cf. Ar. *dā'*, "illness." – VdB reads: *wḏ ḥd lmyṯn ʿl dẖ*, "Et ceci est un retranchement pour Mayṯan Dawẖ."

63 Phot. R 103:22 and copy. (Hu. 513, 2 = Eut. 706 + 707 = Ph. 272f.) H. ⇉ Pls. 6 and 16. VdB, *IT*, p. 255, *TTHE*, p. 133, *TTP*, II, p. 36; Jamme, *TS*, p. 14.

wzn z'(g) wzfry

wẖmy zt fʿl mrḥ ḥm

And Z'G and Zufray have committed adultery.

And this deed stinks worse than a stinking fart.

zn, cf. Ar. *zanā*, "to commit adultery, fornication." The verb is singular, agreeing with the nearer subject (cf. Wright, *Ar. Gram.*, II, p. 294D). – There seems to be a point in the third letter, suggesting that it is to be read as *g* rather than as ʿ. Z'G is new; cf. Ar. *za'aga*, "to cause discord." – *ZFRY* is also new, but *ZFRM* occurs in Sab. (Ry. 334a) and Qat. (*RÉS* 3533); cf. Ar. *zafir*, "greasy, filthy," and *zafīr*, "sighing, moaning" (Wehr). – *ẖmy*, cf. Ar. *ẖamma*, "to stink." – *zt fʿl*: the use of the fem. demonstrative before the masc. noun would seem to be a grammatical error on the author's part. – *mrḥ* is probably the *min* of comparison followed by *rīḥ*, "wind, fart, smell." – Huber and Philby have copied the inscription so that l. 2 in my copy appears as l. 1 in theirs; hence vdB and Jamme read the lines from r. to l. VdB reads: (a) *wẖmy ḏtn ʿlm rḥ ḥm* (b) *wḏn ḏsʿ wḏ(n) fry*, "Et H̱ummy ḏû-Tinn a tracé (ceci), il voyagé le soir, et il a dressé sa tente (ici). Et celui-ci est ḏû-Suʿʿ et celui-là Farayy." – Jamme reads: *wẖmy ḏtfʿl mrḥ ḥm* (2) *w ḏnḏ ʿʿwḏ fry*, "Waẖmay, he of the clan of Tafʿal, has exulted [for] H̱am-(2)aw, he of the clan of Naḏḏ, has protected Farīy from danger."

64 Phot. R 103:20 and copy. (Hu. 512 = Eut. 705 = Ph. 272i.) H. → Pls. 6 and 16. VdB, *IT*, p. 255, *TTHE*, p. 133, and *TTP*, II, p. 36.

bẖyr(t) wḥrb fm *Bi-Khayrat, and he pillaged grain.*

The n. pr. is new. – *ḫrb*, cf. Ar. *ḫaraba*, "to plunder, pillage." – *fm*, cf. Ar. *fūm*, "garlic, wheat, grain." – VdB reads: *lḫy bḫ wḥr bfm*, "Laḫay s'est reposé (ici), et il est revenu à Fam."

65 Phot. R 103:20 and copy. (Hu. 511 = Eut. 704 = Ph. 272h.) H. → Pls. 6 and 16. VdB, *IT*, p. 254, *TTHE*, p. 133, and *TTP*, II, p. 36.

z šzt ṯmt wḍm kʿm

This is ŠZT, an old man, and he (still) hugged (and) kissed.

ŠZT is new; cf. Ar. *šazza*, "to be dry, barren." – *ṯmt*, cf. Ar. *ṯimmah*, "old man." – The sign after *w* is probably a simplified form of *ḍ*, in which case the verb is *ḍamma*, "to embrace, hug." – *kʿm*, cf. Ar. *kaʿama*, "to embrace, kiss." – VdB reads *ḏšḏt ṯmt wḏmkʿm*, "Ḏû-Šâḏḏat de ṮMT et ḏû-Makʿûm."

66 Copy. (Hu. 506 = Eut. 698a = Ph. 272, o.) H. ↓ Pl. 6. VdB. *IT*, p. 253, *TTP*, II, p. 36.

ltqd ḏn ʿrk — *For Taqudd. This is ʿArak.*

TQD is new; ʿRK occurs in Saf. (cf. *RNP*, I, 171). – VdB reads *ltqd ḥn ʿrs*, "A Taqudd miséricorde! ʿIrs."

67 Copy. (Eut. 607 = Ph. 272q, part.) H. → Pl. 6. VdB, *TTHE*, p. 133, and *TTP*, II, p. 36 and Pl. VIII.

z lwzn lḫb kḥd l(r) (?)

This is Lawzān. He lay with Kaḥad ...?

The reading and interpretation are uncertain. Philby's copy has several additional signs. – LWZN is new; cf. Ar. *lawz*, "almond." – *lḫb*, cf. Ar. *laḫaba*, "to lie with."

68 Copy. (Hu. 504 = Ph. 272aa.) H. ← Pl. 6. VdB, *IT*, p. 252, and *TTP*, II, p. 36 and Pl. VIII.

zn mrn mḥ(w)hʿr — *This is Murrān ...*

MRN occurs in Hu. 639 and JS 230 lih. – VdB reads *ḏn ʿml mḥ*, "Celui-ci est ʿAmil, (fils de) Maḥḥ."

69 Copy. (Hu. 503a = Eut. 693 = Ph. 272ab, part.) H. ← Pl. 6. VdB, *IT*, p. 252, *TTHE*, p. 133, and *TTP*, II, p. 36 and Pl. VIII.

ḥfy — *Ḥāfi.*

ḤFY is new; cf. Ar. *ḥafiya*, "to receive hospitably, to have sore feet." – VdB takes the spiral sign above the inscription as *w* and reads *whny*, "Par Hannay."

70 Copy. (Hu. 503b = Eut. 694 = Ph. 272ab, part.) H. ← Pl. 6.

z strt lṯq — *This is the shelter of Lathiq.*

z is here construed with a fem. noun. – *strt*, cf. Ar. *sutrah*, "covering, veil," and Heb. *sitrah*, "hiding-place." For *str* in Saf., see *WSIJ*, p. 167. – LṮQ is new; cf. Ar. *laṯiq*, "damp, moist."

71 Phot. W 5:12. H. ← Pl. 7.

gmr ʿmrl *ʿAmar'il roasted (it).*

The reference is evidently to the long-horned ox (?) depicted alongside the inscription. – ʿMRL = ʿMR'L which is found in Tham. (*HTIJ*, 30, etc.) and Saf. (*CIS*, v, 274, etc.). – *gmr*, cf. Ar. *gammara*, "to roast (meat)."

4 Inscriptions from the Region of al-ʿUlā

A/HISTORICAL BACKGROUND

At the northeastern edge of the oasis of al-ʿUlā lie the remains of ancient Dedan.[1] According to a tradition heard by the Hebrews, and doubtless derived by them from Arab sources, Dedan was a brother of Sheba, both being the sons of Raʿmah (Gen. 10:7). Raʿmah has been identified by some with South Arabian *RGMT* (LXX *Regma*)[2] but the theory requires us to believe that Arabic *g* passed over into Hebrew as ʿayin or ghain, and this seems improbable.[3] The tradition preserved by the Hebrews is usually taken merely as evidence of the existence of close cultural and commercial ties between the Dedanites and Sabaeans, but it may well be that the two peoples had a common origin. One group may have moved from the original homeland, Raʿmah (wherever that was), and established itself at Dedan, the other have moved in a different direction and founded the kingdom of Sheba (Ar. Saba').

Musil[4] thought that Dedan was controlled by the Sabaeans and that It'amar the Sabaean, who paid tribute to the Assyrian king Sargon II (721–05 B.C.), was governor there. Against this is the fact that no inscriptions which can be definitely classed as Early Sabaean have been found at Dedan. It may not be necessary to look for evidence of Sabaeans or of Sabaean control at Dedan. The two peoples may have had an affinity based on common origin and have found it to their mutual advantage to co-operate in developing and controlling the frankincense route.

It is evident from biblical references[5] that Dedan was flourishing in the sixth

1/See p. 38.

2/See, e.g., H. von Wissmann and M. Höfner, *Beiträge zur historischen Geographie des vorislamischen Südarabien* (Wiesbaden, 1961), pp. 227–9.

3/See Albright, *Dedan*, p. [illegible], n. 1.

4/*N. Ḥeǧâz*, pp. 243, 288.

5/For these, see above, p. 38, n. 80.

century B.C.[6] but the references throw no light on its political organization.[7] The large number of inscriptions to be found in and around the oasis testifies to the important role which Dedan played in the commercial and cultural life of ancient Arabia. How far back in time the inscriptions carry us is as yet uncertain. It is inherently probable that if the art of writing was practised at Taymā' in the sixth century B.C., it was practised equally early at Dedan, but no definite proof has yet been adduced for dating any of the Dedanite inscriptions that far back. In my *Study*[8] I drew attention to three inscribed objects (a cylinder seal, a scaraboid, and a gem) which might serve as a basis for dating, but subsequent study of these objects has cast doubt on the Dedanite character of the script which they employ. Van den Branden[9] prefers to call the script on the cylinder seal and on the gem "primitive Thamudic." He allows the script on the scaraboid to be Dedanite and uses Delaporte's dating of it to the end of the eighth or the beginning of the seventh century B.C. as evidence that the Dedanite script was in existence that early. Actually there is nothing indubitably "Dedanite" about the inscription. It could equally well be classified as "primitive Thamudic" or, as I should prefer to call it, "Taymanite."[10] Thus it now appears that none of the three objects mentioned can be used as evidence for dating Dedanite.

There is, however, one inscription about whose Dedanite character there can be no doubt and which seems to offer some light, if only indirectly, on the date of Dedanite. It is JS 138 lih., the funerary inscription of Kabir'il, the only known king of Dedan. It reads as follows: *khf kbr'l bn mtʿ'l mlk ddn wṯrw nʿm bh nʿrgd.* Grimme[11] took *nʿrgd* as the name of a god in spite of the fact that no such god is mentioned elsewhere, and translated the latter part by: "Und es möge (Gott) Naʿrgadd in sie reichlich Gnade spenden." Caskel[12] regards *nʿrgd* as the name of

6/Albright (*Dedan*, p. 9) claims that the reference to Dedan in Gen. 10:7 takes us back to the early first millennium B.C. and that the reference in Gen. 25:3 "can scarcely be later than the ninth century B.C." In my opinion these two passages belong to the secondary J stratum of Genesis and date from the sixth century B.C. (see *JBL*, 84 [1965], pp. 1–19). The references to Dedan in Jeremiah also date from the sixth century. There seems to have been an increased interest in, and knowledge of, Arabia on the part of the Jews at this time.

7/For attempts to separate the Dedanite inscriptions from the Lihyanite, see my *Study*, p. 10, n. 2; Caskel, *LL*, p. 22; and van den Branden, *ID*. The latter would reduce the number of Dedanite texts to seventy.

8/Pp. 49–50.

9/*ID*, pp. 32, 36. He rightly points out that the triangular *z*-sign employed on the cylinder seal is not found in Dedanite: "Ce signe est très ancien et disparaîtra plus tard. On le recontre encore vers le cinquième siècle dans deux textes thamoudéens du premier courant de l'écriture, à.s. JSa 753 et 754 où il figure dans le nom propre Taymʿazîz."

10/The *ẓ*-sign employed on the scaraboid is different from the *ẓ* employed in the Taymanite inscriptions (see Pl. 1) but it occurs in other inscriptions from the Taymā' area (see JS 542 and 545.)

11/*Neubearbeitung*, pp. 277 and 281. 12/*LL*, p. 78.

a person, *ṯrw* as a place-name, and translates: "Naʿr-gadd hat für sie Gunst erfahren (Lohn für ihren Bau erhalten)." If *ṯrw* was a place important enough to be coupled with Dedan in the royal title, it is strange that it does not appear elsewhere in the inscriptions. Van den Branden has offered two slightly different renderings: (1) "A aménagé et s'y trouve bien Naʿrgad,"[13] (2) "Naʿrgadd l'a aménagée (la caverne) et y vit heureusement,"[14] but his interpretations are based on the assumption that the word-divider between *wṯrw* and *nʿm* was incorrectly placed by the engraver and that the proper word-division is *wṯr wnʿm*.

There can be little doubt that *Gadd*, "Fortune," is referred to at the end of the inscription. The interpretation of the word *nʿr*, prefixed to it, is more difficult. Beeston has suggested to me a comparison with Heb. *nōʿar*, "youthful vigour," here regarded as a hypostasized quality of the deity. The root *ṯrw*, as he also points out, is constantly associated with ideas of moisture (cf. *ṯarā*, "moist earth"). "The favour demanded was surely rain, conformably to the deep-seated and ancient Arabian idea of rain on a tomb being a blessing." I would, therefore, suggest the following translation: "The tomb of Kabir'il b. Mataʿʾil, king of Dedan. And may the youthful vigour of Gadd moisten (and) favour it" (i.e. favour it with rain).

The recognition of Fortune as a power operative in human affairs was widespread in the ancient Near East, as is attested by place-names such as Baal-Gad and Migdal-Gad and by the existence of cults of Gadd and Manāt. The occurence in South Arabia of the feminine names GDNʿM and NʿMGD suggests that in that area, as in others, Fortune was revered by women as a Power helpful in childbirth and sickness. The conception of Fortune as the presiding genius of the group gained a great vogue in the Hellenistic and Roman periods and appears frequently in the inscriptions of the Safaitic Arabs of Syria.[15] This might seem to be an argument for dating King Kabir'il of Dedan to the Hellenistic period, but since the cult of Fortune antedates that period, it does not seem possible to use JS 138 by itself for dating purposes. At any rate, the "kingdom" of Dedan must have been of short duration for Kabir'il is the only known king of Dedan.

Another inscription which has a bearing on the subject of Dedanite chronology is JS 349 lih. It reads as follows: *nrn bn ḥḏrw t(q)ṭ b'ym gšm bn šhr wʿbd fḥt ddn br'*[*y*] ..., "Nīrān b. Ḥāḏiru inscribed his name in the time of Gashm b. Shahr and ʿAbd the governor of Dedan, in the reig[n of] ..." Jaussen and Savignac's restoration of the last word as *br'*[*y*] has been accepted by Grimme, Caskel, and van den

13/*ID*, p. 58, no. 24.

14/"Notes thamoudéennes" (*Syria*, 35 [1958]), p. 113.

15/For the twenty-eight references to GDʿWḎ, "the Fortune of (the tribe of) ʿAwīdh," see *CIS*, v, 853, 857, 860, etc.; for references to the Gadd of the tribe of Ḍaif, see *WSIJ*, see p. 151.

Branden and seems probable. Since this expression is used elsewhere only before royal names,[16] it may safely be assumed that the name of a king once stood at the end of the inscription. The reference to a "governor" implies that the king had his headquarters at some place other than Dedan. It would seem to follow that he must have been either a South Arabian king, or a Persian monarch, or one of the Ptolemies.[17]

The fact that the governor is called "governor of Dedan" and not "governor of Liḥyān" is fairly good evidence that the kingdom of Liḥyān had not yet come into being.[18] Furthermore, the employment of the word *fḥt* for "governor" suggests that the inscription belongs to the Persian period since this title seems to have been used in Western Asia only during the time of the Persian Achaemenid empire.[19] Caskel[20] thinks that the term may have lingered on in Arabia after the Persian period and would date JS 349 to the end of the second century B.C. But the very use of *fḥt* implies that the Persians once had a governor in some part of Arabia; otherwise, it is doubtful if the author would have been acquainted with the word.

Whether a dating of the inscription to the Persian period justifies an identification of the Gashm b. Shahr mentioned in the inscription with "Geshem the Arab" who opposed Nehemiah's rebuilding of the walls of Jerusalem in 444 B.C.,[21] and/or with Gashmu the father of Qainu, king of Qedar,[22] is a moot question. The name GŠM was not uncommon.[23] Furthermore, if Gashm b. Shahr were

16/See JS 68, 72, 82, 83, 85, *EDAr.* LXX. For *bsmwy*, used in parallel construction in two Late Lihyanite inscriptions, see the commentary on no. 9 below.

17/The obliteration of the royal name may be a further indication that he was a foreigner.

18/If the inscription comes from the pre-Lihyanite period, it is necessary to revise our ideas about the development of the script and to recognize that a tendency to employ converging lines had already appeared before the Lihyanite period. However, the conversion of an occasional tendency (as exemplified by JS 349) into a formal characteristic does not seem to have taken place until the Lihyanite period. JS 12 lih. (from Madā'in Ṣāliḥ) is evidence that the two types of writing overlapped in part since the author has engraved his inscription twice, first using signs with parallel lines and then using signs with converging lines.

19/See my *Study*, p. 51, also C.-F. Jean and J. Hoftijzer, *Dictionnaire des inscriptions sémitiques de l'ouest* (Leiden, 1962), p. 226.

20/*LL*, pp. 101–2.

21/As I suggested in my *Study*, p. 51.

22/His name, engraved in Aramaic script, appears on a bowl from Tell al-Maskhūṭah in Lower Egypt. See Isaac Rabinowitz, "Aramaic Inscriptions of the Fifth Century B.C.E. from a North-Arab Shrine in Egypt" (*JNES*, 15 [1956]), p. 7, and Grohmann, *Arabien*, pp. 48 and 273.

23/The name is particularly common in Safaitic. Three Safaitic inscriptions (from the Nabataean period) are even dated by a certain Gashm:

(1) *CIS*, v, 269: *lgrm bn nr bn ḫl wrʿy hnḫl bql bḏkr snt gšm wḥn'l*, "By Garm b. Nūr b. Khayl. And he pastured the camels on *baql* in this valley at Dhakīr (?) the year of Gashm and Ḥann'il.'

(2) L 288 *lšʿ bn ḥg bn mlk bn frq bn slm snt gšm wḥ(n'l)*, "By Shaiʿ b. Ḥagg b. Mālik b. Fāriq b. Sālim, in the year of Gashm and Ḥa(nn'il)."

indeed king of Qedar, it is strange that he is not so called in JS 349. Yet the very fact that the inscription is dated by him shows that he was a political figure of some importance. Possibly he was a king, but his royal title was omitted because of the mention of another, more powerful king at the end of the inscription.

Although it is not possible with the evidence currently at our disposal to fix the date of the kingdom of Dedan precisely, there is evidence that the kingdom of Liḥyān which followed it, either immediately or after an interval, dates to the Persian and Hellenistic periods. This evidence is to be found in the inscriptions left by the South Arabian Minaeans at Dedan. These show that the Minaean merchants were established in Dedan as early as the reign of Waqah'il Ṣadiq and Abkarib Yathaʿ,[24] and possibly earlier.

In my early forays into the field of North Arabian research I assumed that the expressions *kbr mʿn mṣrn* and *kbr mṣrn wmʿn mṣrn* in *RÉS* 3535 and 3022 respectively were evidence of the presence of Minaean governors in North Arabia. This, together with the fact that Minaean influence is more noticeable in Late Lihyanite than in Early Lihyanite, led me to the conclusion that the Lihyanite kingdom preceded a period of Minaean political control.[25] The progress of research has demonstrated that this view is no longer tenable. Van den Branden was the first to suggest that the Minaean colony at Dedan was purely commerical in character.[26] This thesis was elaborated still further by Jacques Ryckmans.[27] The discovery of a reference to the *kabīr* of a Minaean colony at the Qatabanian capital Timnaʿ,[28] where Minaean political control cannot be admitted, makes it evident that the *kabīr*s were something other than governors. They were probably the head of the local colony of Minaean merchants and responsible to the local ruler for its good behaviour and for the collection and payment of taxes. The North

---

(3) WH 1276 *lgʿl bn rgl ww(s)q hgl snt gšm*, "By Guʿal b. Rāgil. He drove the herd the year of Gashm."

It is extremely doubtful that this Gashm can be identified with the Gashm by whom JS 349 lih. is dated.

24/See *RÉS*, 3346 and 3697. J. Ryckmans, in his *L'Institution* (p. 265), dated Abkarib no later than 400 B.C., although he would probably be inclined now to lower this date in view of his subsequent dating of Abyadaʿ Yathaʿ to *ca.* 200 B.C. (see *Scrinium Lovaniense*, pp. 56–8). Albright (*BASOR*, no. 129, pp. 22–3) would date Abkarib to the late second century B.C.

25/"The Place of the Minaeans in the History of Pre-Islamic Arabia" (*BASOR*, no. 73 [1939], pp. 6–7).

26/"La chronologie de Dedan et de Liḥyân" (*BOr*, 14 [1957], pp. 12–16); see also Grohmann, *Arabien*, pp. 273–4, and F. Altheim and R. Stiehl, *Die Araber in der alten Welt*, I (Berlin, 1965), chap. 6: Die Liḥyān.

27/"Les 'Hierodulenlisten' de Maʿīn" (*Scrinium Lovaniense*, pp. 51–61, especially pp. 56 and 60).

28/See M. A. Ghul, "New Qatabani Inscriptions – II" (*BSOAS*, 22 [1959], pp. 419–23 and 429–35).

Minaeans and the Lihyanites are, therefore to be regarded as contemporary. Evidence of the cordial relations between the two groups is provided by Eut. 24, which refers to the building of a temple to Wadd (the Minaean Moon-god) at Dedan, and by JS 49 lih., which mentions the presentation of a three-year-old boy by the priest of Wadd to the Lihyanite god Dhū-Ghābat.

J. Pirenne[29] assigns the North Minaean texts to her palaeographic periods C3 to F and would date them from *ca.* 290 to 180 B.C., with the beginning of the Minaean colony being placed *ca.* 320 B.C. The sole basis for this dating appears to be the contention that the script of period E, characterized by terminal swellings, reflects the script employed at Athens beginning in 271 B.C. It seems a precarious foundation on which to erect a system of chronology.

K. Mlaker[30] believed it possible to find a fixed point for Minaean chronology in the Minaean inscription *RÉS* 3022 where there is mention of a struggle (*mrd*) between MḎY ("Media" or "the Medes") and Egypt in the time of Abyadaʿ Yathaʿ, king of Maʿīn. Following the lead of Hartmann and Ed. Meyer, he identified the struggle with Cambyses' invasion and conquest of Egypt in 525 B.C. I myself revived the theory of W. M. Müller[31] that the reference was to the invasion of Egypt by Artaxerxes III Ochus in 343 B.C. since this would be more in conformity with the other evidence that we possess regarding the date of the Minaeans.[32]

Pirenne would identify the struggle with the battle of Raphia, 217 B.C., between Ptolemy IV and Antiochus III since *RÉS* 3022 falls in the latter half of palaeographic period E which she dates from 250 to 205 B.C.[33] J. Ryckmans[34] rejects this identification on the ground that the authors of the inscription speak of having been delivered "in the midst of Egypt" whereas Raphia was on the frontier. He himself believes that the events referred to are those of 202 B.C. and following when Philip V of Macedon and Antiochus III of Syria invaded Egypt. Ryckmans seems to be influenced by the reference in the inscription to a "war (*ḏr*) between the lord of the south and the lord of the north" (*ḏymnt wḏ š'mt*). These expressions remind him of the references in Daniel ii to the "king of the south" (*melek ha-negeb*) and the "king of the north" (*melek ha-ṣāphôn*) and lead him to look for a struggle not too far removed in time from the date of the Book of Daniel (165 B.C.).

Both Ryckmans' theory and that of Miss Pirenne presuppose that the term

29/*Paléographie des inscriptions sud-arabes*, I (Brussels, 1956), pp. 167 and 182.

30/See Maria Höfner, K. Mlaker and N. Rhodokanakis, "Zur altsüdarabischen Epigraphik und Archäologie II" (*WZKM*, 41 [1934]), pp. 94–106.

31/In *MVAG* 3, 1898, pp. 3 and 41.

32/*BASOR*, no. 73 (1939), p. 8.

33/*Paléographie*, I, pp. 212–13 and 217.

34/*Scrinium Lovaniense*, p. 58.

"Medes" could be used to denote the Seleucids.[35] It is well known, of course, that the term was often used by the Hebrews and Greeks to denote the Persians of the Achaemenid period, and by the Safaitic Arabs to denote the Parthians or Sasanids, but there is no evidence that it was ever used to denote a people of non-Iranian origin. Therefore any attempt to date *RÉS* 3022 to the Seleucid period is open to serious objection.

Since the Parthians were never involved in hostilities with Egypt, it is necessary to go back to the Achaemenid period to find a suitable setting for the inscription. An identification of the "Medo"-Egyptian struggle with Artaxerxes' attack on Egypt in 343 B.C. for the purpose of suppressing a revolt would seem best to meet the requirements of the situation.

RÉS 3022 may therefore be taken as evidence that the Minaeans were active in the Egyptian area in the middle of the fourth century B.C. Their presence at Dedan in North Arabia in the reign of Waqah'il Ṣadiq and his son Abkarib Yathaʿ, at least two reigns, and probably more, before that of Abyadaʿ Yathaʿ, is attested by *RÉS* 3346 and 3697, as pointed out above (p. 117). This compels us to carry back the establishment of the Minaean colony at Dedan to the latter part of the fifth century B.C. The absence of Minaean influence on Dedanite inscriptions suggests that the Dedanite kingdom flourished before the establishment of the Minaean colony, while the presence of such influence in the Lihyanite inscriptions suggests that the Lihyanite kingdom arose at least as early as the Minaean colony.

The fact that the Lihyanite inscriptions fall palaeographically into two distinct groups, and the presence of thirty-one Nabataean graffiti at Dedan, led Caskel[36] to suggest that there were two periods of Lihyanite independence, with a period of Nabataean rule (from 9 B.C. to 35 A.D.) intervening. It may be doubted, however, that the differences between the two types of Lihyanite script are of such a character as to warrant the belief that there was a break in the continuity of Lihyanite political life.

The time span covered by the Lihyanite kingdom is somewhat uncertain. The names of at least eight Lihyanite kings can be gleaned from the inscriptions, and these imply a duration of a century and a half, but the list is manifestly incomplete so that a duration of at least two centuries must be considered probable.[37]

35/*Paléographie*, I, pp. 214–15. Miss Pirenne's argument that the use of the term MḎY can be explained by the presence of Asiatic mercenaries in Antiochus' army is unconvincing. Surely the authors of the inscription would be concerned to indicate the identity of the two powers involved rather than the ethnic composition of their respective armies.

36/*LL*, pp. 36, 40–42. See Grohmann, *Arabien*, pp. 46–49 and 272–4, for a survey of the theories regarding the chronological relationship of the Minaeans, Dedanites, Lihyanites, and Nabataeans.

37/W. W. Tarn (*JEA*, 15 [1929], pp. 9–13) suggested that the Lihyanites owed their rise to power to active assistance received from Ptolemy II who campaigned in the northwestern Ḥijāz

A change in the fortunes of Liḥyān is attested by three Nabataean inscriptions (JS 334, 335, 337), the author of which, a certain Masʿudu, calls himself "king of Liḥyān." Since it is inconceivable that a native Lihyanite king would have employed the Nabataean script in preference to Lihyanite, Masʿudu must be regarded as an outsider. Jaussen and Savignac[38] dated the inscriptions on palaeographic grounds to the second century B.C. Albright[39] would date them to the first century B.C., Caskel[40] to the first century A.D. No matter which dating is correct, it is difficult to find a place for Masʿudu in the line of Nabataean kings, the more so when it is recalled that all known Nabataen kings bear the name of either Ḥaretat, Rabb'el, ʿObodat, or Malikho. It is improbable, therefore, that Masʿudu was a Nabataean king. He seems to have been an adventurer acting independently of the Nabataean kings, although his use of the Nabataean script implies that he came from the Nabataean cultural zone north of Dedan.[41] In him we doubtless see the agent responsible for the overthrow of the Lihyanites in the second, or possibly first, century B.C. Masʿudu was apparently robbed of the fruits of victory by the Nabataean kings of Petra who extended their sway southward and incorporated his domain into their own kingdom.[42] The presence of some thirty Nabataean graffiti at Dedan is evidence of the dawn of a new era in the history of the oasis.

B/MINAEAN INSCRIPTIONS

2 Copy (*RÉS* 3721 = JS 47). Pl. 2.

ḥwym	*Ḥuwayyum.*

3 Phot. W 7:27 (*RÉS* 3722 = JS 48). Pl. 2.

sʿd['*l*]	*Saʿad*['*il*]
ḏyfʿn	*of Yafʿān.*

The copy of JS (Pl. cxxii) gives *ḏ* with only one cross-bar but the photo shows two. No. 9 below is by the same person. In the fourth century B.C., one of the

in 277 B.C. The existence of some political link between Liḥyān and Egypt, in the latter part of Liḥyān's history at least, is indicated by the fact that two of the late Lihyanite kings bear the name TLMY (= Ptolemy). Jaussen and Savignac dated the rise of Liḥyān to the third or second century B.C., as did Levi Della Vida in his article on "Liḥyān" in the *Enc. of Islam*, 1st ed.

38/*Mission*, II, p. 221.

39/*Dedan*, p. 7, n. 2. See also van den Branden in *BOr*, 14 (1957), p. 14.

40/*LL*, p. 42, n. 125.

41/Or does the fact that his inscriptions come from Khabu al-Gharbī near Taymā' indicate that he came from that direction?

42/It is unlikely that the Nabataean kings would have allowed a viceroy of theirs at Dedan to bear the title of "king."

Minaean *kabīrs* at Dedan was a member of the Yafʿān tribe (cf. Hal. 536, 578 = Gl. 1155 = *RÉS* 3022). This doubtless accounts for the presence of many Yafʿānite tribesmen at Dedan, as is attested by their inscriptions (cf. JS 17, 18, 23, 42, 48, 57, 64, 67, 68, 72, 76, 85, 101, 107, 109, 132, 137, 138, 143, 149, 162, 170(?), 172 min. and 50, 196, 197(?), 216 lih.).

4 Phot. R 105:15A (*RÉS* 3727 = JS 53). Pls. 2 and 25.

yfʿ	*Yāfiʿ*
bn mrr	*b. Marār.*

The reading of JS. – The other inscriptions below this are illegible.

5 Phot. 105:16A (*RÉS* 3732 = JS 58). Pl. 2.

ʿbdt	*ʿAbdat*
ḫbʾt	*of Khabiʾat.*

The reading of JS. – The relative particle *ḏ* is often omitted before the name of the family or tribe but see *ḏy ḫbʾt* in the Sab. inscription *CIS*, IV, 695. The form of the *ḫ* is noteworthy.

6 Phot. R 105:16A (*RÉS* 3733 = JS 59). Pl. 2.

ʿbdwd mn	*ʿAbdwadd from* (*the tribe of*)
grmnhy	*Garmanāhy.*

JS suggested that *mn* has here the force of *bn*, "son," and this interpretation seems supported by the fact that *GRMNHY* is the name of an individual in JS 68 min. However, there is no other instance, I believe, of *mn* being so used, although the preposition *bn* ("from") is commonly used for *mn* in SAr. Hence it seems preferable to take *GRMNHY* as the name of a tribe, and *mn* as the preposition "from."

7 Phot. R 105:16A (*RÉS* 3736 = JS 62). Pl. 2.

grmn	*Garmanāhy.*
hy	

Cf. Nab. *GRMʾLHY* (see J. Cantineau, *Le Nabatéen*, II [Paris, 1932], p. 79).

8 Phot. R 105:16A (*RÉS* 3735 = JS 61). Pl. 2.

ḫḍn	*Khaḍan*
grmt	*of Girmat.*

JS read *Ḫaḍan Ğirmat.* – GRMT occurs in Saf. (cf. *RNP*, I, 63) but *ḪḌN* is found only here.

9 Phot. R 105:16A (*RÉS* 3738 = JS 64). Pl. 2.

sʿdʾl ḏyfʿn Symbol	*yrb ḏbwsn*
Saʿadʾil of Yafʿān Symbol	*Yarubb of Bausān.*

See no. 4. – JS take the sign after *yf'n* as the letter *ḥ* and read the following name as *ḤYRB*, a name which occurs nowhere else. The sign is noticeably larger than the other letters of the inscription and this makes it probable that it is a symbol without phonetic value. – YRB occurs in Qat. (Gl. 1606, 34), YRBM in Sab. (Hal. 615). – JS read the last name as Dabūsān but our photo shows that the initial sign is *ḏ*. BWSN occurs as a family or tribal name in JS 178 min., and ḎBWSN in Qat. (*RÉS* 3566, 28). The inscription is therefore of interest because it provides the first clear evidence of the presence of Qatabanians at Dedan. The family of Yaḥar mentioned in JS 249 lih. may also be of Qatabanian origin (cf. SE 80, 2). For evidence of friendly co-operation between Minaeans and Qatabanians, see M. A. Ghul in *BSOAS*, 22 (1959), pp. 429–33. For co-operation between the Minaeans and Ḥaḍramis, see J. Ryckmans in *Scrinium Lovaniense*, pp. 60–1.

10 Phot. R 105:9A and copy. Pl. 2.

yḥm'l ḏqḥl ḏbyt

Yaḥmi'il of Qaḥal who spent the night (*here*).

JS 83 is by the same author but lacks *ḏbyt*. – The family of QḤL is not mentioned elsewhere. – The verb *byt* (Ar. *bāta*) appears several times in Tham. in the contracted form *bt* (see vdB, *IT*, p. 512), in Saf. as *byt* (see, e.g., *CIS*, v, 28 and *WSIJ*, no. 139) but does not seem to occur in SAr.

11 Copy. Pl. 2.

ġlb	*Ghālib*
'ḥrm	*of 'Aḥram.*

ĠLB occurs in the Delos inscription (*RÉS* 3952, Hadr.) and in Qat. (cf. *RNP*, I, 174). – The family or tribe of 'ḤRM appears in JS 122 min. and in *EDAr.* XVII, 7, in the latter text being preceded by the particle *ḏ*.

C/DEDANITE AND LIHYANITE INSCRIPTIONS

1–5 Phot. R 105:24A and copy. On the way up the mountain behind al-Khuraybah. D(edanite) or E(arly) L(ihyanite). Pls. 24 and 25.

1 *zdy bns m(b)ṭ*	*ZDY his son* ...(?)
tm yṯmt	*Taym of Yathmat.*

The name ZDY is not met with elsewhere. Possibly it is an error for ZYD, which occurs frequently in Minaean. – *bns* = *bn* with the Min. 3rd person sing. suffix. – *mbṭ* (or *mkṭ*) is difficult. – The YṮMT family is mentioned in four Minaean inscriptions at Dedan (JS 26, 111, 112, 174). The inscription is of interest because the language is Minaean but the script is Lihyanite. For Lihyanite texts exhibiting Minaean script-influence, see my article, "The Place of the Minaeans in the History of Pre-Islamic Arabia" (*BASOR*, no. 73 [1939], pp. 3–9). It would appear that after the collapse of the Minaean kingdom, some of the Minaean residents of Dedan continued to reside there.

2 D or EL.

dln *DLN*

The inscription appears to be framed on either side by a vertical stroke; see no. 5. The name, which is new, recurs in no. 3.

3 D or EL.

z ldln lrm *This is for DLN by RM.*

See no. 2. The name RM is new.

4 D or EL.

lšnḫ *By ŠNḪ.*

The name is new; cf. *šannaḫa*, "to remove the thorns (of a palm tree)."

5 D or EL.

btt hnʿm bn mtʿ

The cutting of ha-Naʿam b. Mataʿ.

The inscription is framed by a vertical stroke at each end. – *btt*, cf. Ar. *battah*, "a cutting," and *batāt*, "provisions." – HNʿM is a new name, but NʿM is common. – MTʿ occurs as a tribal name in Min. and Qat. (cf. *RNP*, I, 303).

6 Phot. R 105:19A and copy (*EDAr.* 34 = JS 79). EL. Pls. 24 and 25.

(a)	(b)
1 *mrrh wḥṭlh bnw*	(i) *hnfy*
2 *nṭr 'ḫḏw hqb*	(ii) *y wgrm*
3 *r ḏh hm w'ḫwhm f*	(iii) *lwš'*
4 *(m)rr*	(iv) *ḏt l*
	(v) *mrrh wḥṭlh*
	(vi) *wn's*

1 *Murārah and Ḥiṭlah, the sons of*	(i) *Ha-Nafy*
2 *Nāṭir, have taken possession of this*	(ii) *and Garm*
3 *tomb, they and their brother, in*	(iii) *have denied this*
4 *perpetuity.*	(iv) *wish to*
	(v) *Murārah and Ḥiṭlah*
	(vi) *and Nu'ās.*

The last two lines of inscription (b) are engraved below inscription (a). – For

MRRH, see *RNP*, I, 132. – ḤṬLH, cf. Ar. *ḥiṭl*, "wolf" (Salmoné, p. 143). JS and Grimme (*Neubearbeitung*, p. 312) read ḤḌRH but see JS 72, 3 for the form of the *ṭ*. – NṬR is found in Min. (JS 96, 2; 135, 3). – *'ḫḏw*, cf. Cantineau, *Le Nabatéen*, II, p. 59. – *'ḫwhm* could be either "their brother" or "their brothers." – *fmrr* is taken by JS as the conjunction *f* followed by a n. pr. This is improbable since elsewhere the conjunction *w* is used before proper names. It is more likely that *f* is the prep. *fī*, followed by *murūr*, "uninterrupted sequence" (Wehr). – HNFY appears to be the Lih. form of Min. NFY (JS 75). It recurs in JS 80, 193, 256, 259, 302 and *EDAr.* LVII. For the isolated *y* at the beginning of line 2, see the remarks of JS. – GRM is found in Min., Tham., and Saf. (cf. *RNP*, I, 63; II, 44). – *lw*, cf. Ar. *lawā*, "to twist, repudiate, deny." JS read *mrmlw*, "Marāmlaw," but such a name is improbable. The author evidently felt that a word-divider was unnecessary at the end of the line; similarly at the end of line 3. – *š'*, cf. Ar. *šay'*, "thing," from *šā'a*, "to wish." To be grammatically correct, the article should have been used before *š'*; cf. *hnqbr ḏh* in no. 7. – N'S is found in Sab. (*CIS*, IV, 68, 1). – It is evident from (b) that the tomb designed for the sons of Nāṭir was later appropriated by ha-Nafy and Garm.

7 Phot. W 8:36, R 105:17A and copy (*EDAr.* 35 = JS 81). D. Pl. 24.

lntnb'l	*This tomb belongs to*
bn wny hn	*Natanba'al b. Wany.*
qbr ḏh ḥm	*It has been protected*
'ly ymn	*on the right*
w'ly šm['l]	*and on the left*
mn ṯrq(h)	*from thieves.*

NTNB'L: The *b'l* is no doubt Ba'alsamīn, whose worship at Liḥyān is attested by JS 64. – For the n. pr. WNY, see no. 16 below and Jamme, *Notes*, p. 19. This WNY may be the same person as the WNY b. FSY of no. 16. – *hnqbr ḏh*: The article in Lihyanite was *h* before ordinary consonants, *hn* before all gutturals except *ġ* (see JS 49). Here, where the article is separated from the noun, the *n* has been retained in the writing. The Lihyanite demonstrative comes after the noun, as in Hebrew, but unlike Hebrew usage it does not take the article. – *ḥm* is taken by JS as the passive of *ḥamma*, "to decree, appoint," and rendered by "il a été disposé," but more probably it is to be explained from Ar. *ḥamā*, "to defend, protect." – *šm...* is manifestly the correlative of *ymn* and hence to be restored as *šm'l*; cf. Ar. *šimāl*, "left." – JS read the last word as *ṯrqr* but the root is unknown in Arabic. E. Ullendorf (*Orientalia*, 24 [1955], p. 431) suggested that it was the name of some disease. The photograph lends some support to the reading *ṯrqh*; cf. Ar. *saraqah*, "theft, thieves." – Following *ṯrqh* there are faint traces of a word-divider and the letter *s*. See no. 14. The entrance to the tomb was enlarged at a later date with the result that the inscription has suffered some slight damage.

8 Copy. Two metres to the right of no. 7. D. Pl. 24.

'(w)s'l *'Uways'il.*

The cross-bar of the *w* is missing (as in Thamudic inscription no. 48) giving to the letter the appearance of ʿayin. *'WS'L* occurs in Min. (JS 23 and 324 lih., the latter a Minaean text).

9 Phot. W 8:32 (JS 83). EL. Pls. 24 and 25.

1 ...
2 *š wk* ...
3 *m šms* ... *hṣl*
4 *mn hḏ(h)n* ...
5 *'bhm ḫrḥḏġbt fr*
6 *ḏyhm w'ḫrthm wsʿ*
7 *dhm snt ʿšrn wtsʿ*
8 (29) *br'y gltqs*

1–2 ...
3 ... *these two*
4 *statues* ...
5 *their* (*divine*) *father ḪRḤ-dhū-Ghābat. So may he*
6 *favour them and guide them and bless*
7 *them. The twenty-ninth* (29) *year*
8 *in the reign of GLT-Qaus.*

The inscription is engraved on a square pedestal with recessed top, designed to receive a statue. For the statues found at the site, see JS, *Mission*, II, p. 57, and Plates XXIX–XXXI. The copy of the inscription given above is based on the photograph of JS since most of the pedestal is now buried in the sand. Line 1 is completely obliterated. Of line 2 only *š wk* . . . can be discerned on the impression and copy of JS (Pls. LXXV and CXII). The three letters are all that remains of the names of those who presented the statues. JS's restoration [*w*ʿ]*mšms* at the beginning of l. 3 is doubtful since the name ʿMŠMS does not occur elsewhere. A possible restoration is [ḤR] MŠMS which occurs in Min. (JS 137). The restoration *hdqw* or *hwdqw* before [*hṣl*]*mn* can be supported by reference to *hdqt hṣlmn* in JS 62 (cf. also JS 49, 50, 61, 63), but instead of *hḏh* the dual form *hḏhn* should be read. JS 82, 2 supports the restoration of *nḏr* (not *ḏnḏr* as Grimme read) but it is to be regarded as the substantive *nuḏur*, pl. of *naḏr*, "votive-offering," rather than a verb. The attempt to find a reference to ʿAglibūn (= Palmyrene ʿAglibol) at the end of l. 4 is very precarious. The only letter which is certain is *g*. The idea contained in this line may have been that the statues were presented as votive-offerings for the adornment of the temple of the god. JS interpret the words *'bhm ḫrḥḏġbt* of l. 5 to mean "their father Ḫaraḥ, the proprietor of (the place) Ghābat." But the formula consisting of the three verbs *rḍy* (Ar. *raḍiya*), *'ḫrt* (cf. Ar. *ḫarita*, "to be an expert guide"), and *s'd* is always used with a god as the subject, expressed or implied (see JS 62, 63, 75, 82–4). This makes it highly probable that ḪRḤḎĠBT is a divine name. A god ḎĠBT (Dhū-Ghābat) appears frequently in the inscriptions, but such a name is a title meaning "He of Ghābat" and is not the god's real name. The latter may well have been ḪRḤ. The root *ḫrḥ* has been found only once elsewhere in ancient Arabic, in Qat. *mḫrḥw* (Gl. 1693, 13 = *RÉS* 3858), "canals" (?). N. Rhodokanakis (*Ḳat. Texte*, II, [*SBWA*, 198 (1922), Bd. 2 Abh.], pp. 43, 94) explains it from Ar. *ḫr'* (cf. Ar. *ḫara'a*, "to slit, split," Syr. *ḥ'rīā*, "ditch, canal").

The inscription is dated to the twenty-ninth year of the *r'y* of GLTQS. The expression *br'y* appears elsewhere in JS 72, 83, 85, *EDAr.* VIII, LXX; *r'y* without *b* in JS 68. In two Late Lihyanite texts (JS 54 and 77) it is replaced by *bsmwy*. Both expressions are without parallel in other Arabian inscriptions and seem to be an attempt to render a foreign concept. Müller (*EDAr.*, pp. 60–61) and Grimme (*Neubearbeitung*, p. 304) translate *smwy* by "himmlischen." Müller did not venture a translation of *br'y* but Grimme (pp. 301ff.) renders it by "unter der Regierung." It seems probable that both terms are an attempt to render the Hellenistic conception expressed by *epiphaneia*, the word used, for instance, of the accession of the divine Caligula (37–41 A.D.) and of deities manifesting themselves to worshippers (cf. H. G. Liddell and R. Scott, *Greek-English Lexicon*, new ed. [Oxford, 1940], p. 669). The *smwy* of the king must mean something like his "elevation to heavenly status," i.e. his deification at his accession. Hence *bsmwy* may be rendered "(dated) by the epiphany of." *br'y* is used in parallel construction but seems to mean simply "oversight, reign." Caskel believes that the dates in Early Lihyanite inscriptions (such as this is) are reckoned from the Syrian provincial era which began with Pompey's conquest in 64 B.C. Hence he dates the inscription to 36 B.C. (p. 41). But it is more probable that the Lihyanites dated their inscriptions by the regnal years of their kings, as did the Nabataeans. The exact position of GLTQS in the Lihyanite king-list is difficult to determine. For attempts to arrange the kings in chronological order, see my *Notes*, p. 308; Caskel, *LL*, p. 41; and Albright, *Dedan*, pp. 6–7.

The inscription is so closely related in content and function to JS 82, both occurring on pedestals designed to receive statues, that it is natural to assume that they must be almost contemporary. But JS 82 is dated in the thirty-fifth year of (MN)' Laudhān b. han-'Aus whereas JS 83 is dated in the twenty-ninth year of GLTQS. If GLTQS reigned before MN' Laudhān, there is a minimum of thirty-five years between the two inscriptions. If MNʿ Laudhān reigned first, there are at least twenty-nine years between them. In either case it seems unlikely that sons of an individual named ḪRḤ-dhū-Ghābat set up statues and an inscription in honour of their father twenty-nine (or thirty-five) years after they had set up similar statues and an inscription. It is much more probable that the dedications were made to a divine father. (For the conception of a community as the sons of a god, see G. Ryckmans, *Religions*, p. 329.) Grohmann (*Arabien*, p. 65) retains the incorrect readings MLTQS for the royal name.

10 Phot. W 7:34A. LL. Pl. 24.

mr'lh	*Mar'allāh*
kḥl	*of Kuḥayl.*

MR'LH occurs several times in Lih. The Nab. orthography is 'MR'LHY. The name KḤL is new; cf. Ar. *kuḥayl*, "blood-horse."

11 Phot. R 105:21A (JS 314). EL. Pls. 24 and 25.

mr'lh	*Mar'allāh*
bn ṣlmgd	*b. Ṣalmgadd.*

It is unlikely that the element *ṣlm* in the second name is the Taymanite god Ṣalm. More probably it is the substantive *ṣalm* (= Ar. *ṣanm*), "image." For GD, "Fortune," see above, p. 115.

12 Phot. R 105:21A. Below no. 11, to the left. EL. Pls. 24 and 25.

bḥš mn llh(?) rtb(h)

Buḥaysh from LLH(?) arranged it.

BHŠ occurs in Tham. (Ph. 279h). The reading of the two letters after *mn* is uncertain. – *rtb*, cf. Ar. *rattaba*, "to arrange, dispose." The reference is probably to the drawing of two camels below the inscription.

13 Phot. R 105:15A (JS 186, Pl. cxxxii = Doughty, Pl. xiv, fol. 25 = *EDAr.* 71). Pls. 24 and 25.

mtʿ'l bn ḏrḥ'l
hnʿm ḥwl
ʿḏ'rl htndd

Mataʿ'il b. Dharaḥ'il.
May the power of ʿAdar'il be graciously disposed (toward him) *on the day-of-assembly*!

Mataʿ'il's funerary inscription is so unusual as to suggest that he was a person of some importance. Although not called a king, it is probable that he was the father of Kabir'il, king of Dedan, whose tomb-inscription was discussed above (pp. 114–15). – *hnʿm*, cf. Ar. *naʿama*, iv, "to make pleasant, bestow favours on, be graciously disposed toward." The word "God" may be implied before the optative as in JS 73:5–6 and 75:4, but more probably *ḥwl ʿd'rl* is the subject. Although there is room for several letters after *ḥwl* (cf. Ar. *ḥawl*, "power," or *ḥawla*, "around, about"), the photograph lends no support to the view of Grimme (*Neubearbeitung*, p. 284) and Caskel (*LL*, p. 78) that one or more letters have been erased.

The interpretation of the inscription offered above differs radically from the interpretations proposed by Grimme and Caskel. The former translates: "Matta''il, Sohn des Ḏaraḥ'il, hat (freundschaftlich) überlassen [dieses] Zwischenstück dem Wadd'il, Sohne des Natandad." Caskel renders by: "Mataʿ-il b. Ḏaraḥ hat für [seinen] Transport nach Uruk – Natan-Dād Gunst (Lohn) ausgesetzt." Van den Branden (*ID*, p. 62) reads: "Mata''il b. Ḏaraḥ'il a fait du bien autour de (lui) ... les gens de Uruk-Natandud."

In my opinion the key to the proper understanding of the inscription lies in recognizing that the last word is to be read *htndd* rather than *ntndd*. (See Doughty's copy in *Doc. épig.*, Pl. XIV. D. H. Müller, *EDAr.*, no. LXXI, reads the first letter as *ḥ*.) *htndd* is composed of the definite article and the *maṣdar* of either *nadda*, VI, "to disperse, flee," or *nadā*, VI, "to assemble." The significance of the term is to be found in the Qur'ānic expression *yawm at-tanādi*, "the day of assembling," i.e. the Day of Resurrection (cf. 40:34). According to Lane (p. 2778), the expression *yawm at-tanāddi*, "the day of men's dispersing themselves, and betaking themselves in different directions," was also used.

ʿd'rl was read *ʿd'rk* (ʿAd'arak) by JS, but what they and Caskel took to be a *k* is really *l* followed by a word-divider (see Doughty's copy). The author's use of a word-divider in lines 1 and 2 makes it improbable that he neglected to use it in line 3. The failure of JS and Caskel to allow for a word-divider in this line is a fundamental weakness in their treatment of it. Grimme's reading *[w]d'[l]bntndd* is quite impossible. *ʿd'rl* must be a name ending in *'il*. It is either a misspelling of *ʿdr'l* (ʿAdar'il) or the spelling indicates a pronunciation with long *ā*-vowel after the *d*, ʿAdār'il. In view of the reference to the Day of Assembly and the fact that the inscription is a tomb-inscription, as well as the fact that angels' names end in *-'il*, it seems likely that in *ʿd'rl* we have an Aramaic (Nabataean?) form of *ʿIzrā'īl* who appears in the eschatology of Islam as the Angel of Death (cf. *ERE*, iv, 616–17; *Enc. of Islam*, 1st ed., "ʿIzrā'īl"). The Islamic form of the name is generally believed to be of Jewish origin, but the only Jewish angel who might serve as a prototype is ʿAsrī'ēl who presided over Gehinnom. Possibly Jewish ʿAsrī'ēl, Islamic ʿIzrā'īl, and Dedanite ʿD'RL (ʿAdār'il) all derive ultimately from Egyptian Osiris, ruler of the abode of the dead, but the exact source from which the Dedanites acquired the name remains to be determined. At any rate the inscription gives us our first insight into the religious beliefs of some of the pre-Islamic Arabs regarding the Hereafter. – The significance of the large circle at the end of the inscription is not clear; it is manifestly an integral part of the inscription for it stands within the same cartouche.

14 Phot. W 8:34 and copy (JS 318). LL. Pl. 24.

ršm bn sʿ	*Rashm b. Saʿdallāh.*
dlh	

See JS. The photograph does not support their interpretation of the sign at the end of the inscription as *w*. It is probably a numerical sign indicating the age of the deceased; cf. the form of the Nab. numeral 5.

15 Phot. R 105:16A. EL or LL. Pl. 24.

'rš	*'Irāsh.*
bḥtr	*b. Ḥatr.*

'RŠ occurs in both Lih. and Tham. (cf. *RNP*, I, 47; II, 35). The reading of the second name is not quite certain; cf. Ar. *ḥatr*, "small gift."

16 Phot. R 105:23A and copy. D. Pls. 24 and 25.

wny bn fsy	*Wani b. FSY*
tqṭ mʿ	*has inscribed his name with*
ḏmʿly frḍyh	*Him-on-high. So may He favour him*
wsʿdh wʾḫrth	*and bless him and guide him.*

This WNY may be the one mentioned in no. 7. – FSY is new. – *tqṭ* seems to be the vth form of *qaṭṭa*, "to cut, carve." It recurs in JS 103, 119, 147, 149, 182, 185, 339 lih. and JS 251, 539 tham. – It is unlikely that *ḏmʿly* is the name of a person since blessings are invoked only upon Wani. Possibly it is to be explained as the rel. pron. *ḏ* + *min ʿạlay*, "He who is above"; cf. Ar. *maʿālīhi*, "His Excellency." The idea of having one's name inscribed with God (if that is the meaning of the inscription) recalls Moses' words in Exod. 32:32, "But now, if thou wilt forgive their sin – and if not, blot me, I pray thee out of the book which thou hast written."

17 Phot. W 8:35 and copy. EL or LL. Pl. 24.

... nḍr ...	*... Naḍr ...*

A fragment of a monumental inscription found lying on the surface by Dr. Vidal. For Naḍr, cf. *RNP*, I, 144.

18 Phot. W 9:13 and copy. On summit of the mountain east of Dedan. D or EL. Pls. 24 and 25.

nšr bdṯ . . .	*Nashr b. DṮ . . .*
tqṭ	*has inscribed his name*
f(ḫ)r . . k	...

See no. 16. For NŠR, cf. *RNP*, I, 145, 397.

5 Inscriptions from the Madā'in Ṣāliḥ Area[1]

A/HISTORICAL BACKGROUND

It is usually assumed that Ḥegrā was a Nabataean foundation but the presence there of seven monumental Minaean inscriptions (JS 1–5, 33, 34) and twenty-nine Lihyanite graffiti is evidence that the site was occupied before the Nabataean period.[2] The Lihyanite-Minaean occupation must have ended in the second, or first, century B.C. with Mas'udu's overthrow of the kingdom of Liḥyān.[3] However, there is no specific reference to the presence of Nabataeans at Ḥegrā until 24 B.C. when Strabo (*Geography*, XVI, 4, 24) states that Aelius Gallus, on the way back from his campaign in South Arabia, came to *Egra*, situated in the territory of Obodas, king of the Nabataeans. Since Dedan, twenty-four kilometres (by road) to the south, was inhabited by a non-Nabataean population, the Nabataeans soon concentrated on the development of Ḥegrā as a centre that was peculiarly their own, doubtless to the detriment of Dedan.[4] The large number of magnificent tombs which they have left at Ḥegrā testifies to the prosperity which accrued to them as a result of their control of the northern end of the frankincense route. Since all the dated Nabataean inscriptions at Ḥegrā come from the first century A.D. (except one from 1 B.C.), it is evident that the city reached its apogee in that period.

The Roman annexation of Nabataea in 106 A.D. did not spell the extinction of the Nabataean people or of the Nabataean script. Inscriptions in Nabataean continued to be written down to the early fourth century A.D.

It is usually assumed that the indigenous population of the Ḥegrā area belonged to the Thamūd tribe, but if that were so, it is odd that they have left so few

1/See pp. 37, 42–54.

2/Grohmann (*Arabien*, p. 44) suggests that it was built by the Minaeans.

3/See above, p. 120.

4/Possibly the Nabataean graffiti near al-'Ulā and the stone with Nabataean dressing at al-Khuraybah (see p. 39) are the work of Nabataeans who took up residence in Dedan after the fall of the kingdom of Liḥyān.

inscriptions (about forty) in the immediate neighbourhood of the city.[5] The only one of these which can be dated is a bilingual Nabataeo-Thamudic inscription,[6] which comes from 267 A.D. There is no reason for believing that the Hijazi type of Thamudic script ceased to be used immediately after this, but it is unlikely that it continued in use much beyond 300 A.D.

B/THAMUDIC INSCRIPTIONS

72 Copy. H. → 30 km east of Madā'in Ṣāliḥ.[7] Pl. 7.
Sign. *ʿt ʿf hbkrtn*. Sign.
ʿAtī cured the two young she-camels.
The inscription is accompanied by a drawing of two camels. The sign at the end of the inscription seems to have no phonetic value. This raises the possibility that the sign at the beginning has no phonetic value either, the two signs serving merely as a frame for the inscription (see "Dedanite and Lihyanite Inscriptions," no. 5). – ʿT = ʿTY (cf. Ar. *ʿatī*, "haughty, unruly"). For other occurrences of the name in Tham. see no. 74 and vdB, *IT*, p. 541 (where Hu. 475 is to be deleted). – *ʿf*, cf. Ar. *ʿafā*, III, "to restore to health, cure, guard."

73–77 Above the water-channel south of the Dīwān, Madā'in Ṣāliḥ.[8] Copy. For previous discussions of the inscriptions, see vdB, *IT*, pp. 420–1.

73 (Doughty 6 = Hu. 577 = Eut. 792 = JS 1bis.) H. ↓ Pl. 7.
wbn'l šm lḥbyb
And Bin'il was on the look-out for Ḥubayb.
BN'L occurs in Sab. and Saf. (cf. *RNP*, I, 221 and *CIS*, V, 537, etc.). – *šm*, cf. Ar. *šāma*, "to be on the look-out." – The form *ḥbyb* occurs only here. It could be either the n. pr. Ḥubayb or the subst. *ḥabīb*, "lover." – Littmann (*TS*, p. 68) reads *wbn'r šml ḥbyb*, "Und Bn'r bedeckte ein Liebchen mit dem Mantel," giving to the straight-line sign two different values, *r* and *l*. VdB (*IT*, p. 421) reads "Et Bin'il (fils de Šimāl (fils de) Ḥubayb," but *bn*, expressing filiation, is never omitted in late Thamudic texts.

74 (Doughty 6 = Hu. 575 + 576 = Eut. 790 + 791 = JS 3 + 2.) Copy. H. ↓ Pl. 7
wddt fʿt fktmt
w'n fln

5/See vdB, *IT*, pp. 410–26.
6/See Nabataean inscription no. 91 and Pl. 33.
7/See above, p. 37.
8/See above, p. 50.

I love the mouth of ʿAtī, and I have concealed (my name).
I am So-and-So.

For *wdd f*, see no. 47. VdB (*IT*, pp. 421, 429) takes *wddt* as the pl. of *wdd* and renders by "amitiés," but Littmann's view (*TS*, pp. 68–9) that it is a verb, Perf. 1st sing., seems more probable. His interpretation of *ktmt* as a verb ("vergarg [meinem Namen]") instead of a n. pr. (so vdB) is supported by JS 12 + 13, *wdd fʿslt wktmt smy*, "He loves the mouth of ʿAssālah. And I have concealed my name." The change of person is strange but not impossible (see Thamudic inscription no. 36). – For ʿT, see no. 72. – The inscription presupposes a widespread knowledge of reading and writing.

75 (Doughty 6 = Hu. 574 = Eut. 789 = JS 4.) Copy. H. ↓ Pl. 7.

wddt fʿḏrf

I love the mouth of ʿUdhārif.

ʿḎRF may be derived, by metathesis, from Ar. *ʿuḏāfir*, "tall, strong (camel)." – VdB (*IT*, p. 420) reads *wddt fgḥrf*, "Amitiés à Gaḥr et ..." – Littmann (*TS*, p. 68, no. 101) reads *wddt f ʿḏf*, "Ich grüsste ʿAdāf," but this reading omits the *r*.

76 (Doughty 6 = Hu. 573 = Eut. 788 = JS 5.) Copy. H. ↓ Pl. 7.

nʿmt ʿn btms — *May she favour Tamuss*!

Cf. Ar. *naʿama ʾallāhu bika ʿain^{an}*, "May God favour thee!" (Hava, p. 783). Whether "she" refers to a goddess or to a human female is not clear. – TMS occurs in Lih. (JS 315). – Littmann (*TS*, p. 68) reads *nʿmt ʿšbt ms*, "Es war im zarten Grün ein Lotusbaum(?)." – VdB (*IT*, p. 420) translates, "Naʿamat est une aide dans l'infortune."

77 (Doughty 6 = Hu. 578 = Eut. 786 + 787 = JS 7 + 6.) Copy. ↓ Pl. 7.

wddt fʿṣm — *I love the mouth of ʿAṣim,*
wktmt — *and I have concealed* (my name).

So Littmann (*TS*, p. 68). – VdB (*IT*, p. 422) reads "Amitiés à ʿAṣam, et Katamat." – For the *ṣ*-sign, see Jamme, *TS*, p. 57

6 Inscriptions from the Upper Wādī as-Sirḥān

A/HISTORICAL BACKGROUND

At present there are some twenty Arab settlements and Bedouin camps in the upper reaches of the Wādī as-Sirḥān.[1] They are known collectively as "the salt villages" (Qurayyāt al-Milḥ). Their ancient history is unknown, but the *wādī* must have been under the control of either the dominant power in North Arabia or the dominant power in Transjordan and Syria. The Nabataeans eventually controlled it, the *wādī* serving as "the connecting lifeline between the two widely separated parts of the Nabataean kingdom."[2] The presence of Nabataean inscriptions at Ithrā[3] and at or near Sakākah[4] and al-Jawf[5] supports this view. Excavation would doubtless unearth further evidence of Nabataean occupation.

The indigenous population was probably closely related to that in the Ḥegrā area and may be conveniently grouped with it under the label "Thamudic." The script employed by the "Thamūd" in the Wādī as-Sirḥān, while similar to that employed by the "Thamūd" of the Ḥegrā area, developed certain peculiarities of its own (see Pl. 1) and has in the present work been labelled "Tabuki" since it seems to have radiated from the Tabūk oasis.

Most of the inscriptions found at Ithrā are inscribed on small pieces of limestone. The pieces seem to have come from the sanctuary there, but how they had been disposed in the sanctuary must remain a matter of conjecture.

B/THAMUDIC INSCRIPTIONS

(*i*) *Ithrā*[6] (*nos. 78–92*)

78 Phot. R 107:9 and copy. T. → Pls. 7 and 17.

lḥnnt bn skrn By *Ḥanānat b. Sakrān.*

ḤNNT, cf. ḤNNH in JS 252 lih.

1/See pp. 56–9.
2/Nelson Glueck in *BASOR*, no. 96 (1944), p. 7.
3/See Nabataean inscription no. 130, p. 160.
4/See Nabataean inscriptions nos. 1–15, pp. 142–4.
5/See Nabataean inscriptions nos. 16–21, pp. 144–6.
6/See pp. 59–60, 62.

79 Phot. R 107:9. On the same stone as no. 78. T. Pls. 7 and 17.

l'krtn bn šrqt — *By 'Akratān b. Shariqat.*

'KRTN is new; cf. Ar. *'akrat*, "curly." Possibly 'SRTN should be read. – ŠRQT occurs in Saf. (*WSIJ*, nos. 949 and 967); cf. Ar. *šaraqa*, "to sip, suck in."

80 Phot. R 107:10 and copy. T. Pl. 7.

lb(n)m(r) bn ḥrb — *By b. Nimr(?) b. Ḥarb.*

The reading of the first name is uncertain.

81 Phot. R 107:21 and copy. T. Spiral direction, beginning at lower left. Stone 16 × 20 × 3.6 cm. Pls. 7 and 17.

l('db) bn n'rt bn zd ḏ'l '(n'm) wndm 'l (')ḫh w'l (')ḫt(h) w'l ṣll w'l 'bd w'l km w'l 'ys w'l mlk w'l 'ys w'l m'n w'l mġṯ w'l ḥb'l w'l ḥn w'l kḥsmn

By ('Adīb) b. Na'rat b. Zayd of the tribe of 'A(n'am?). And he grieved for his brother and for his sister and for Ṣalāl and for 'Abd and for Kamm and for 'Iyās and for Mālik and for 'Iyās and for Ma'n and for Mughīth and for Ḥabb'il and for Ḥann and for Kaḥaysumān.

The reading of the first name is not quite certain. – N'RT occurs in Saf. (*CIS*, v, 2390). Possibly NGRT should be read. – The name of the tribe is almost illegible. – *ndm 'l* occurs several times in Saf. (*CIS*, v, 2240, 2947, 3144, 4988, 5050, and L 669). – For ṢLL, cf. *RNP*, I, 183. – KM occurs in Lih. (JS 371). – For KḤSMN, see *WSIJ*, pp. 24 and 190.

82 Copy. T. Upper line r. to l., lower line l. to r. Stone 13 × 16 × 1.5 cm. Pl. 7.

[l . .] š hdf(y) [w]wgm 'l 'ḫ[h] . . m ḏ'l fgn wsby

[By . .]sh ha-DF(Y). [And] he grieved for his brother . . M of the tribe of FGN. And he was taken prisoner.

For *wgm 'l*, see *JAOS*, 73 (1953), pp. 41–2. – The tribe, or family, of FGN is mentioned here for the first time. – The verb *sby* (Ar. *sabā*), here in the passive, occurs in Saf. (WH 1247, unpublished).

83 Phot. R 107:20 and copy. T. Boustrophedon, beginning with top line. Stone 14 cm long and *ca.* 2 cm thick. Pls. 8 and 17.

lkhl [w]bhš wslm wnbhn w'qrb w'ys ws(n) wġyr

For Kāhil [and] Buhaysh and Sālim and Nabhān and 'Aqrab and 'Iyās and Sīn and Ghayr.

Most of the names are common in Saf. NBHN occurs in Tham. (see *HTIJ*, nos. 363 and 461); cf. Ar. *nabhān*, "wakefulness, wariness," and *abū nabhān*, "fox." – SN occurs in *CIS*, v, 1190, etc.; the reading is not quite certain since part of the stone is broken away. Possibly the beginning of the inscription should be restored to read *lkhl*[*wwgm* *'l*] *bhš*.

84 Phot. R 107:22 and copy. T. Spiral direction, beginning with lower line r. to l. Pls. 7 and 17.

lmr bn mḥlm	*By Murr b. Muḥallim*
ḏ'l grm wwgm	*of the tribe of Garm. And he grieved*
'l 'bh w'l	*for his father and for*
'ys w'l yġṯ	*'Iyās and for Yaghūth*
w'l ġyr'l	*and for Ghayyar'il.*

The names are common in Saf. This is the first mention of the family or tribe of Garm. For the magical sign composed of seven parallel lines, see my *Study*, pp. 6–7; Littmann, *TS*, p. 120; and vdB, *HT*, p. 68, n. 223.

85 Phot. R 107:24 and copy. T. Spiral direction, beginning in centre. Stone 4 × 5.5 × 1 cm. Pls. 8 and 17.

qhr bn 'smnt — *Qāhir b. 'Awsmanāt.*

QHR, cf. Ar. *qāhir*, "conqueror"; the name may occur in Harding, *NST*, no. 8. – 'SMNT is found in Lih. and Tham. (Littmann, *TS*, p. 67 and *HTIJ*, p. 51). The *m* has an unusual form. A hole has been drilled through the stone, suggesting that the inscription was tied to some object.

86 Phot. R 107:25 and copy. T. ← Stone 6.7 × 3 × 3 cm. Pls. 8 and 17.

. . . (*t*)*wd* . . . — ?

87 Phot. 107:27 and copy. T. ← ? Stone 3 × 1.7 × 1 cm. T. ? Pls. 8 and 17.

. . . *mnh* . . . — ?

88 Phot. R 107:26 and copy. T. → ? Stone 5.5 × 4 × 3 cm. T. ? Pls. 8 and 17.

. . . *nš* . . . — ?

89 Phot. 107:28 and copy. T. → ? Stone 5.3 × 2 cm. Pls. 8 and 17.

. . . (')*wq* — ?

90 Phot. R 107:29 and copy. T. ← ? Stone 10 × 6 × 2 cm. T. ? Pls. 8 and 17.

ldb — *By Dubb.*

DB occurs in Tham and Saf. (*RNP*, I, 64).

91 Phot. R 107:23 and copy. On a jar fragment. T. ← Pls. 8 and 17.

. . . *ḏgn*(*m*) . . . — ?

92 Phot. R 107:30 and copy. T. ⇄ Stone 16 × 8 × 3 cm. Pls. 8 and 17.

(*l*)'(*dbn*) *wtšwq* ... — *By 'A*(*dbān?*). *And he longed for ...*

(ii) South of Ithrā (nos. 93–97)

93 Copy. T. ↓ Pl. 8.

lsmm bn 'lh *By Samām b. 'Alih.*

For the names, see *RNP*, I, 151 and 37.

94 Copy. T. ↑↓ Pl. 9.

lbgt bn gdyn wḥgn

By Baggat b. Gadyān. And he crooked (a staff).

BGT occurs in Saf. (cf. *RNP*, I, 48). – GDYN is new; cf. Ar. *gady*, "kid." – *ḥgn*, cf. Ar. *ḥagana*, "to bend, crook (a staff)."

95 Copy. T. → Pl. 9.

lġṯ bn ʿzz *By Ghawth b. ʿAzīz.*

96 Copy. T. → Pl. 9.

lgrf bn ḥn'l *By Gurayf b. Ḥann'il.*

GRF occurs in Eut. 130 and in Saf. (cf. *RNP*, I, 63 and vdB, *IT*, p. 7). – ḤN'L is common in Saf.

97 Copy. T. ⇄ Pl. 9.

lglm bn 'b'ns wrmy

By Galm b. 'Ab'anas. And he was wounded.

GLM occurs in Saf. (*CIS*, v, 699). – 'B'NS is found in both Qat. and Saf. (see *RNP*, I, 253; II, 22; and *WSIJ*, p. 136). – The verb *rmy* (cf. Ar. *ramā*, "to shoot, hit") is no doubt in the passive.

(iii) From an old cemetery north of Ithrā (no. 98)

98 Copy. T. Pl. 9.

lmġyr b ... *By Mughayr b. ...*

For the name, cf. *RNP*, I, 174.

(iv) From the ḥarrah beyond Ithrā[7] *(nos. 99–101)*

99 Copy. T. Pl. 9.

slḫ lsn ?

Cf. Saf. *slḫ rwḥ* (*CIS*, v, 35 and 5050).

7/See p. 63.

100 Copy. T. Pl. 9.

lʿk(r)b bn mgnn hdr

This camping-place belongs to ʿK(R)B b. Magnān.

ʿKRB is new and without a known root in Ar. The identity of the third letter is, however, uncertain. – MGNN occurs in Qat. (cf. *RNP*, I, 123).

101 Copy. T. → Pl. 9.

lʾfl bn ʾws *By ʾAfil b. ʾUways.*

ʾFL occurs in Saf. (cf. *RNP*, I, 46). ʾWS is common.

(*v*) *Al-Qarqar*[8] (*no. 102*)

102 Phot. R 107:15 and copy. T. Spiral direction, beginning at the lower left corner. Pl. 9.

lm ... gwtrẖlf(nḏ) ..... ʾnṣr w.ẖ.gm

The inscription is so badly defaced that it seems impossible to make any sense of it.

8/See pp. 63–4.

7 Inscribed Stone at Turaif

THAMUDIC INSCRIPTIONS

103 Copy. T. → Pl. 9.

l'sn bn g(f) *By 'Awsān b. G(F).*

The last sign is not quite clear; it may be *l*. GL occurs in no. 50 and is common in Saf. The inscription is thought to have been brought to Turaif from Badanah.

104 Copy. T. ⇆ Pl. 9.

l's bn ḫl(f) ... llh wgls

By 'Aws b. Khal(af) ... and he set (it) up.

gls, cf. Ar. *gallasa*, "to set up"; see *WSIJ*, nos. 688, 715, and 798.

III Nabataean, Palmyrene, and Hebrew Inscriptions

J.T.MILIK and J.STARCKY

1 Inscriptions nabatéennes

Le catalogue qui suit a été préparé sur la base des photographies et de quelques copies transmises aux éditeurs par W. L. Reed et F. V. Winnett. Elles représentent la moisson épigraphique nabatéenne récoltée au cours de leur expédition en Arabie (oasis d'el-Jauf, Taimâ, el-'Ulâ, el-Ḥijr, villages du Wādī es-Sirḥān), en avril-mai 1962.

Toutes les inscriptions sont transcrites, et souvent commentées, à l'exception des textes funéraires de Hegra dont la photographie est insuffisante (sauf notre n° 79). La plupart ont été reprises sous forme de fac-similés, pls. 26–31; pour plusieurs nids d'inscriptions on a respecté la situation réciproque des graffites sur le rocher. Quelques inscriptions sont reproduites en photographie, pls. 32–34.

Aire de cette récolte :

A/Région d'el-Jauf	21
B/Région de Madā'in Ṣāliḥ	
(i) A 30 km à l'est de Madā'in Ṣāliḥ	17
(ii) El-'Ulâ	12
(iii) El-Ḥijr	79
C/Ithrā (Wādī es-Sirḥān)	1
	130

De ce total, 68 numéros sont inédits et 39, déjà connus, reçoivent ici un premier déchiffrement, ou une lecture améliorée, ou une interprétation nouvelle. Pour les graffites de Hegra, on s'est efforcé de comparer et d'identifier les copies anciennes réunies dans le *CIS* à celles du Père Savignac et aux photographies de W. L. Reed et de F. V. Winnett.

En plus, un des deux éditeurs publie ici une inscription palmyrénienne inédite, et l'autre, deux inscriptions juives de Dedan, dont une inédite.

Un premier essai d'identification des inscriptions a été fait par W. L. Reed et F. V. Winnett ; l'essai plus poussé, le premier déchiffrement et des éléments du commentaire sont dus à J. Starcky. Ils ont été ensuite revus par J. T. Milik, qui est le principal responsable du texte dans son état actuel.

A/RÉGION D'EL-JAUF

(*i*) *El-Qal'ah* (*n*os *1–14*)

Rocher à 6 km environ au nord de Sakākah; avec des inscriptions thamoudéennes 1–11. Photographie d'ensemble R(eed) 101:18A.

1 Phot. 101:19A et copie; notre copie, pls. 10 et 26.

šlm wtrw br ʿnmw — *Paix, Witrû fils de Ǵānimû.*

A la fin un signe, identique au waw, qui n'est pas dû à la même main. – Même personnage au nº 4 (une autre main) et au nº 14 (même main qu'au nº 1). – Nous conservons ici la traduction reçue de *šlm* par « paix ». En fait, il ne s'agit pas, à notre avis, du substantif *šalām*, mais de l'adjectif verbal *šalim*, qui ici a valeur de permansif : qu'un tel « soit (durablement) sain et sauf ».

2 Phot. 101:20A et copie. Pls. 10 et 26.

'wš'lhy br ʿwydw — *'Auš'ilāhî fils de ʿAwîdû.*

3 Phot. 101:21A et copie. Pls. 10 et 26.

rbyb'l br — *Rabîb'el fils de*
dmsps šlm — *Damasippos, paix.*

Le personnage nommé ici ne semble pas un inconnu. Diverses inscriptions de Hegra mentionnent un stratège Rabîb'el : Jaussen et Savignac, *Mission*, I, p. 196, nº 34 (« Malikû le stratège fils de Rabîb'el le stratège »); nº 43 (« Rabîb'el le stratège »); nº 84 (« Damasî fils de Rabîb'el le stratège »). Ce nom ne se rencontre pas ailleurs en nabatéen, et notre Rabîb'el a toutes chances d'être le même personnage, avant sa nomination à la préfecture de Hegra. Le nom grec de Damasippos est en effet tout aussi rare dans notre domaine : toujours à Hegra, une inscription nomme « Ǵānimû le stratège, fils de Damasippos » (*Mission*, I, p. 206, nº 40). Or le même « Ǵânimû fils de Damasippos » avait été stratopédarque du district de Dûmat, c.à d. du Jauf et du désert environnant (*RB*, 1957, pp. 196–215), et on peut envisager de faire du nom de *dmsy* (du graffite Sav. nº 84) un hypocoristique de Damasippos (*RB*, 1957, p. 204). Par ailleurs nos graffites nº 1 et nº 4 qui encadrent notre graffite 3 mentionnent deux fils d'un certain Ǵānimû, à savoir Witrû et Guraišû. On est naturellement tenté d'établir une parenté entre ces divers personnages. L'inscription *RB* 1957 est de 44 ap. J.-C. et Sav. nº 34 est de 72. Le plus simple est de considérer Ǵānimû et Rabîb'el comme frères; le premier était stratopédarque de Dûmat quand le second, sans doute son cadet, était encore sans fonction. Damasî et Rabîb'el seraient également frères, l'aîné portant le nom de son grand-père. Witrû et Guraišû seraient les neveux de notre Rabîb'el.

4–5 Phot. 101:22A et copie. Pls. 10 et 26.

4 *šlm wtrw wgryšw bny ʿnmw*

Paix, Witrû et Guraišû fils de Ġānimû

5 *šlm* mn*kw br šlmn*

Paix, Malikû fils de Šalāmān (ou *Šalmān*)

mn au n° 5 : abîmé, mais assez certain.

6 Phot. 101:18A. Pl. 26.

šlmw

dkyr .f . y br

A lire dans l'ordre l. 2, l. 1; *Que soit commémoré ... fils de Šalimû*, ce qui suppose que ce graffite est postérieur aux graffites tham. n° 8 et 9. – Le premier nom propre, non déchiffré, revient au n° 7.

7 Phot. 101:18A. Pl. 26.

dkyr gz/d'	*Que soit commémoré G . . .*
br .f.y	*fils de ...*

8 Phot. 101:25. Pl. 26.

brdw br ʿbdw	*Burdû fils de ʿAbdû*

Le nom de *brdw* est connu en safaïtique, *brd*, et en grec, *Bordos*; cf. J. T. Milik dans *Syria*, 35 (1958), p. 242.

9 Phot. 101:18A. Pl. 26.

dkyr šlmw	*Que soit commémoré Šalimû*
br šlmn	*fils de Šalāmān*

10 Phot. 101:18A. Pl. 26.

dkyr ʿnmw	*Que soit commémoré Ġānimû*
br zbyn*w*	*fils de Zabînû* (?).

On est tenté de lire *g* au début du patronyme, mais la liaison avec la lettre suivante est alors inhabituelle.

11 Phot. 101:18A. Pl. 26.

A gauche de la l. 1 du n° 10, séparé par un trait de division.

qbylw	*Qubailû(?)*
br	*fils*

qbylw semble meilleur que *qbynw*, *qnynw*. Le patronyme n'a été, semble-t-il, jamais écrit.

12 Phot. 101:18A. Pl. 26.

dkyr ʿ...

13 Phot. 101:18A. Pl. 26.

šlmw br ʿnmw — *Šalimû fils de Ǵānimû* (?)

14 Phot. R(eed) 101:28A et W(innett) 2:5. Pl. 26.
A une certaine distance du nid des graffites 1–13, sous le dessin d'un chameau.

šlm wtrw br ʿnmw — *Paix, Witrû fils de Ǵānimû*

Le même personnage qui a gravé l'inscription n° 1.

(*ii*) *Sakākah* (*n° 15*)

Sur le rocher portant les graffites tham. 12–23.

15 Phot. W 2:15. Pls. 11 et 26.

qdrw br šlmn — *Qadarû fils de Šalāmān*
tmmt — *Tammamāt.*

Écriture assez particulière et bien ancienne. – Le nom *qdrw* est probablement un homonyme de l'éthnique Qedar; en sabéen on a le nom de tribu *qdrn* (*CIH* 493 et 495). Le nom propre *Tmmt* est attesté dans une inscription inédite, trouvée par MM Harding et Winnett près du H-4.

(*iii*) *El-Jauf* (*n° 16*)

16 Bloc endommagé à gauche, remployé dans un mur près du Qaṣr Mārid; long. 64 cm, haut. 14 cm.
Dans une *tabula ansata*, inscription de trois lignes, assez abîmée. Probablement vue par A. Musil, *Ar. Des.*, pp. 470, 515. Phot. 102:31, assez floue; reproduite ici, pl. 32.

1 *dnh qbrʾ dy bnh šlytw br šltw br mny br šltw br mny*
br . . . . n br mny lnfšh wlbnwhy
2 *.l . . . yldh ʾḥrh ʿlm ʿd ʿlm byrḥ sywn šnt tltyn wḥmš*
lḥrtt mlk nbṭw rḥm ʿmh
3 [ ]*vacat lʾ šlm ...*

N.B. L'incertitude de lecture n'est pas notée ici par le corps romain des lettres; voir le commentaire.

[1]*Ceci est le tombeau qu'a bâti Šulaitû fils de Šalitû fils de Mannay fils de Šalitû fils de Mannay fils de . . . . n fils de Mannay pour lui-même, pour ses enfants,* [2]*pour toute sa progéniture* (*et*) *postérité, éternellement et pour l'éternité, au mois de Siwān de l'an trente-cinq d'Arétas roi des Nabatéens, qui aime son peuple.* [3]*... Ô paix ...*

L. 1 : Les noms propres dans la généalogie sont assez incertains : *šlytw* et *šltw* pas attestés, préférables à *ʿlytw* et *ʿltw*, à cause du deuxième *šltw* où le shin est presque sûr. *Mny* assez assuré, surtout le premier et le deuxième; sur ce nom, de personne et de tribu, en saf. et tham., cf. Milik : *Studii Biblici Franciscani Liber Annuus*, IX (1958–9), p. 350.

L. 2 : Le premier mot reste énigmatique : on s'attendrait à *wlbnth*; *klh klh* (cf. *RÉS*, 1144) semble trop long. – *yldh* ou *wldh*. – *ʿlm* est un adverbe, comme en *CIS*, II, 788. – La date, juin/juillet 26 ap. J.-C., est tout à fait certaine, bien que plusieurs lettres soient abîmées. Le fondateur du tombeau étale sa généalogie jusqu'à la septième génération, ce qui placerait l'arrivée de cette famille à Dûmat vers 150–25 av. J.-C.

L. 3 : La formule *lʾ šlm* introduit ici la signature du constructeur (ou des constructeurs) du tombeau. En tout cas, la gravure est de la même main que l'inscription principale.

L'importance de ce texte funéraire est due au lieu de la trouvaille, l'actuelle Dûmat el-Jandal, l'Adummatu des chroniques assyriennes, la Dumah biblique, oasis principale du Jauf. Nous avons mentionné plus haut la dédicace datée de l'an cinq de Malichos II (44 ap. J.-C.), provenant du même lieu et déchiffrée par le Père R. Savignac (*RB*, 64 [1957], pp. 196–215). Le nouveau texte atteste donc le contrôle de ce chapelet d'oasis par le prédécesseur de Malichos, ce qui implique un trafic caravanier avec le golfe Persique.

Les deux inscriptions, comparées aux textes contemporains de Hegra, se distinguent par l'allongement très marqué de certaines lettres; c'est la transposition sur pierre du style calligraphique des scribes de Pétra et de Hegra. Les papyri nabatéens de la mer Morte en donnent de beaux spécimens pour le règne de Rabbel II (cf. *Supplément* au *Dict. de la Bible*, VII [1964], col. 927, fig. 696 (I, 4) et col. 931 sq). Par la nouvelle inscription du Jauf, nous savons maintenant que ces formes étirées sont déjà le fait de la chancellerie d'Arétas IV.

(*iv*) *Jabal Abu'l Jays* (*nos 17–21*)

17 Phot. 4A:8 et copie. Pl. 26.

1	... *ʿbd*	... *a fait*
2	*dnh šnt* 20 + 100(?)	*ceci, l'an* 120(?).
3	*bly dkyr ʿwydw*	*Ô que soit commémoré ʿAwîdû*
4	*br šlymw*	*fils de Šulaimû*
5	*khnʾ*	*prêtre.*

L. 1 : Les trois ou quatre premières lettres sont un nom propre; peut-être *ršw*, *Rašû*, égal au tham. *Rš*, attesté dans la région par les graffites tham. 2 et 11.

L. 2 : La date reste incertaine, à cause de l'ordre inusité : dizaines – centaines, mais les signes pour « 20 » et « 100 » sont bons, cf. le tableau dans *Revue Numismatique*, 1958, pp. 16 sq : l'an 120 de l'ère de l'éparchie répond à 225 ap. J.-C.

L. 5 : Lecture *khn*' d'après la copie; sur la photographie, le bas des lettres est coupé.

18 Phot. 4A:4. Pl. 26.

šlmw br	*Šalimû fils de*
šlmn dkyr	*Šalāmān, qu'il soit commémoré.*

19–21 Copies. Pl. 26.

19 šnnw

20 šnnw *br 'm*yw

21 mḥršw
br ḥbyw

Toutes ces lectures sont très incertaines.

B/RÉGION DE MADĀ'IN ṢĀLIḤ

Nous groupons dans ce chapitre les inscriptions photographiées (et quelques-unes copiées) sur la route de Taimâ à Hegra (i), ainsi qu'à Dedan (ii) et à Hegra même (iii).

(i) 30 km à l'est de Madā'in Ṣāliḥ (nos 22–38)

22 Phot. 6:30, reproduite ici pl. 32.

Deux lignes du nabatéen, où aucun mot n'est de lecture et d'interprétation certaine ou vraisemblable, sauf *dkyr* au début de la première ligne. Au milieu de la deuxième, peut être un nom propre *gšrwn*.

23 Phot. 6:32, 6:33 (partie gauche de l'inscription), 104:35A, et copie. Pl. 27.

*dkyr ʿmrw qyn*y *br*h

A comprendre : *Que soit commémoré ʿAmrû, (commémoraison faite par) Qainay son fils.*

Lecture alternative pour l'avant dernier mot *ʿšyny*, l'écart entre les deux premières lettres étant dû à l'arête de la roche; cf. palm. *ʿšylt/Osailathos*, J. Cantineau, *Inventaire des inscriptions de Palmyre* (Beirut, 1931), VII, 5 (*CIS*, II, 4618). Mais l'alternance *l/m* fait difficulté, faute d'une labiale.

24 Phot. 6:34 et copie. Pl. 27.

dkyr zydmnwtw br d [. . . .]

Que soit commémoré Zaidmanôtû fils de D . . .

25 Phot. 104:33 et copie. Pl. 27.

zydmnwtw br d . . [. .]

A droite un chameau. – Même personne qu'au numéro précédent. Le patronyme peut se lire Dyn[ys] « Dionysios ».

Le nom de la déesse *Mnwtw* doit se vocaliser, à notre avis, *Manautû* ou, au cas de réduction de la diphtongue, *Manôtû*, en s'inspirant de la graphie défective nabatéenne *Mntw*, *CIS*, 320F; saf., tham. et lihy. *-mnt* dans les noms propres. La forme arabe tardive *Manātu* représente une adaptation phonétique arabe de *Manôtu*; *Manawātu*, par contre, une pluralisation secondaire, la même qu'on retrouve dans *'Ilāt et 'Allāt*.

Nous avons ici la première attestation nabatéenne de *zydmnwtw*, déjà connu en lihyanite sous la graphie *zdmnt*.

26–29 Phot. 104:36A. Pl. 27.

26 *zydw br zydw* — *Zaidû fils de Zaidû.*

27 *dkyr nšlw* — *Que soit commémoré Našlû.*

28 Phot. et copie.

nšlw šlm — *Našlû, paix.*

Même personnage qu'au n° 27, bien que le nun ressemble à un 'ain.

Pour le nom *nšlw* et sa transcription grecque *Naslos* : J. Cantineau, *Le Nabatéen* (Paris, 1932), II, p. 127; tham. et. saf. *nšl*.

29 *'nmw šlm* — *Ǵānimû, paix.*

30–31 Phot. 105:2 et copie. Pls. 27 et 32.

30 *'mryw ww* . [. .] *'ḥwhy šlm*

31 *šlm dygns br*
hn'w

'Amrayû et W . . . son frère, paix.
Paix, Diogenès fils
de Hāni'û.

Au n° 30 le nom du frère est incertain : deuxième lettre, *b/n/l*; puis une ou deux lettres abîmées par le dessin d'un petit chameau.

32–36 Phot. 105:3. Pl. 27.

32 *gdw* — *Gaddû.*

33 *bnt br šḥrw* — *Banat fils de Šaḥrû*(?).

Une lecture *štrw* ne donne pas d'étymologie satisfaisante.

34 *'fklw br hny'w* — *'Afkallû fils de Hunai'û(?)*

'Afkallu, nom propre dérivant du nom d'office *'fkl'*, est connu par ailleurs (Philby, carnets inédits).

35 *šlm tymw br* [...] — *Paix, Taimû fils de ...*

36 *šlm ʿdrw br t . . .* — *Paix, ʿAdrû fils de T . . .*

Le patronyme est probablement *t*ymw.

37 Copie. Pl. 28.

Lecture désespérée.

38 Copie. Pl. 28.

[šl]m ḥnṭln — *Paix, Ḥanṭalān.*

(*ii*) *El-ʿUlâ* (*n*[os] *39–50*)

Rocher dans la marge méridionale de la grande oasis.

39–48 Phot. 105:12, assez floue. Pl. 28.

Nous mettons entre parenthèses les parties des inscriptions invisibles sur la photographie, ou bien en dehors de la photo.

39 Sav(ignac, *Mission*, II, inscr. nab. n°) 208

ʿmw — *ʿAmmû*

40 Sav. 209.

šlm m(*ʿyrw*) — *Paix, Muġairû.*

41 Sav. 211.

'spsn' 'kys

A noter l'absence de *br*. Le nom *'spsn'* est peut-être identique au nom de lieu *Spasinou Charax* (Charax de Mésène). Un tel nom convient à un esclave, d'où notre interprétation :

'Aspasinâ (*esclave d'*) *Akios.*

'*kys*, peut-être un soldat, a laissé son nom dans la région, Sav. 228.

42 Sav. 212.

dkrt 'lt '(*lʿz*) — *Que 'Ilat se souvienne d'al-ʿAzz*
br bʿtw bš(*lm*) — *fils de Baʿatû, en paix.*

'al-ʿAzz, avec R. Savignac, ce qui est conforme au fait que tous les noms arabes des Nabatéens relèvent de parlers arabes à article *al-*. Mais on peut aussi envisager ici le n.pr. théophore sud-arabique 'Il-ʿazz, transcription grecque *Eleazos*.

43 Sav. 214.

šnyf(*w br n ḥ/ṭṣ*) — *Šanîfû fils de N . . .*

Le nom de *Šanîfû* a encore été relevé entre Hegra et Taimâ, Sav. 354. Il est attesté dès le huitième siècle, vers 733 : Sanipu (*s* assyrien pour *š*), nom d'un roi ammonite, *ANET*, p. 282; W. F. Albright, *Notes on Ammonite History*, *Miscellanea Biblica B. Ubach* (Montserrat, 1953), p. 136, note 26, en arabe on a Šanîf et en safaïtique *ŠNF*, E. Littmann, *Saf. Insc.*, n° 400 et 1128, et index.

44 Sav. 215.

dkyr zydw br (tymw)

Que soit commémoré Zaidû fils de Taimû.

45 Sav. 216.

rbyb'l šlm — *Rabîb'el, paix.*

Je ne tiens pas compte des deux éraflures qui précèdent ce graffite, et qui sont lues « aleph + point » (abréviation de *'srtg'*, stratège!) par le Père Savignac. – *šlm* pas copié par lui.

46 Sav. 217.

šly šlm — *Šullay, paix.*

47 Sav. 218.

Sa lecture, *tpṣ' 'lt šlm Tafṣâ (fils de) 'Ulat*, est difficilement la bonne. Je ne vois pas le début (une ou deux lettres), ni le petit trait du 'ain, et le mem à la fin me semble ouvert. Je propose, à titre de suggestion,

(tf)ṣ' brt šlm(w) — *Tafṣâ fille de Šalimû.*

48 Traces d'autres graffites.

49 Phot. 7:29A. Sav. 222.

(š)lm mlkw — *Paix, Malikû.*

50 En bas à gauche

šlm (...)

A gauche du n° 49, l'inscription hebraïque n° 1 (voir le chapitre 3 ci-dessous).

(*iii*) *El-Ḥijr* (*n°s 51–129*)

Nous suivons l'ordre des prises photographiques de Reed (A) et de Winnett (B), sauf lorsqu'il y a double prise des mêmes inscriptions.

Photographies de Reed

51–55 Phot. 105:37A. Pl. 28.

CIS 264 (copie Doughty) = 272–6 (Hub.) = 296 (Euting) et Sav. 50–3. Équation avec copies de Huber déjà vue par Savignac, les deux autres par Chabot, *RÉS*, n° 1171.

51 *CIS* 264, ligne 1 = 272 = 296, 1 et Sav. 50
bly dkyr ḥwrw br 'wšw bṭb
Ô que soit commémoré Ḥûrû fils de 'Aušû, en bien.

52 *CIS* 264, 2 = 273 = 296, 2 et Sav. 51.
dkyr ḥyw br š'd'lhy
Que soit commémoré Ḥayyû fils de Śa'd'ilāhî.

53 *CIS* 264, 3 = 274 = 296, 3 (pas copié par Savignac).
'bd'ysy br whbw šlm
'Abd'îsî fils de Wahbû, paix.

Noter *šlm* écrit en deux registres, comme souvent; de même *qdm* au n° 54. – Notre lecture; Chabot, in *RÉS*, n° 1171 : *'bd'y* ... Le trait vertical au début de l'inscription n'est pas un waw, mais un signe d'insertion ou de séparation (les n°ˢ 52 et 54 sont du même personnage).

54 *CIS* 264, 4 = 275 = 296, 4 et Sav. 52.
šlm ḥyw mn qdm dwšr'
Paix (*à*) *Ḥayyû devant Dûšārâ.*

55 *CIS* 264, 5 = 276 = 296, 5 et Sav. 53.
šlm tymw 'lym ḥlfw
Paix, Taimû serviteur de Ḥalafû.

56 Phot. 106:4. *CIS* 221, Sav. 20. Texte de fondation du tombeau B23 (nomenclature de Savignac).

57 Phot. 106:5, reproduite ici, pl. 32. *CIS* 234, Sav. 40.

dnh mškb'	*Ceci est le lieu des banquets* (*sacrés*)
dy 'ḥd 'nmw	*qu'a pris en possession Ġānimû,*
'srtg' br	*stratège, fils de*
dmsps	*Damasippos.*

L. 1 : Sur le sens de *mškb'*, voir J. T. Milik, *Discoveries in the Judaean Desert* (Oxford, 1962), III, pp. 248sq, n° 108. Ll. 2–4 : Sur le personnage, voir ci-dessus le commentaire au n° 3.

58–60 Phot. 106:7.

58 Sav. 122.

l' dkyr ḥyn	*Ô que soit commémoré Ḥayyān.*

59 Sav. 124.

šlm 'bwdw br . . . 'w	*Paix, 'Abûdû fils de . . .'û.*

Le patronyme reste énigmatique (voir fac-similé, pl. 29) : *zbynw*(?) Savignac; *'zy'w*(?) Starcky; *'m'w*(?) ou *hny'w*(?) Milik.

60 Pl. 29.
šlm 'bdw (...) *Paix, 'Abdu* (...).

61–62 Phot. 106:8.

61 Sav. 123.
dkyr 'wtw br mn't
Que soit commémoré Ǵautû fils de Mun'at.

62 Pl. 29. Sav. 125.
dkyr ḥmlgw fsl' *Que soit commémoré Ḥamlagû, sculpteur.*
Le même sculpteur revient plus loin, au n° 93. Savignac n'a pas lu ce nom de métier. Le même nom en Sav. 68 (qui lit *ḥmlfw*) et probablement en Sav. 67 (qui lit *tmlhy*) : il a sans doute dédoublé un même graffite, dont il ne donne qu'une seule copie, n° 68. Le graffite Sav. 68 est à identifier à *CIS* 241 (Doughty) d'après Chabot, *RÉS* 1165.

63–64 Phot. 106:9. Pl. 29.

63 Sav. 126.
dkyr whb'lhy br blw bṭb
Que soit commémoré Wahb'ilāhî fils de Balû, en bien.
Le patronyme, non lu par Savignac, se retrouve en Sav. 350.

64 *dky*
Inscription laissée inachevée : *Que soit commémo⟨ré ...⟩.*

65–66 Phot. 106:11. Pl. 29.

65 *bly dkyr* [... *br*] *Ô que soit commémoré ... fils*
qdm br myd'*w* *de Qadm fils de Maida'û.*
Le nom *Qdm* est déjà connu : nab. *Qdmw*, saf. *Qdm*.

66 *'nytw br* *'Unaitû(?) fils*
myd'w *de Maisa'û.*
'nytw ou *'lytw*, vocalisation incertaine; *myd'w*, égal à *myd'*, et *Maidaou* attestés dans le Ḥaurân (J. Cantineau, *Le Nabatéen*, II, p. 113). – Ce sont donc les proscynèmes d'un homme et de son neveu, chacun ayant gravé de sa propre main.

67–76 Phot. 106:12. Pl. 32.

67 *šlm wdkyr zydw* nḥrg' *br m'nw bṭb l'lm*
Paix et que soit commémoré Zaidû, ..., fils de Ma'nû en bien, pour toujours.

Lecture assez assurée, sauf pour le nom de métier ou d'office. Je suggère, pour la lecture proposée, l'interprétation « esclave sacré, hiérodule », à partir du mot *ḥrg* (*CIS* 350, 3 : Pétra), synonyme de *ḥrm* dans les inscriptions funéraires de Hegra. Le schème à préformante *n-* est ici substantival; peut-être dissimilation de *mḥrg*. – On a le participe *ḥ́ryg* au n° 79.

68–70 Très abîmées.

68 Illisible.

69 *šlm ...* — *Paix ...*

70 *šlm zydw* — *Paix, Zaidû.*

71 Sav. 92.

dkyr tymmnwtw — *Que soit commémoré Taimmanôtû.*

72 *CIS* 283 (pas transcrit) et Sav. 93. L'équation vue par Chabot, *RÉS* 1180.

šlm tymmnwtw — *Paix, Taimmanôtû.*

Même personnage qu'au n° 71, lu *Tymmnwty* par Savignac.

73 *wdkyryn ḥlṣt wm .... bṭb wbšlm*

et que soient commémorés Ḥaliṣat et M[... et ... et ...], en bien et en paix.

74 *CIS* 282. Sav. 94.

šlm gmyrw — *Paix, Gamîrû.*

-w semble préférable à *-n* de Savignac.

75 *CIS* 285.

bly šlm 'šlm br ...

Ô paix, 'Ašlam fils de ...

L'aleph n'est pas clair sur la photo. Lecture du *CIS* : *bl' šlm 'šl br bny ...*

76 *šlm ḥyw br š'd'lhy*

Paix, Ḥayyû fils de Ša'd'ilāhî.

Même personnage qu'au n° 52.

77–78 Phot. 106:13. Pl. 29.

77 *CIS* 286. Sav. 87.

šlm ṣ'bw br 'dynt

Paix, Ṣa'bû fils de 'Udainat.

78 Sav. 90 (sans copie).

šlm tdy br — *Paix Tadday fils.*

L'inscription n'a jamais été achevée.

79 Photos R 106:15 (reproduite ici, pl. 33) et « W no number ». Photographies assez bonnes du texte de fondation du tombeau E1 (décrit *Mission*, II, p. 97). Inscription *CIS* 200 (pl. XXIX : ph. estampage Doughty) et Sav. 30 (*Mission*, I, pp. 190–2 et pl. XX : ph. estampage).

Voici ma lecture, faite sur des photos de l'estampage Savignac et sur ces deux prises de vue directes. Elle est beaucoup plus complète que celle de Savignac.

1 *dnh kfr' dy ʿbdw mnʿt whgrw bny ʿmyrt*
2 *br whbw lnfšhm wyldhm w'ḥrhm wdy hn*
3 *yhw' b'tr mnʿt dnh ʿwyh dy* yz[b]n 'w y*mškn*
4 *ḥlqh mn kfr' hw f'yty ḥlqh* ḥryg *l'ḥr hgrw*
5 *d' whn yhw' b'tr hgrw d'* lmʿ*bd kwt f'yty ḥlqh*
6 *ḥ*ryg *l'ḥr mnʿt dnh w'yty ʿm kl mzbn yth ldwšr'*
7 *'lh' ksf slʿyn 'lf ḥd ḥrty wl*mr'*n' ḥrtt*
8 *kwt ksf slʿyn 'lf ḥd ḥr*ty [wlmnwtw ?] *'lht'* ksf
9 *slʿyn ḥmš m'h* wd' *mn* ywm [... *byrḥ* ... *šnt*]
10 *ʿšr wšt lḥrtt ml*[*k*] *nbṭ*[*w rḥm ʿm*]*h*

[1]*Ceci est le tombeau qu'ont fait Munʿat et Hagarû, enfants de ʿAmîrat* [2]*fils de Wahbû, pour eux-mêmes et leurs enfants et leur postérité; et si* [3]*après* (la mort du) *Munʿat susdit, se trouvait quelqu'un* (de ses héritiers) *qui tenterait de vendre ou de mettre en gage* [4]*sa part de ce tombeau, sa part sera bien de mainmorte pour la postérité de la susdite Hagarû.* [5]*Et si quelqu'un faisait pareillement après* (la mort de) *la susdite Hagarû, sa part*[6] *sera bien de mainmorte pour la postérité du Munʿat susdit. Et chacun qui vendrait le* (*tombeau*) *sera redevable à Dûšārâ* [7]*le dieu, de la somme d'un millier de drachmes arétiennes, et à notre seigneur Arétas,*[8] *un millier de drachmes arétiennes également,* [*et à Manôtû?*] *la déesse, de la somme*[9] *de cinq cents drachmes. Et ceci à partir du jour* [..., *du mois* ..., *de l'an*][10] *seize d'Arétas, roi des Nabaté*[*ens, qui aime son peup*]*le.*

80 Photos R 106:18 et W 12:5. *CIS* 222 et Sav. 37 : texte de fondation du tombeau E19.

A la l. 2 lire *'hdly 'Ahdalî*, avec J. Cantineau, *Le Nabatéen*, II, p. 57, contre *'hkly* du *CIS* (qui n'exclut pas *'hd/rly*) et de Savignac.

81 Photos 106:20 et 12:10A. *CIS* 204 et Sav. 27 : tombeau C17.

82 Phot. 106:21. *CIS* 213 et Sav. 24 : tombeau C6.

Photographies de Winnett

83 Phot. 9:19. *CIS* 205 et Sav. 12 : texte de fondation du tombeau B10.

84 Phot. 9:20. *CIS* 226, Sav. 13 : à l'intérieur du tombeau B11.

85 Phot. 9:21. Pl. 29. *CIS* 266, Sav. 44.

bly šlm ḥnṭln	*Ô paix (à) Ḥanṭalān.*

Je copie le yod autrement que Savignac.

86–88 Phot. 9:22. Pl. 29. Ces trois graffites sont gravés à gauche d'un loculus.

86 Sav. 48 et *CIS* 237, mais seulement la copie Huber; la copie Doughty est égale à Sav. 170; cf. Chabot, *RÉS* 1161 : « on peut douter de l'identité de deux copies ».

šlm br ʿbdmnwty	*Šalim fils de ʿAbdmanôtî.*

Le patronyme a été lu correctement par Chabot (*loc. cit.*) contre *ʿw/zdm nwty*(?) de Savignac. – Le *-y* semble préférable à *-w*; opp. n°s 71–72.

87 Au-dessous du précédent, graffite tracé à grands traits, assez fins, dont la ligne principale a été martelée.

tym'lhy br '. . . .	*Taim'ilāhî fils de 'A . . .*
ʿbd	*a fait (ce loculus?)*

88 Au-dessus du précédent, à trait à peine visibles : [*ʿbd* (...) *a fait* (...) Le nom propre est en dehors du cadre le la photographie. L'auteur de ce graffite a-t-il contesté le travail de Taim'ilāhî et martelé son nom ?

89–90 Phot. 9:24. Sav. 18.

90 *wdkyr ʿd mn hw'*
ktb ktb' d' bṭb wbšlm

89 *dkyr bny' hn'w w'ḥbrw-*
h dy *bnw qbrw 'm kʿbw*

89 *Que soit commémoré le constructeur Hāni'û et ses compagnons, qui ont construit le tombeau de la mère de Kaʿabû*;

90 *et que soit commémoré, en plus, celui qui*
a écrit cette inscription, (tous) *en bien et en paix*.

Lectures de Savignac à écarter : n° 90, l. 1 *gzmn* (n. pr.), l. 2 *wšlm* (notre *b* est distinct, malgré sa ligature avec le *š*); 89, l. 1 *'ḥynd*(?) n. pr., l. 2 *hm*(?) *bny* (*m* final peu probable, car non bouclé en bas, mais notre *y* a une forme inusitée).

91 Photos 9:24, 9:25, et 9:26. Lignes 5–9 de la bilingue nabatéo-thamoudéenne *CIS* 271 (quelques mots du nab.) et Sav. nab. 17, tham. 1. Pl. 33.

A la fin de la l. 8, lire *d* ou *dy* et non pas *w* de Savignac. A la l. 9, *mn yqbr w'ʿly mnh*, lecture de Chabot, *CRAIBL*, 1908, pp. 270–2, acceptée par Savignac, *Mission*, I, p. 481, contre *mn yʿyr d' ʿly mnh* à la p. 172 (lecture reprise par distraction par J. Cantineau, *Le Nabatéen*, II, pp. 38sq et passim).

92 Phot. 9:31 et copie. Sav. 56.

ʿbdʿbdt br 'rybs 'ḥd 'tr' dnh

ʿAbdʿubdat fils de 'Arîbas a pris possession de ce lieu-ci.

Il s'agit du lieu pour réunions sacrées et non pas d'une concession funéraire, à laquelle on aurait ensuite préféré – selon Savignac – l'emplacement du tombeau B7, dont notre personnage est fondateur (inscr. *CIS* 212 et Sav. 9).

93–95 Phot. 9:32 (sous-exposée) et copies. Mes copies (pl. 30) à main levée.

93 *CIS* 278, 1 et Sav. 62 (sans copie).

ḥmlgw fsl'	*Ḥamlagû sculpteur.*

Le nom pr. est sûr : lecture Chabot, *RÉS* 1177, contre *ḥflgw* de Savignac. Même artisan qu'au n° 62. Son fils, *ḥlf'lhy br ḥmlgw*, est le graveur de l'inscription funéraire *CIS* 206 = Sav. 19, datée de l'an 35 d'Arétas IV. Notre Ḥamlagû a donc fleuri aux premières années de notre ère.

94 *CIS* 278, 2–3 et Sav. 63.

dkyr mnʿt	*Que soit commémoré Munʿat,*
ḥwy'	*le ...*

Le nom de métier *ḥwy'* est inconnu par ailleurs. – Noter qu'à côté de *Ḥamlagû* du n° 62 apparaît *Ǵautû fils de Munʿat*, n° 61, sans doute fils du Munʿat du n° 94.

95 *CIS* 279, Sav. 64.

dkyr ḥyw br	*Que soit commémoré Ḥayyû fils de*
mqt	*Māqit.*

96–97 Phot. 9:35 et 9:36. Pl. 30. *CIS* 239, Sav. 73.

96 *'fls br hn't br ʿnmw dkyr bṭb*

'Aflos fils de Hāni'at fils de Ǵānimû, qu'il soit commémoré en bien.

Cette lecture me semble certaine, contre *'fnm/s brt mtnw bnt...* du *CIS*, *'fnm/s br hgbt br ʿnkw m ...* de Savignac. Le nom propre *'Aflos* (prononcé peut-être *'afnus* comme *Mankû* pour *Malikû*, *ḥnyfw* pour *ḥlyfw*, etc.) revient à Maqʿad Ǧindî, graffite Sav. 13 (grec) : *Aphlos*, à côté du nab. *tymw br 'fls*, Sav. 243. *Taimû fils de 'Aflos* signe encore à Mebrak Nāqah, Sav. 176.

97 Au-dessus de la finale du graffite précédent.

'nw ou *'bw*

Graffite inachevé ?

98–100 Phot. 9:37. Pl. 30.

98 Sav. 74 (sans copie).

šlm ʿbdw br ʿṣbw	*Paix, ʿAbdû fils de ʿAṣbû,*
bṭb	*en bien.*

99 Inscription antérieure au n° 98; le premier nom du n° 99 a été détruit par le *bṭb* du n° 98.

šlm ḥ(f?)l[w br] ʿbdw

Paix Ḥuffālû(?) fils de ʿAbdû.

Le nom *ḥflw*, grec *Hyphphalos*, est attesté dans le Ḥaurān, Littmann 92 (*RÉS* 1094). Savignac réunit les deux : *šlm ʿbdw br ʿqbw [br ʾf?]tḥ bṭb.*

100 *ḥyn* — *Ḥayyan.*

101–102 Phot. 9:38. Pls. 30 and 33.

101 Sav. 72 et *CIS* 263 (non transcrit) : copie Doughty, pl. XL, répétée sur la même planche, en bas à gauche et marquée du n° 259, ce qui est une erreur, car le n° 259, transcrit à la p. 276, se trouve toujours à la même pl. à dr. du faux 259.

šyʿ"lqwm ʾlhʾ — *Šaiʿ"alqaum le dieu.*

Lecture désormais certaine.

102 Plus bas, un graffite abîmé :

*mnk*w *br ...* — *Maliku(?) fils de ...*

103 Phot. 10:4.

Débris de graffites nabatéens.

104–106 Phot. 10:5A.

104 Pl. 30. Sav. 71.

ʾft*ḥ fslʾ br*	*ʾAftaḥ, sculpteur, fils*
ʿbdʿbdt fslʾ	*de ʿAbdʿubdat sculpteur.*

Cette lecture me paraît certaine, malgré le mauvais état de conservation; l. 1 Sav. *šlm lḥrs zybw [br]*; Chabot, *RÉS* 1113, *šlm ltd/rsys br..* – ʾAftaḥ fils de ʿAbdʿubdat, l'un des principaux sculpteurs de Hegra, a construit sept tombeaux, datant de la fin du règne d'Arétas IV (Sav. 7, 19, 32, etc.).

105 Il semble qu'on ait, en palimpseste, sous la deuxième moitié de la première ligne de 104, un graffite illisible, qui paraît commencer avec le yod, situé entre le lamed et l'aleph. Ce graffite aurait comporté trois lignes.

106 *CIS* 240, Sav. 69. Le bas des lettres n'apparaît pas sur la photographie.

tyrw br . . [. .] — *Tairû fils de ...*

Cette lecture du *CIS* est meilleure que celle de Sav. *dkyr wbrh.* – *tyry* (et peut-être *tyrw*) : souvent à Pétra; plusieurs exemples inédits.

107–110 Phot. 10:11A. Pl. 30.

107 Sav. 77 (sans copie; seulement *brt w'lt*).

šlmt brt	*Šalimat fille de*
w'lw br 'glḥ	*Wa'ilû fils de 'Aglaḥ*
wqynw brt w'lt	*et Qainû fille de Wa'ilat.*

108

ʿdrw br	*ʿAdrû fils de*
ʿmnw wqynw	*ʿAmanû et Qainû*
br ...	*fils de ...*

Le dernier nom reste incertain : *dnyḥw* ?

109 Doughty, *Doc. épig.*, pl. v, fol. 8, en bas à droite.

ʿbdmnkw	*ʿAbdmalikû*
fsl' šlm	*sculpteur, paix.*

Le même personnage a répété ailleurs sa signature, mais sur une seule ligne : c'est *CIS* 230 (pl. xxxix, est. Doughty) = *CIS* 254 (pl. xl, copie Doughty = *Doc. épig.* pl. iv, fol. 5, avant dernier texte) et Sav. 140 (pl. xxviii, copie). A ce dernier numéro, Savignac renvoie à « un graffite identique, aux abords du Diwān, cf. n° 75 ». En fait, il s'agit de son n° 76, où il transcrit : *ʿbdmlkw psl' ʿbd.* Ce qui suppose que Savignac a lui aussi lu notre graffite, et qu'il l'a ensuite confondu avec ses graffites 140 et 76, d'autant que ses n°s 75–79 sont publiés sans copies. Les éditeurs du *CIS* ont bloqué sous le même n° 230 l'estampage de Doughty (Sav. 140) et sa copie à main levée, qui est notre numéro.

110 On perçoit d'autres graffites illisibles sur cette photographie.

111 Phot. 10:12A. Pl. 30. Sav. 82 + 81 (sans copies); Sav. 81 est égal à *CIS* 259 (Doughty), d'après Chabot, *RÉS* 1169.

Une très longue inscription, cinq lignes d'écriture irrégulière, en grande partie délavée par les intempéries. La partie droite des quatre premières lignes est hors du cadre de la photographie.

1 (*dnh m*)*sgd' dy ʿbdw tymw br* šbw *wtymw br*
2 . . . . *wʿbdrb'l br* šbw *wḥlfw*
3 [*bn* *l'lh ṣ?*] *ʿbw 'lh*[' . . . .] . . . .
4 [. . . . . . . ʿ]*l ḥy* . . . .
5 *ʿbdt* . . . .

[1]*Ceci est le lieu de culte qu'ont fait Taimû fils de Šabbû(?) et Taimû fils de* [2] *... et ʿAbdrabb'el fils de Šabbû(?) et Ḫalafû* [3]*[fils de ..., pour le dieu de Ṣa]ʿbû(?), dieu ...* [4][...] *pour la vie ...*[5] *ʿUbdat ...*

Sav. 82 : *dnh msgd(y)' dy ʿbd*; 81 : *tymw br šb . . . r tymw br/{w?} ʿbdw.*

Ll. 1 et 2 : *šbw*, ou bien *šnw*, *šly . . .*

L. 3 : La restitution du nom de la divinité, vénérée ici par le groupe de cinq hommes, me semble assez certaine.

Je retrouve le même dieu comme titulaire d'un temple au Ḫubṯâ à Pétra. Voir G. Dalman, *Neue Petra-Forschungen* (Leipzig, 1912), n° 92; *RÉS* 1434 (bibliographie); J. Cantineau, *Le Nabatéen*, II, pp. 9–10; R. Savignac : *RB*, 42 (1933), pp. 409–10.

Cette dédicace du temple a été faite par un *Wahb'ilāhî* originaire de *Swdy* (*Sôdâ*, mod. Suweida au Gebel ed-Drûz), sous le règne de Rabbel II, et antérieurement à son année dix-sept, 86 ap. J.-C. Après études répétées des photographies et des copies exécutées par J. Starcky, je lis à la l. 5 :

l'lh ṣʿbw 'lh' dy [b]'ṣl ḥbt'

pour le dieu de Ṣaʿbû, qui (réside) à ... de Ḫubtâ.

En plus, je retrouve la même divinité nabatéenne dans l'inscription palmyrénienne *CIS* II, 3991, lue par Chabot :

ʿbd whblt / br 'bmrt / [l]'lh ṣʿb[w] / dy mqr'
gd' / [']nbṭ ʿl ḥywh / [wḥy'] br[h . . .].

Sur l'estampage, vu au Cabinet du *CIS* (Paris), le lamed au début de la l. 3 est visible, mais non l'aleph à la fin de la l. 4 : le mot *gd* est donc à l'état construit. Le aleph au début de la l. 5 est discernable; *'nbṭ* : orthographe phonétique (et puis arabe) de *nbṭ*. L. 6 : [*wḥy*]*y br*h[. . .].

On a donc ici une mention très intéressante du « dieu de Ṣaʿbû qui s'appelle Fortune des Nabatéens », *'lh ṣʿbw dy mqr' gd 'nbṭ.*

112 Phot. 10:14A. Pl. 30.

CIS 299 (Huber et Euting), Sav. 78 (sans copie).

ʿdrw br nḥšṭb šlm

ʿAdrû fils de Naḥašṭāb, paix.

Le nom propre *Naḥašṭāb*, « Bonne Fortune » (*Eutyches*, *Fortunatus*, etc.) est maintenant bien attesté dans l'onomastique palmyrénienne, nabatéenne, nord et sud-arabiques, dans les transcriptions grecques, jusqu'à l'époque byzantine.

113–114 Phot. 10:15A.

113 Pl. 31. A droite d'un double bétyle.

ytʿw *Yitaʿû*

Ce n'est peut-être pas, de l'avis de Starcky, le nom propre *yt'w* mais le nom du dieu attesté, en dehors des anthroponymes, par une seule inscription grecque du Ḥaurān sous la forme *Ethaos*; cf. D. Sourdel, *Les Cultes du Hauran* (Paris, 1952), p. 85.

114 A droite, débris de graffites, dont

šlm '. . .	*Paix 'A . . . .*

115–120 Photos 10:17A, 18A, 19A. Pl. 31 (nos 115–18).

115 *CIS* 260 (Doughty, Euting) et Sav. 80 (sans copie).

šybw br šmšw	*Šaibû fils de Šamšû,*
šlm	*paix.*

šybw avec le *CIS*, contre *qynw* de Savignac.

116 *šlm 'bdrb'l* — *Paix 'Abdrabb'el.*

117 *CIS* 301 (Euting). A gauche, plus haut que les précédents :

š' . . w br 'mry	*Š . . . fils de 'Amray.*

Le début est abîmé par le graffite arabe.

118 *CIS* 300 (Huber, Euting) et Sav. 79 (sans copie). Sous le précédent.

šlm zbdw br	*Paix Zabdû fils*
'šdw	*de 'Ašadû.*

119 Deux longues lignes, à gauche des nos 115–16 et sous le no 118.
A la première ligne on devine :
šlm . . . . br tymw br . . ln

120 A gauche du no 119, l. 1.
h . . .

121 Phot. 10:20A. Pl. 31. *CIS* 262 (Doughty), non déchiffré.
dkyrt 'swd' brt ...
Que soit commémorée 'Aswadâ fille de ...

122–123 Phot. 10:21A.

122 Pl. 31. *CIS* 261 (Doughty) = *CIS* 281 (Huber), pas lus.
dbrh br zbr šlm
Les lettres daleth et resh semblent être distinguées. Les noms paraissent nouveaux dans l'onomastique nabatéenne. Starcky propose *'bdy br zbd.*

123 Au-dessous du précédent, graffite très abîmé.

124–127 Photos 10:24A, 25A, 26A, 27A, 28A. Pl. 31.

124 A droite d'un trou.

šlm' *Šalmâ*

125 A gauche du trou.

šly nwl' *Šullay le tisserand.*

Ce nom de métier se rencontre pour la première fois en nabatéen.

126 *CIS* 257 (Doughty).

qbr tlmwn br *tdy*

Tombe de Talmôn fils de Tadday.

Talmôn : cf. *Talmû* et *Talmai*, tous dérivés de *Ptolomaios*. Le second *br* semble être écrit par les deux traits obliques. *Tadday*, transcription grecque *Thaddaios*, diminutif *qattay* de *Theodoros* etc., déjà au nº 78.

127 Sous le précédent.

šlm f'rn br šly *Paix, Fa'rān fils de Šullay.*

Le premier nom est très fréquent au Sinaï, c'est l'homonyme du nom de l'oasis principale. Le patronyme Šullay est gravé à gauche des irrégularités de le roche. Fa'rān doit être le fils du Šullay du nº 125.

128 Phot. 12:3A. *CIS* 225 et Sav. 35 : texte de fondation du tombeau E16.

129 Phot. 12:12A. *CIS* 223 et Sav. 26 : texte du tombeau C14.

C/WĀDĪ ES-SIRḤĀN

130 Ithrā. Phot. 106:36 et copie. Pl. 31 (copie à main levée) et pl. 33 (phot.).

dy ʿbd nšrw ʿbd'
br ḥrmw dy mn 'l q-
myrw

Qu'a construit Našrû, esclave,
fils de Ḥarmû, de la tribu de Qu-
mairû.

La même tribu revient probablement dans les inscriptions safaïtiques, *'l qmr* (qu'on peut vocaliser *Qamar*, *Qumair*, etc.) ; cf. p. ex. Littmann, *Saf. Inscr.*, 254 et 255; *CIS*, v, 8, 9, 1414, 1868, 1870, 1952, 2802, 4278, 4384, 4834, 4844–5, 5050; *WSIJ* 840 et 841.

2 Inscription palmyrénienne[1]

1 El-Qarqar (Wādī es-Sirḥān). Phot. 107:16. Pl. 31.

Pierre calcaire; six lignes gravées au vilbrequin. La photographie est surexposée et une partie des lettres n'apparaît pas.

[byrḥ] sywn	[*Au mois de*] *Siwān*
[šnt](4)85	[*de l'an*](4)85
[dkyr]*bgšw br*	*que soit commémoré Bagešû fils de*
qml' [br]	*Qāmilâ* [fils de]
*š'*d *bṭb*	*Ša'd en bien.*
f[s]*l br*h	*A gravé son fils*(?).

Ll. 1 et 2 : La trace qui précède les signes « 20 » ne semble pas appartenir à un signe de « cent ». Celui-ci sera sous-entendu, comme il arrive parfois en palmyrénien. Ici c'est trois cents ou quatre cents. Je penche pour quatre cents, ce qui donne 174 ap. J.-C. L'écriture relève en effet de la cursive, et celle-ci n'apparaît guère avant le second siècle. C'est à l'époque antonine et flavienne que les Palmyréniens se sont montrés particulièrement actifs dans le désert oriental : bilingue d'Umm el-'Amad, milieu du deuxième siècle (*Syria*, 12 [1931], pp. 101–15), inscription d'Umm eṣ-Ṣelabiḥ, de 225 (*Syria*, 14 [1933], pp. 179–80), inscription trouvée près de la station de pompage T-1, fin du deuxième siècle (*Syria*, 40 [1963], pp. 48–55, avec carte), stèle bilingue du Musée de Bagdad, datant de 128/129 ap. J.-C. et provenant probablement de la même région (*Syria*, 40 [1963], pp. 42–6).

J'ai publié une pierre funéraire en écriture cursive provenant de la frontière syro-jordanienne ou syro-irakienne, dont la date me paraît être Ṭebet 471 plutôt que 371, donc 160 plutôt que 60 (*Mélanges de l'Université Saint Joseph*, XXVIII [1949–50], pp. 45–51). J. T. Milik préfère la lecture 371. Cette date, qui s'accorde mal à ce que nous savions il y a encore peu d'années de l'apparition de la cursive palmyrénienne, est aujourd'hui possible. Fuad Safar vient en effet de publier une série de pierres avec inscriptions palmyréniennes cursives, trouvées dans le

1/Par J. Starcky.

Wādī Ḥaurān à une cinquantaine de km à l'ouest de l'Euphrate (*Sumer*, XXI [1965], pp. 9–27). Or celles qui portent une date sont d'Adar 409 = 98 ap. J.-C. Cela repose la question de la date de l'inscription analogue publiée par J. Teixidor et provenant de la dépression de la Qaʿara, donc de la même région (*Syria*, 40 [1963], pp. 33–42). Il signale d'ailleurs à Palmyre même un buste funéraire dont l'inscription est cursive et dont la date répond à 113 ap. J.-C., *CIS* 4374 (*loc. cit.*, p. 46).

La date de 174 que je préfère pour l'inscription de Qarqar n'est donc pas pleinement assurée, d'autant que le troisième siècle n'est pas non plus absolument exclu (274 ap. J.-C.).

Ll. 3–5 : Les noms propres sont assez assurés et tous connus par ailleurs (Qāmilâ répond en saf. *qml*, cf. tham. *qmlt* et *qmln*).

L. 6 : La restitution *psl* est d'autant plus conjecturale qu'en palmyrénien on dit *glp* pour « sculpter, graver ».

S'agit-il d'un soldat, d'un caravanier ou d'un ouvrier agricole ? Par sa phraséologie, notre texte ressemble à ceux qu'a publiés F. Safar : « au mois de ... en l'an ... que soit commémoré un tel en bien ». Son intérêt principal est le lieu où il a été trouvé : c'est l'inscription palmyrénienne la plus méridionale du désert de Syrie, dans la zône où expirait le contrôle nabatéen (au cas où notre inscription est antérieure à 106 ap. J.-C.).

3 Inscriptions hebraïques[1]

EL-ʿULÂ

Pour les inscriptions hebraïques d'el-ʿUlâ, voir Savignac, *Mission*, II, pp. 641–4 et pl. CXXI, inscr. hébr. n°s 1–8.

1 Phot. 7:29A. Pl. 31 (fac-similé) et pl. 34 (photographie). Sav., inscr. nab. n° 223, qui ne transcrit que la l. 2.

dh ʾbyšlw[m]	*Ceci est ʾAbîšalôm*(?)
br šwšnh	*fils de Šôšannah.*

Le pronom féminin *dh* est à comprendre au sens neutre : cette chose-ci, c'est à dire la signature. – Le premier nom est incertain. Curieuse indication de matronymie; cf. N. Avigad, *IEJ*, 7 (1957), p. 243, n. 53; Milik, *Recherches d'épigraphie* ... (sous presse).

2 Phot. 7:35A. Pls. 31 et 34.

brkh	*Bénédiction*!
lʿṭwr br	*à ʿAṭûr(?) fils de*
mnḥm wrb yrmyh	*Menaḥem et rabbi Yeremiah.*

Ces deux inscriptions, ainsi que Sav. hébr. 3 et 5 (pronom *hdh*), sont en araméen et datent de l'époque byzantine. Les autres, par exemple Sav. hébr. 1 et 8, sont rédigées en arabe.

1/Par J. T. Milik.

IV Archaeological Records

W.L.REED

1 An Arabian Goddess

The discovery of a stone plaque incised with what appears to be a representation of an ancient Arabian goddess (see Fig. 38) is of unusual interest in view of the fact that comparatively little is known about the manner of representing goddesses in pre-Islamic Arabia.[1] The find was made on the highest point of Jabal Ghunaym, a mountain situated about eight miles southeast of Taymā' and clearly visible from the oasis (see p. 29). Many of the rocks on the summit bear ancient inscriptions invoking the god Ṣalm (see pp. 29 and 192), a fact which suggests that the summit once served as an open-air sanctuary or "high-place" for some of the festivals of ancient Taymā'. Unfortunately in none of the inscriptions is there any mention of a goddess which might help in identifying the figure depicted in the drawing. On a vertical rock face just below the summit are drawings of the heads of several divinities (see pp. 31–4), but none of these resembles the goddess on the plaque. If the drawing is contemporary with the inscriptions, as seems probable, it may date from as early as the sixth century B.C. (see pp. 91–3) and Figs. 36, 37). The drawing was found lying face down, a circumstance which saved it from erosion by sand and weather throughout the centuries. A sherd (see p. 176) discovered in the vicinity resembles the "granite" ware of Taymā' (see p. 175) and appears to come from a large, heavy jar, used perhaps for the storage of water.

The stone[2] is irregular in shape, having maximum measurements of 24 cm in height and 23 cm in width. It varies in thickness from 2.5 to 4 cm. We were not able to identify with certainty the type of rock formation from which it came, but it seems to be a fairly hard type of sandstone, tan in colour, somewhat lighter

1/For representations of South Arabian goddesses, see Jacqueline Pirenne, "Notes d'archéologie sud-arabe," III, IV, and V (*Syria*, 39 [1962], pp. 257–62; 42 [1965], pp. 109–46, 311–41). For a representation of Allāt found at Jabal Ramm, see *RB*, 43 (1934), p. 584 and Fig. 7, and Grohmann, *Arabien*, p. 78. A similar representation of some divinity is to be seen opposite the entrance to the Majlis as-Sulṭān at Madā'in Ṣāliḥ (see JS, *Mission*, I, p. 410 and Figs. 201–3).

2/The stone was catalogued as Register no. 103 and shipped with the pottery to Riyadh University (see p. 172, n. 1).

in shade than most of the stones in the vicinity.[3] There are no chisel marks on the surface, except for those made in the process of inscribing the figure, and none on the outer edges and sides.

The back of the stone bears three signs (see Pl. 23). The first two, reading from right to left, may be Taymanite *b* and *l* (see Table of Scripts, Pl. 1); the third does not appear in Taymanite, a fact which suggests that all three signs constitute a *wasm* (individual or tribal mark of ownership).[4] This interpretation was actually suggested to us by Amir ʿAbdallāh ash-Shunayfī when we returned to Taymā' and showed him the stone.

Directly below the signs the stone protrudes 1.5 cm in a horizontal segment which is about 6 cm from top to bottom and extends to the right edge and to about 2 cm from the left edge. This protruding segment may have been merely a part of the original shape of the stone, or it may have been roughly formed to serve as a means of attaching the stone to a wall. The presence of many rocks on the summit may be an indication that a sacred building or enclosure once stood there, but the rocks now lie in such jumbled confusion that it is impossible to discern the line of any wall.

The figure depicted on the stone is seated on a four-legged chair or throne the legs of which terminate in claws such as those of a lion. The breasts of the figure are clearly discernible, indicating that we are dealing with a goddess rather than a god (see p. 31). The hairline is also that of a female figure. The absence of facial features, such as eyes, mouth, and nose, might suggest that the artist had a veiled figure in mind. However, the single vertical line near the centre of the facial area may indicate rather that he was influenced by superstitions concerning the "evil eye" which led him to avoid any attempt to represent facial features.[5]

The goddess appears to be holding in her right hand a cord to which is attached a vessel of some kind, perhaps a basket or other container suitable for offerings. In her left hand she holds aloft a staff or sceptre, the symbol of authority. The

3/Philby (*Midian*, p. 88) describes the rock formation of Jabal Ghunaym as "highly ferruginous sandstone, blackened by weathering and streaked with veins of pink and yellow rock."

4/See the extensive collection of *wasms* in Henry Field, *Camel Brands and Graffiti from Iraq, Syria, Jordan, Iran, and Arabia*, Supplement to *JAOS*, no. 15 (1952). G. Lankester Harding, *Archaeology in the Aden Protectorates* (H.M. Stationery Office, London, 1964), p. 57, identifies a sign, similar to the one at the right, as a "water-sign" and suggests that other marks may have been used to give the distance or depth at which water could be found in the district.

5/Z. Mayani, *L'Arbre sacré et le rite de l'alliance chez les anciens Sémites*, p. 34, Fig. 3. See also G. Lankester Harding, *Archaeology in the Aden Protectorates*, Pl. LV, no. 2, where one of the two figures appears to be that of a female whose facial features are not represented. However, in view of the fact that the human figure was sometimes represented with facial features in pre-Islamic Arabia, one can only speculate as to the reasoning that lay behind the artist's manner of representing the face of the goddess at Jabal Ghunaym. Cf. Charles M. Doughty, *Travels*, I, p. 296, for an example from Taymā' of a human figure represented with eyes, and JS, *Mission*, I, Fig. 80, p. 122, for a petroglyph from Madā'in Ṣāliḥ with "représentations humaines en style bédouin ..."

rounded head of the sceptre gives it the appearance of a mace similar in type to those used in battle; many examples of the type have been found in Palestinian tombs, and it is often represented in Near Eastern art.[6]

Below the sceptre is an object having the appearance of an incense burner. Above it the artist seems to have attempted to portray smoke ascending. Unlike the incense burners currently in use in the region, which are made with a solid base and four vertical supports for the burner (see Fig. 31), this appears to be a bowl-shaped container with a single stem and base.[7] Directly to the left of the incense burner are two parallel lines of uncertain significance. On the opposite side of the goddess there is another enigmatic sign.

In regard to the original purpose or function of the inscribed stone, one can only speculate. Was it a sacred stone which came from a temple in Taymā'? Or was it merely a casual drawing on a conveniently flat stone, the attempt on the part of some individual to draw from memory the image of some goddess which he had seen in a sanctuary at Taymā'? Although there is no certain answer to these questions, the presence of the stone at an open-air sanctuary on the summit of Jabal Ghunaym argues in favour of the view that it was an object of veneration and not just a casual drawing.

The identification of the goddess presents a difficult problem. Many goddesses were revered in the ancient Near East, and the caravans which passed through Taymā' must have brought back a knowledge of some of them. One thinks of goddesses like Astarte, Qudshu, and Anath,[8] also of the figurines and moulded plaques of the nude goddess which were made in Palestine and Syria as early as

6/See James B. Pritchard, *The Ancient Near East in Pictures Relating to the Old Testament* (Princeton, N.J., 1954), p. 346, for an index of numerous representations of maces. Figure 698 is a scene on a cylinder seal representing an enthroned goddess holding in her left hand an upraised mace. In this scene the mace is more ornate than the one from Jabal Ghunaym, and a "pail" is held by one of the attendants rather than by the goddess. There are numerous references in biblical literature to the sceptres of both deities and military leaders. Among those that may shed some light on the role of the ancient Arabian goddess are the references to the "mighty sceptre" (*maṭṭēh ʿōz*) and the "glorious staff" (*maqqēl tiph'ārāh*) of Moab's king and her deity, Chemosh (Jer. 48:13, 17). The "royal sceptre" and the "sceptre of equity" are symbols of the power and justice of the king (Ps. 45:6) and also of Yahweh (cf. L. E. Toombs' article on "Scepter" in *The Interpreter's Dictionary of the Bible* [Abingdon Press, New York and Nashville, 1962]).

7/For examples of ancient incense burners from South Arabia, see Richard LeBaron Bowen, Jr., and Frank P. Albright, *Archaeological Discoveries in South Arabia* (Baltimore, 1958), pp. 150–3, Fig. 96. Unlike the representation on the stone from Jabal Ghunaym, these are rectangular in shape, having four legs, as in the type currently in use in Sa'udi Arabia (see Fig. 31).

8/Although there are no exact parallels to our inscribed stone from Jabal Ghunaym, features such as the bare breasts, the long hair, the sceptre in hand, and a seat or throne are well known from other representations; cf. I. E. S. Edwards, "A Relief of Qudshu-Astarte-Anath in the Winchester College Collection" (*JNES*, 14 [1955], pp. 49–51); Marie-Thérèse Barrelet, "Les Déesses armées et ailées" (*Syria*, 32 [1955], pp. 222–60).

the Middle Bronze Age and which were especially popular during the Iron Age.[9] Such Iron Age figurines have been found at Mt. Nebo and at other sites in Moab, a region with which the people of Taymā' must have had many contacts in ancient times as they do today.[10] In view of Nabonidus' association with both Taymā' in Arabia and Ḥarrān in Syria, it is of interest that the goddesses of Syria were sometimes represented by plaques or figurines.[11] It is impossible, however, to identify these figurines with any of the well-known goddesses.[12] The problem of identification is further complicated by the fact that there was a fluidity in the functions attributed to the various goddesses.

A possibility which must be considered is that the goddess from Jabal Ghunaym is Allāt since she seems to have been one of the most popular goddesses in ancient North Arabia. In linguistic areas where the definite article was *hn* (**han*) her name appears as *hn'lt* (**han-'ilāt*), "the goddess" par excellence. An illustration of this is found in the Aramaic inscription of the fifth century B.C. engraved on a silver bowl which Qainu bar Geshem, king of Qedar, presented to the goddess at her shrine at Tell al-Maskhūṭah (about twelve miles west of Isma'ilia in Egypt).[13] See also the n. pr. 'WSHN'LT (**'Aws-han-'ilāt*, "the gift of the goddess") in an inscription from Thaj.[14] In areas where the definite article was *'al* her name appears as *'Allāt*, which is a contraction of *'al-'ilāt*). However, our ignorance of the original attributes of *han-'ilāt/'al-'ilāt*[15] makes precarious any attempt to identify the Jabal Ghunaym goddess with her.

9/See, for examples, W. F. Albright, *The Excavations of Tell Beit Mirsim*, II, *AASOR*, XVII (1938), pp. 43f., 70ff., Pls. 25, 26, dating from the Middle Bronze and Late Bronze periods. "Astarte figurines" dating from 700 B.C. to 450 B.C. were excavated at Tell en-Nasbeh; cf. C. C. McCown, *Tell en-Nasbeh* (Berkeley, 1947), pp. 245f., Pls. 85, 86.

10/See Nelson Glueck, *Explorations in Eastern Palestine*, III, *AASOR*, XVIII–XIX (1939), pp. 32f. and Fig. 18 for figurines found in Moab and designated by the general term "Astarte figurines," although different goddesses may have been so represented.

11/See Harald Ingholt, *Rapport préliminaire sur sept campagnes ed fouilles à Hama en Syrie* (Copenhagen, 1940), Pls. XVIII, XXXVIII.

12/J. B. Pritchard, in his excellent study of Palestinian figurines in relation to the literary references to the various goddesses, reached the conclusion that "there is no direct evidence connecting the nude female figure represented on the plaques and figurines of Palestine with any of the prominent goddesses. The meaning of the figure may have been so well understood by those who made and used the figurines that contemporary writers did not find it necessary to refer to it" (*Palestinian Figurines in Relation to Certain Goddesses Known through Literature* [New Haven, 1943], p. 86).

13/Isaac Rabinowitz, "Aramaic Inscriptions of the Fifth Century B.C.E. from a North Arabian Shrine in Egypt," *JNES*, 15 (1956), pp. 1–9.

14/G. Ryckmans, "Inscriptions sud-arabes" (4e série) (*Muséon*, 50 [1937]), no. 155. See also now the names .. RMHN'LT (**[Ga]rm-han-'ilāt*) and HN'BD (**han-'Abd*, cf. Saf. H'BD) in Jamme, *Sabaean and Ḥasaean Inscriptions from Saudi Arabia* (Studi Semitici; University of Rome, 1966), nos. 1043 and 1044, although Jamme prefers to regard the element *hn* as Ar. *hawn*, "quietness, gentleness."

15/See p. 78.

Another possibility is that she is the goddess Asherah who, as we know from the Taymā' Stone (ll. 3 and 16), was worshipped at Taymā' in the sixth century B.C.[16] The worship of this goddess was widespread in the ancient Near East. Under the name of Athirat Yam she appears at Ugarit, where she is the consort of El and the mother of seventy gods.[17] In Canaan she appears as Asherah and is conceived as a fertility goddess. She was worshipped in the form of a wooden idol (cf. Exod. 34:13, Deut. 7:5, 12:3, 16:21; Judges 6:25–26; I Kings 16:33; etc.), probably a female figure in appearance. This idol was usually located on a "high-place" and was often associated with altars, sacred pillars, incense burners, and other cultic paraphernalia.

The appearance of Asherah at Taymā' (where her name occurs in the Aramaic form 'ŠR') is evidence of the close commercial contacts of the oasis with Syria and other lands of the eastern Mediterranean. Perhaps the scarcity of wood in North Arabia led the desert artist to use stone rather than wood for his representation of her. It may be that in the inscribed stone from Jabal Ghunaym we have an illustration of what is meant by the "graven image of Asherah" (*pesel ha-'asherah*) which King Manasseh is reported to have placed in the temple at Jerusalem. Not enough is known about the manner of representing Asherah to establish any links between the Jabal Ghunaym drawing and that particular goddess, but it is inherently probable that the drawing depicts a local goddess and we know that Asherah was one of the goddesses of Taymā'.

16/For a discussion of the date of the Taymā' Stone and of the deities mentioned on it, see pp. 28, 92–3; see also G. A. Cooke, *A Text-book of North Semitic Inscriptions* (Oxford, 1903), pp. 195–9, and W. L. Reed, *The Asherah in the Old Testament* (Fort Worth, Texas, 1949), p. 79.

17/Reed, *op. cit.*, pp. 69–96, where material has been collected relating to epigraphic evidence bearing on the Old Testament references to the Canaanite goddess Asherah.

2 The Pottery

A/INTRODUCTION

One of the objectives of the expedition was to collect and study sherds from as many sites as possible in the hope that they would indicate the main archaeological periods of sedentary occupation in ancient North Arabia and the main types of ceramic ware used in that region.

Sherds were collected at ten of the sites visited. Specimens suitable for photographing came from five of these, namely, Sakākah, Taymā', Madā'in Ṣāliḥ, al-Khuraybah, and Ithrā (see map, p. 2 and Figs. 81–85). No sherds were found at Turaif, Badanah, ʿArʿar, or an-Nabk since these are comparatively recent settlements (see pp. 3, 5, 62). At the older sites of Tabūk and al-ʿUlā it was not practical to conduct a search or to investigate the possibility that ancient pottery and inscribed stones might be found in the homes of some of the local residents. In the Wādī as-Sirḥān, at the villages of al-ʿIsāwiyah, Kāf, Manwā, al-Qarqar (Karkar), no sherds were found in spite of the helpful efforts of the local residents. However, they brought for our inspection a number of inscribed stones, and also directed us to the ruins at Ithrā. For the Late Byzantine and Early Arab sherds found at al-Ḥadīthah, see p. 63. At aṭ-Ṭuwayr, Qārah, and Muwaysin, in the al-Jawf region, no sherds were found, but our guides were not very familiar with these places and it is possible that sherds may yet be discovered at them.

Although approximately two thousand specimens of ancient Arabian pottery were collected,[1] the number is small when compared with the large collections which have been made at ancient sites in the Fertile Crescent. The difference is

1/Of this number, about 160 sherds were considered sufficiently distinctive to preserve for further study; these were catalogued in the Register, copies of which are available from Winnett and the writer. This collection, together with a list indicating the provenance of each sherd, was sent to Riyadh University in the hope that it would receive attention in the newly established Department of History and Archaeology. For the disposition of the specimens from the upper Wādī as-Sirḥān region, see p. 64.

to be explained by the fact that North Arabia contains no large *tells* like those in Palestine, Syria, and Iraq. Furthermore, the ancient settlements in the desert were few and far between, while the difficulty of transporting ceramic vessels by donkey or camel rendered pottery of little use to nomads. This all combined to limit the quantity of pottery in use in North Arabia. Settled communities appear to have existed in the northern part of the peninsula as early as the eighth century B.C. and possibly much earlier (see p. 88) and it is highly probable that they made and used pottery.

A study of the sherds collected was rendered difficult by the fact that many of them had suffered considerable erosion from sand and water. Furthermore, the recording and preliminary study had to be done in haste because of the time-limitation on our visas. Photographs of the sherds were made at an-Nabk and Turaif under less than ideal conditions, and there was no time to make drawings. Our conclusions must therefore be regarded as tentative at a number of points.

Some of the pottery types are similar to those already known from Palestinian sites and this suggests that they had been imported from places in the Fertile Crescent (see Figs. 81 and 82). Other sherds, such as those at Taymā' (see Figs. 84 and 85), appear to have no parallels with known types, and may be local products. Final conclusions regarding the chronology of these wares will have to await the excavation of key, stratified sites, but it is possible that some of this material is pre-Nabataean in date, even from Iron I or II, to judge from some similarity to the heavy, coarse ware containing grits that was excavated at Tell el-Kheleifeh (Ezion-geber, King Solomon's seaport) near ʿAqaba, and at other Jordanian and Palestinian sites.[2] A number of parallels with materials from Dhībān (Moabite Dibon), where Winnett and the writer directed two seasons of excavations, were apparent in the Nabataean and Early Arab wares.[3]

The following discussion of the pottery is arranged according to the order in which the sites were visited. It will be helpful to the reader to refer to the appropriate sections of the Journal and to the introductions to the chapters dealing with the inscriptions for information regarding the history of each site as known from ancient literary sources and from the reports of modern explorers.

2/The writer wishes to express his appreciation to several persons who have been most helpful in preparing this report. All members of the expedition shared in collecting the sherds; Fred Winnett and Rick Vidal assisted with the cleaning, cataloguing, and preliminary study of the material. From the photographs of the sherds the following archaeologists were able to suggest a number of parallels with materials discovered at excavations which they have directed: President Nelson Glueck, Hebrew-Union College, Iron Age pottery from Tell el-Kheleifeh; Dr. Gus Van Beek, Smithsonian Institution, pre-Islamic pottery from Hadhramaut, South Arabia; Professor Peter J. Parr, Institute of Archaeology, University of London, Nabataean pottery from Petra.

3/See Fred V. Winnett and William L. Reed, *The Excavations at Dibon (Dhībān) in Moab*, *AASOR*, XXXVI–XXXVII (New Haven, 1964).

B/POTTERY FROM THE JAWF AREA

The sites investigated in this area included al-Qalʿah, about four miles from Sakākah, the region of Qaṣr Zaʿbal at the northern edge of Sakākah, and the environs of Qaṣr Mārid in al-Jawf.[4] Sherds were found only at the last two sites. The absence of sherds at al-Qalʿah is to be explained by the fact that it was not a permanent settlement but simply a rest area for caravans. The large outcropping of rock provided some shade and a suitable surface for recording inscriptions and drawings (see above, p. 7).

In Sakākah the only sherds found were near the base of the sandstone hill called Burnus, about twenty metres west of Qaṣr Zaʿbal. Of the nine sherds that were catalogued, none could be identified with certainty as pre-Islamic (see Fig. 83:3, 5–8). Patterns of incised lines on some of the vessels and rows of indentations on others are characteristic decorations on much of the pottery at several of the sites visited (for the specimens from Sakākah, see Fig. 83:3, 5). It is probable that the moulded sherds (Fig. 83:6–8) are fragments of lamps dating from the Islamic period, but they are so fragmentary as to make it impossible to determine whether they are Early of Mediaeval Arab in date.[5] The presence of Thamudic and Nabataean inscriptions at Sakākah, as well as the petroglyph of the "dancing girls," and the large stepped "pool" (see pp. 8–11) suggest the presence there of a pre-Islamic settlement but the problem is one to which only the archaeologist can provide an answer. The *qaṣr* is no longer occupied and offers a promising site for excavation.

At al-Jawf the search for sherds in Qaṣr Mārid was disappointing. A few sherds were found in the vicinity of the abandoned well north of the *qaṣr*. Those that could be identified came from a large, two-handled jar bearing wavy-line incisions and rows of indentations covered in a rather irregular pattern with black and dark red glaze. Comparisons with Palestinian materials suggest that they are Mediaeval Arab in date. An archaeological sounding at Qaṣr Mārid, now no longer occupied, would be helpful in determining whether or not the present structure rests on foundations dating to the Nabataean or Iron Age periods. Such an undertaking might well be combined with a work of restoration on the outer walls, and with an intensive exploration of the ruins (apparently abandoned dwellings and shops) north of the *qaṣr*.

4/For other sites visited in the region but where no sherds were found, see p. 12.

5/For parallels with Early Arab ware from Dibon in Moab, and similar sherds from Abū Ghōsh and Khirbat al-Mafjar in western Palestine, see Winnett and Reed, *Excavations at Dibon*, Part I, Pls. 15, 16; Part II, Pls. 60, 67. Perhaps because of the scarcity of suitable materials for preparing colour paints, painted vessels of the Islamic period in North Arabia are less common than those with incised patterns as decoration.

C/POTTERY FROM THE TAYMĀ' AREA

In contrast with the above mentioned sites where the sherds were few and difficult to locate, several hundred were found at Taymā'.[6] All were collected on the slopes of the ancient city walls or about a mile south of the modern oasis where our camp was established (see p. 22). Considerable sand has drifted against the city wall, but one of the gateways can still be detected and a number of sherds were found in this area. Archaeological soundings at the gateway and in the adjacent region where a vertical section of the city wall is still visible (see Figs. 22–27) would doubtless answer the question as to whether or not this is the location of the Taymā' built by King Nabonidus (see pp. 88–93).

The amount, variety, and excellent quality of the pottery at Taymā' (see Figs. 84 and 85) are of special interest because of the historic importance of the city. The painted sherds (see Fig. 84:2–4, 7–8) bear some resemblance to Early Arab ware (see n. 5), but they differ in that the pottery is better fired (see Fig. 84:2–4, 7), contains grits (see Fig. 84:3, 4), and is decorated with patterns not usually found on Early Arab pottery.[7] One sherd (Fig. 84:8), possibly pre-Islamic in date, is a dark red ware containing black grits and is decorated with white paint in a pattern comprised of a dot and three concentric circles. The "cross-hatch," "trellis," or "lattice" decoration on two sherds (Fig. 84:2, 7) bears a very close resemblance to pottery of the Iron I and II periods at Dhībān,[8] and at other Moabite and Edomite sites explored by Nelson Glueck.[9] In view of the probability that caravans travelled during the Iron Age between Taymā' and the cities of Moab and Edom, located on the King's Highway (see Numbers 20:17–18; 21:22) east and southeast of the Dead Sea, one is not surprised to find this similarity. Until excavation is undertaken at Taymā', and until further work is done in ancient Moab and Edom, the chronological pattern of Iron Age pottery in these regions will remain uncertain. However, it seems quite probable that some of the sherds found at Taymā' are pre-Nabataean, possibly Iron I or II.

Of special interest at Taymā' was the pottery which we have designated "granite ware" because in texture and colour it resembles some types of granite

6/Of sherds collected at Taymā' forty-six were catalogued under Register numbers 116–61, and thirteen flints (no. 119) of a Neolithic type were found out of context on the surface with the sherds.

7/The presence of one sherd (Register no. 116) bearing the blue-green glaze typical of the Mediaeval Arab period is evidence for a later occupation in the region of the ancient city walls.

8/See Winnett and Reed, *Excavations at Dibon*, Part II, Pl. 78:5, 13.

9/See *AASOR*, XIV (1934), p. 20, Pl. 23:25; XV (1935), pp. 129f., Pl. 27A; XXV–XXVII (1951), Part II, p. 468 (where Glueck lists a number of parallels), Pl. 61. He classifies a sherd from Tell al-Ghazalā, in the Jordan Valley near Deir 'Alla, as Late Bronze–Iron Age I (p. 468).

(see Fig. 85). The sherds come from large bowls or jars. The ware varies in colour from reddish to pinkish orange and contains a high proportion of black, white, and brown grits. Two of the sherds (Fig. 85:5, 1) bear wheel marks which give the appearance of ribbing, but it is quite a different type from that known from the Byzantine-Arab periods in Palestine. In the absence of close parallels one can only conjecture that the sherds may belong chronologically with the painted sherds of the Iron Age periods and be of local manufacture.[10]

When one looks to South Arabia for possible parallels, he meets with considerable uncertainty in the matter of chronology. G. Lankester Harding has published some specimens from his survey of the Aden Protectorates which resemble in a few features both the coarse, heavy ware of Taymā' and the painted "trellis" pattern. Although he is properly cautious about chronology, he suggests that some of the pottery, such as that from Subr in the Aden region, may be as early as the fifth or sixth century B.C.[11] Whether or not any of the Taymā' pottery is to be dated to the period of Nabonidus (see above, pp. 88–93) can only be determined when an excavation in the ancient parts of the oasis is undertaken.

Our search for sherds on the summit of Jabal Ghunaym, about fourteen kilometres south of Taymā', was disappointing, especially because of the presence there of ancient inscriptions and petroglyphs, and a stone plaque bearing a representation of a female figure, probably the goddess of Taymā' (see pp. 29–31 and 167–71). Only one sherd (Register number 205) was found, the plain rim of a large jar made of the "granite" ware, pinkish in colour with many grits, similar in texture to the sherds found at ancient Taymā' (see Fig. 85:2, 7). Because the ascent of Jabal Ghunaym is difficult, it is unlikely that large quantities of pottery were ever carried to the summit, but a more careful search for sherds than we had time to conduct might well uncover additional specimens.

D/POTTERY FROM THE REGION OF AL-ʿULĀ

The pottery discovered in this region came from the surface of the *tell* at al-Khuraybah, ancient Dedan, northeast of al-ʿUlā (see pp. 38–42). The *tell* is

10/In 1962 the writer had an opportunity to inspect the pottery in the small museum in Aden. Some of the coarse, grey ware, except for the colour, bears a resemblance to the Taymā' "granite" ware. However, the provenance of much of this material is unknown and the dates are very uncertain.

11/See G. Lankester Harding, *Archaeological Survey in the Aden Protectorates* (H.M. Stationery Office, London, 1964), p. 20; see also pp. 12, 24; Pls. VII, 67; XVII, 16, 25; XXI, 10, for possible parallels with Taymā' pottery and Harding's view that some of the material he discovered may date "from the seventh or even the eighth century B.C." (p. 12). The presence of pre-Islamic pottery in the Hadhramaut region of South Arabia is reported by Dr. Gus Van Beek (see "An Archaeological Reconnaissance in Hadhramaut, South Arabia – A Preliminary Report," *Smithsonian Report for 1963*, pp. 521–45, by Gus W. Van Beek, Glen H. Cole, and Albert Jamme).

literally covered with sherds, many of which were doubtless "excavated" by the residents of al-ʿUlā in the process of removing some of the stones of ancient Dedan for use in new buildings. From the hundreds of sherds collected, more than forty were catalogued (Register numbers 162–204), and seven were photographed (Figs. 83:1, 2, 4; 84:1, 5, 6, 9).

As might be expected, most of the pottery is Early and Mediaeval Arab in date and is characterized by glaze decoration, some pieces of light blue, and by a fairly porous type of ware painted with black, brown, and dark red lines. Several fragments of small vessels made of stone, probably a type of alabaster, were found with the sherds. One sherd (Fig. 84:5) bears a type of "trellis" or "cross-hatch" pattern and may be as early as the Taymā' ware decorated with this pattern, but the texture of the ware suggests that it is Early Arab in date.[12] Probably from the same period are three other painted sherds (Fig. 84:1, 6, 9), although, as excavations in Moab have demonstrated, this type of pottery is characteristic of the Byzantine period also.

Unpainted sherds from al-Khuraybah (Fig. 83:1, 2, 4) may well be pre-Islamic in date. Two sherds (Fig. 83:1, 2), incised with parallel lines and wavy-line decorations on body and rim, are probably of local manufacture and cannot be dated with certainty, although the medium coarse, pinkish ware of the vessels may indicate that they are not pre-Islamic in date.

Of special interest is one sherd (Fig. 83:4) of coarse, dark brown ware incised with the fragments of two or more early Arabian letters. One of these is a Taymanite 'alif; the identity of the others is less certain. Unfortunately no drawing of this sherd was obtained. The writer is indebted to Dr. Nelson Glueck who examined the photograph and suggested a possible parallel from his excavations at Tell el-Kheleifeh near Aqaba.[13] His specimen, the first to be found in a controlled excavation, is from a jar, and bears two South Arabic letters inscribed in a manner similar to those on our sherd from al-Khuraybah. Glueck thinks the characters on the jar from Tell el-Kheleifeh are Minaean, but Albright (*Dedan*, p. 3 and n. 3) regards them as "proto-Dedanite." The jar was found in the Iron I level and may be from the tenth–ninth centuries B.C. It is thought that such jars, inscribed with South Arabic letters, perhaps the owner's mark, were used in the incense trade which flourished for many centuries between South Arabia and the seaports of the Red Sea and the cities of the Fertile Crescent.[14] The inscribed

12/See Winnett and Reed, *Excavations at Dibon*, Part II, Pl. 61:8.

13/See Nelson Glueck, *The Other Side of the Jordan* (New Haven, 1945), pp. 105–8, Fig. 56. The writer is also indebted to Dr. Gus Van Beek for the privilege of examining the sherds from the excavations at Ezion-geber that are stored at the Smithsonian Institution. The publication of this material, promised by Glueck for the near future, will provide an important source for the study of pottery, not only in ancient Edom, but also in both North and South Arabia.

14/Glueck, *ibid.*, p. 108.

sherd from al-Khuraybah, an important centre on the incense route, may be the earliest found at this site.[15]

The absence of Nabataean sherds should not be taken to indicate that Nabataean influence failed to reach Dedan. It is probable that if we had had more time to search, some Nabataean specimens would have been discovered dating from the same periods as the Nabataean graffiti on the cliffs directly east of al-Khuraybah (see p. 120), and the stone bearing diagonal dressing characteristic of Nabataean masonry (see p. 39).

Although the depth of the *tell* at al-Khuraybah is low, being only about fifteen to twenty feet, and there has been some disturbance of the stratification both by the construction of the Ḥijāz Railway through its western edge and by recent quarrying for building-stones, the remains are sufficiently impressive to warrant an excavation. Until such work is undertaken the ceramic chronology of the district will remain uncertain, but the surface finds suggest that the city flourished as early as the Iron Age and continued to be occupied, at least intermittently, until the mediaeval period when it was abandoned.

E/POTTERY FROM THE MADĀ'IN ṢĀLIḤ AREA

In view of the fact that reports by early visitors to Madā'in Ṣāliḥ, such as Doughty, Huber, Euting, Jaussen, and Savignac, contain no descriptions of its ancient pottery, we were especially pleased to have the opportunity of making a study of the ceramic ware from this impressive region. Our investigation represents only a very modest beginning in the light of the vastness of the archaeological remains, which are similar in many respects to those at Petra but extend to much greater distances on all sides of Ḥegrā, one of the "cities of Ṣāliḥ."

The number of sherds was not as great or as concentrated as at Taymā' and al-Khuraybah. It is probable that many have been buried by drifting sand in the open areas and at the bases of the tombs cut in the faces of the cliffs (see Figs. 54–59, 68, 70 and colour plate 3B). We scrupulously resisted the temptation to probe into the sand for sherds which might reveal more of the history of the site. Of the three hundred or more sherds collected in this region, only about thirty-five were distinctive enough to catalogue (Register numbers 206–40). From this collection eleven, all Nabataean, were photographed (see Fig. 81).

The pottery discovered came from two areas, one outside the entrances to the tombs at Qaṣr al-Bint (see pp. 37, 45), the other south of the railway station at

15/For a discussion of the dates of the Minaean inscriptions in the vicinity of al-Khuraybah, see pp. 117–19.

Ḥegrā (see pp. 50, 53). In spite of a rather careful search for sherds in the region of Jabal Ithlib, at the Dīwān or Majlis as-Sulṭān (see Fig. 61), and the impressive array of tombs south of the railway station and west of the railway, not a single sherd was discovered, although many must lie beneath the surface (see p. 53).

The sherds at Qaṣr al-Bint (see Fig. 81:2, 5–11) were doubtless thrown outside the entrances to the tombs when the latter were last cleared of their contents. All the sherds are the exquisite "egg-shell" painted ware so well known from Petra and other Nabataean sites in ancient Edom and Moab. The sherds (Fig. 81:1, 3, 4) found in the open area near "mushroom rock" (see p. 50), which must have been a residential area at one time, are of Nabataean type like those found at Qaṣr al-Bint. In this region south of the Madā'in Ṣāliḥ railway station, there were three small mounds or *tells* rising about three metres above the level terrain. On the surface of the *tells* were many fragments of "egg-shell" Nabataean ware, unpainted Nabataean ware, and some blue-green glazed ware typical of the Mediaeval Arab period.[16] No sherds that could be identified as pre-Nabataean were found, although the presence of Minaean and Lihyanite inscriptions at Ḥegrā is evidence that the site was inhabited before the arrival of the Nabataeans (see p. 130).

It is evident that the region containing these small *tells* would be a promising place to excavate. Since our exploration of the district, the importance of this region at "mushroom rock" has been confirmed by Mr. 'Ādil 'Ayyāsh, Archaeological Adviser to the Department of Antiquities, Ministry of Education, at Riyadh. Working for a period of thirty-five days in early 1966 with a party from Riyadh, Mr. 'Ayyāsh reports the mapping and recording of the monuments at Madā'in Ṣāliḥ. Of special interest is his statement that a detailed map was made of the "residential area" (which apparently included the three small *tells* which

16/Only one sherd (Register no. 211) decorated with blue-green glaze was found in this region south of the Madā'in Ṣāliḥ railway station. A date in the Mediaeval Arab period is proposed on the basis of its similarity with glazed pottery from numerous Palestinian sites. However, as Dr. Vidal has pointed out, the possibility of it being "Parthian" and having similarities with glazed pottery from Jāwān near the Persian Gulf must be considered. Samples of the green glazed ware have also been found at Dura-Europus dating from the first century B.C. to the third century A.D., and from the same general chronological periods at Seleucia on the Tigris; cf. Frederick R. Matson, "Technological Notes on the Ain Jawan Pottery," and Florence E. Day, "Historical Notes on the Ain Jawan Pottery," in *BASOR*, Supplementary Studies, nos. 7–9 (1950), pp. 57–68; Neilson C. Debevoise, *Parthian Pottery from Seleucia on the Tigris* (University of Michigan Press, 1934), pp. 7–11, 28–34; Nicholas Toll, *The Excavations at Dura-Europus*: Final Report IV, Part I, *The Green Glazed Pottery* (Yale University Press, 1943), pp. 5–6. Until excavations can be conducted at the *tell* of Madā'in Ṣāliḥ and additional specimens recovered, the identification of the glazed pottery found there must remain uncertain; it can probably be determined only by laboratory tests on the glaze, but a tentative conclusion that it is Mediaeval Arab in date is a reasonable one.

we inspected), and that he had discovered the line of the ancient city wall enclosing this area, about five to six hundred metres in diameter.[17] It was further reported by Mr. ʿAyyāsh that the city wall was constructed of mud-brick (now badly disintegrated), resting on stone foundations, and that it was reinforced with square towers, one of which is rather well preserved.

The importance of the Nabataean pottery at Madā'in Ṣāliḥ lies, in part, in the fact that it is almost identical with specimens known from other parts of the Nabataean kingdom. One of the sherds (Fig. 81:1), from a small, unpainted bowl of a thin, well-fired ware, is almost identical with bowls excavated at Dhībān,[18] and could have been made by the same potter. The painted "egg-shell" ware is also identical with that found at Dhībān,[19] Petra,[20] and other Nabataean sites such as Khirbat at-Tannur in Edom, excavated and explored by Nelson Glueck.[21] This type of ware is usually dated between 100 B.C. and 100 A.D. The writer is especially indebted to Peter J. Parr, Archaeological Institute, University of London, for examining the photographs of our sherds. He believes that the specimens cover both his early and later periods at Petra (Fig. 81:11, an example of the early style; Fig. 81:4, 5, examples of the later style[22]).

F/POTTERY FROM THE UPPER WĀDĪ AS-SIRḤĀN

In spite of the fact that the villages in the upper Wādī as-Sirḥān were important caravan stations on the route between Damascus and the cities of North Arabia (see map and pp. 56, 59), pottery was not discovered in the same quantity as at Taymā' and al-Khuraybah.[23] However, about two hundred sherds were found,

17/Reported to the writer in a letter dated February 20, 1966. Further information about these discoveries will be awaited with much interest.

18/Winnett and Reed, *Excavations at Dibon*, Part II, Pl. 68:1, 2, 3.

19/See *ibid.*, Part II, Pls. 62B, 68, and also 68A:6 for an illustration of terra sigillata sherds found both at Dhībān and Madā'in Ṣāliḥ.

20/Peter J. Parr, "Excavations at Petra, 1958–59," *PEQ*, 1960, pp. 124–35; "The Beginnings of Hellenization at Petra" (*Le Rayonnement des Civilizations Grecque et Romaine sur les Cultures Périphériques*, Huitième Congrès International d'Archéologie Classique [Paris, 1965]), pp. 527–33, Pl. 131, 132.

21/Nelson Glueck, *The Other Side of the Jordan*, Fig. 111; *Explorations in Eastern Palestine*, II, *AASOR*, XV (1935), Pls. 31A, 31B; *Deities and Dolphins* (New York and Toronto, 1965), pp. 6, 291.

22/In a letter to the writer, dated May 16, 1966, Parr stated that our sherds from Madā'in Ṣāliḥ "seem to cover exactly the same range as at Petra, including both my early and late styles." His view that there may be some connection between the Late Nabataean and Early Byzantine ware seems quite convincing on the basis of sherds from Dhībān, but no examples of Byzantine ware of this type were found at Madā'in Ṣāliḥ. Our moulded sherd (Fig. 81:8) is a typical Nabataean one, although there is no basis for dating it early or late.

23/The Early Arab or Late Byzantine sherds from al-Ḥadīthah came from the vicinity of a cemetery located about two miles south of the village (see p. 63). The explanation for the absence

most of them at Ithrā (see Fig. 82) and a few from the summit of Jabal as-Saʿīdī (see p. 62 and Figs. 76, 77). The Nabataean sherds in the vicinity of Qaṣr as-Saʿīdī attest its occupation during that period (see p. 62), but because of the apparent shallowness of debris on the summit of the *jabal,* it would be difficult to determine the date of this fortified citadel by means of excavation.

The sherds from Ithrā span the archaeological periods from Nabataean to Mediaeval Arab. Typical of the latter is the sherd (Fig. 82:16) decorated with green glaze. Most distinctive are the fragments of lamps (Fig. 82:8–15) which are Nabataean in date and probably imported from other Nabataean towns to the north such as Petra and Dibon.[24] Because lamps of this type have been found in levels at many Palestinian sites, they are often designated as "Herodian" and are dated to the first century A.D.[25] Of special interest is the fact that similar lamps have been found at Qumran and in the caves of the Dead Sea Scrolls nearby.[26] It is evident that such lamps were exported from Palestinian centres, not only to large cities but also to places as remote as Ithrā. The discovery of fragments of them in the rooms and near the foundations of the building at Rās al-ʿĀnīyah in Ithrā (see pp. 59–60) is evidence that the building was occupied during the Nabataean period. Whether or not the building was a Nabataean temple like the one at Khirbat at-Tannur could probably be determined by a small excavation which might also answer the question as to whether or not it was built at the site of an Iron Age sanctuary, as was the temple at Khirbat at-Tannur.[27]

Further confirmation of a Nabataean date for the building at Rās al-ʿĀnīyah may be seen in the character of the other sherds found there. They include "egg-shell" painted ware (Fig. 82:4, 5), rims (Fig. 82:2, 3), and bases (Fig. 82:18, 20, 21). Less certain in date are the examples of ribbed ware (Fig. 82:1, 7, 19) which would not be inappropriate in a Nabataean context but might also be Byzantine or Early Arab.[28] One of the sherds (Fig. 82:22) appears to be the base

---

of sherds in some of these villages, where one would expect to find them, may lie in the fact that there has been more drifting of sand in this region than at al-Khuraybah or in ancient Taymā'.

24/See Winnett and Reed, *Excavations at Dibon*, Part II, Pls. 56:6, 7; 69:1–6.

25/For other examples of this type of lamp, see James B. Pritchard, *The Excavation of Herodian Jericho, 1951, AASOR*, XXXII–XXXIII (1958), Pl. 49:1–6; Paul W. Lapp, *Palestinian Ceramic Chronology, 200 B.C.–A.D. 70, ASOR*, Publications of the Jerusalem School, Archaeology, III (1961), pp. 193–6; Robert H. Smith, "The Household Lamps of Palestine in New Testament Times" (*BA*, XXIX, no. 1 [February 1966], pp. 1–27).

26/See D. Barthélemy and J. T. Milik, *Discoveries in the Judaean Desert*, I (Oxford, 1955), Pl. III; M. Baillet, J. T. Milik, and R. de Vaux, *Discoveries in the Judaean Desert of Jordan*, III (Oxford, 1962), Pl. VII, 1.

27/Nelson Glueck, *The Other Side of the Jordan*, pp. 180–200; *Deities and Dolphins*, Plans A and H.

28/One small sherd (Fig. 82:6) has a pattern of parallel lines, unusual for Nabataean bowls, but the thin, well-fired texture is characteristic of that period.

of a limestone cup similar to those found at Dhībān, Herodian Jericho, al-Jīb (ancient Gibeon), and other Palestinian sites (see p. 60).[29]

Also from Rās al-ʿĀnīyah came fragments of ostrich eggs and one coin (Fig. 82:17), which was so eroded that it could not be attributed with certainty, but its size and general features are similar to those of Nabataean coins (see p. 60). On the basis of the pottery it is certain that the Qurayyāt al-Milḥ, especially Ithrā and Jabal as-Saʿīdī, were occupied by Nabataeans during the first century B.C. and the first century A.D.,[30] and that the neighbouring villages of Kāf, al-Qarqar, Manwā, and probably al-Ḥadīthah were inhabited during the same period.

It is clear from the above survey that a great deal has still to be learned about the pottery of North Arabia, especially in the pre-Nabataean periods, before a pottery-sequence can be established, but at least a beginning has been made. A clear picture will only emerge when more extensive surveys are undertaken and, in particular, when some of the ancient sites have been excavated.

29/A fragmentary specimen is published by James B. Pritchard from Herodian Jericho, *The Excavation of Herodian Jericho*, Pl. 52:5; he notes also a parallel from Wādī Murabbaʿat. Such cups are designated "measuring cups" by Y. Yadin ("The Excavation of Masada – 1963/64, Preliminary Report," *IEJ*, 15, nos. 1–2 [1965], Pl. 24B).

30/For the Nabataean inscription from Ithrā, see p. 160.

3 Pottery Catalogue

FIGURE 81 Nabataean sherds from Madā'in Ṣāliḥ.[1]

1 (216) Rim, bowl, thin and well-fired ware.
2 (229) Rim, bowl, "egg-shell," reddish ware with dark brown paint.
3 (218) Body, bowl; see no. 2.
4 (217) Body, bowl; see nos. 2, 3.
5 (234) Body, bowl; see nos. 2–4.
6 (232) Body, bowl; see nos. 2–5.
7 (236) Body, bowl; see nos. 2–6.
8 (235) Body, pressed or moulded, very thin and hard ware, buff.
9 (231) Body, bowl; see nos. 2–7.
10 (237) Body, bowl; see nos. 2–7, 9.
11 (239) Body, bowl; see nos. 2–7, 9, 10.

FIGURE 82 Sherds and coin from Ithrā in Wādī as-Sirḥān.[2]

1 Body, ribbed ware; Byzantine or Mediaeval Arab.
2 Rim fragment.
3 Rim, jug, handle attachment; Nabataean.
4 Body, bowl, "egg-shell," reddish ware, with dark brown paint; see Fig. 81; Nabataean.
5 Body, bowl; see no. 4; Nabataean.
6 Body, bowl; see nos. 4, 5; Nabataean.
7 Body, ribbed; Byzantine or Mediaeval Arab.

1/The numbers in parentheses are the Register numbers. Copies of the Register are available from Winnett and Reed. The numbered sherds, together with a list indicating the provenance of each, are at Riyadh University. All sherds in this figure are from Ḥegrā; nos. 1, 3, 4 were found south of the railroad station in the vicinity of "mushroom rock" (see Fig. 67); the others were collected in the vicinity of Qaṣr al-Bint (see Fig. 41).

2/The sherds in this figure are from the area of the foundations of a Nabataean sanctuary located about one-half kilometre east of the *qaṣr* in Ithrā (see Fig. 74). No Register numbers were assigned to them; they were placed in the small museum of Amir ʿAbdallāh as-Sudayrī in an-Nabk.

8 Lamp, rim of filling-hole; Nabataean-Roman.
9 Lamp, rim of filling-hole; Nabataean.
10 Lamp, rim of filling-hole; Nabataean.
11 Lamp fragment; Nabataean.
12 Lamp, body; Nabataean.
13 Lamp, rim of filling-hole; Roman period, "Herodian" type.
14 Lamp, body fragment at filling-hole; Roman period, "Herodian" type.
15 Lamp, fragment of body; Nabataean.
16 Body, jar, green glaze; Mediaeval Arab.
17 Coin; badly eroded, but size and general features are typical of Nabataean coins.
18 Base, buff ware.
19 Body, broad ribbing.
20 Base and body fragment.
21 Base, jar; Nabataean-Roman.
22 Limestone, bottom of cup; Nabataean-Roman.

FIGURE 83 Inscribed sherds from Sakākah and al-Khuraybah.[3]
1 Khuraybah (190). Body, medium coarse, pinkish ware, incised concentric lines, wavy-line decoration below.
2 Khuraybah (191). Wide rim, medium coarse, pinkish ware, wavy-line incision on rim, another wavy-line incision below rim and concentric-line incisions on body; see no. 1.
3 Sakākah (114). Body, line of wedge-shaped indentations on body.
4 Khuraybah (203). Body, coarse, dark brown ware, fragments of two South Arabic letters.
5 Sakākah (108). Body, dark brown ware, black inside, incised wavy line.
6 Sakākah (112). Lamp, medium coarse, grey ware, moulded (?).
7 Sakākah (113). Lamp, medium coarse, grey ware, moulded; see no. 6.
8 Sakākah (115). Body, medium coarse grey ware, moulded; see nos. 6, 7.

FIGURE 84 Painted sherds from Taymā' and al-Khuraybah.[4]
1 Khuraybah (200). Rim, bowl, buff fine ware, dark brown paint on rim and side, and lines extending down from band inside.
2 Taymā' (137). Rim, bowl, medium fine ware, reddish slip outside and inside, black painted decoration outside.

3/The sherds from Sakākah were found about twenty metres west of the *qaṣr* at the foot of the sandstone outcrop (see Fig. 6). The sherds from al-Khuraybah in Figs. 82 and 84 were found in the vicinity of the "reservoir" of Ṣāliḥ (see Fig. 47).

4/The sherds from Taymā' in Figs. 84 and 85 were found in the vicinity of the ancient city wall west of the modern oasis near the expedition's camp (see Figs. 22–27).

3 Taymā' (150). Rim, bowl, cream coloured ware, light brown paint outside, small grits.
4 Taymā' (147). Rim, bowl, medium fine ware, small grits, brown paint.
5 Khuraybah (183). Body, bowl; medium coarse, buff ware, black paint inside, "cross-hatch" pattern.
6 Khuraybah (196). Body, jar, medium coarse, pink ware, slip inside, concentric lines with pattern extending below bottom line, dark brown paint.
7 Taymā' (145). Rim, bowl, fine buff ware, black and dark red paint outside, and black bands of paint on inner and outer edges of rim.
8 Taymā' (157). Base, bowl, dark red ware, black grits, white paint outside in pattern of dot and three concentric circles.
9 Khuraybah (184). Rim, bowl, medium coarse, reddish ware, grits, black and red painted decoration inside.

FIGURE 85 "Granite" ware sherds from Taymā'.
1 (123) Rim, bowl, reddish ware, black, white, and brown grits, "granite"-like appearance.
2 (121) Rim, bowl, very hard, heavy, pinkish-orange ware, black and coloured grits, light ribbing outside.
3 (120) Base, bowl, heavy, pinkish-orange ware, black and coloured grits; see no. 2.
4 (125) Body, bowl, heavy, reddish ware; black, white, and brown grits, ridge on outside and traces of dark red slip or burnish.
5 (130) Body, bowl, reddish ware, black and white grits, wheel marks inside, concentric grooves outside.
6 (124) Body; see no. 2.
7 (122) Body, heavy, hard, pinkish-orange ware, black, white, and coloured grits.
8 (117) Body, hard, black, white, and coloured grits, broad and light ribbing.

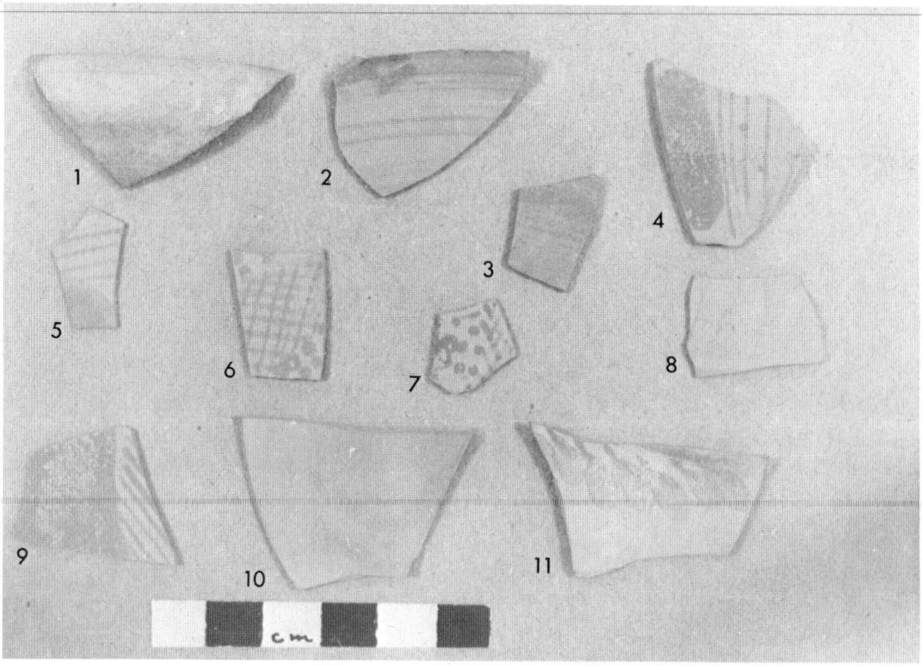

FIGURE 81 Nabataean sherds from Madā'in Ṣāliḥ

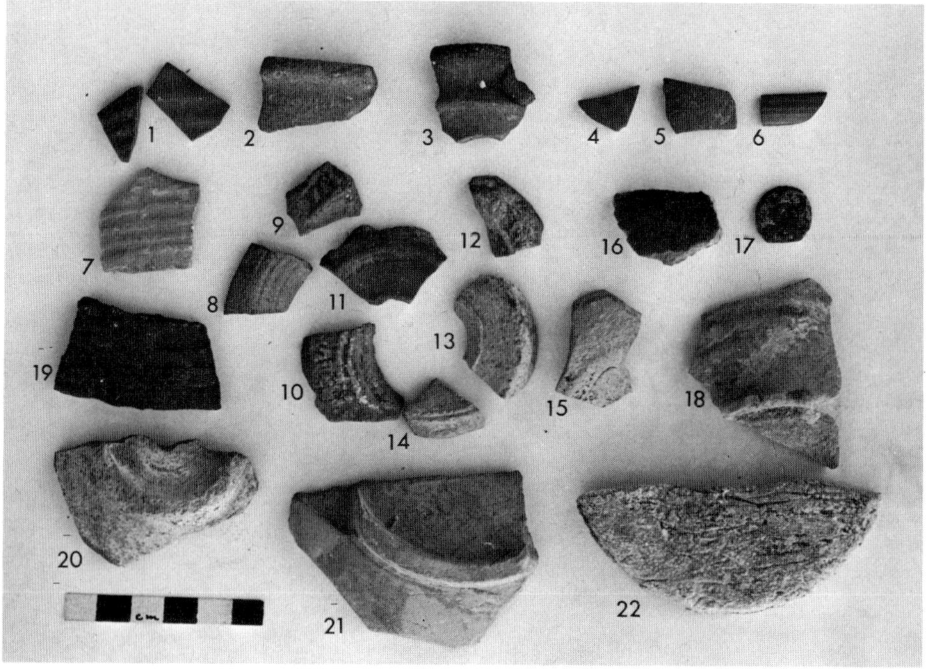

FIGURE 82 Sherds and coins from Ithrā in Wādī as-Sirḥān

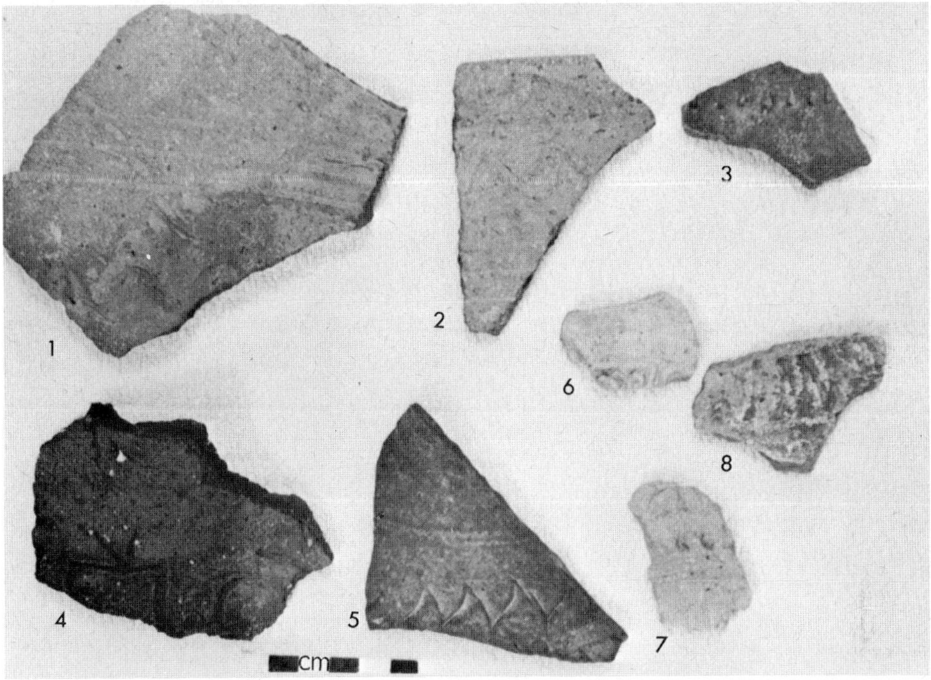

FIGURE 83 Inscribed sherds from Sakākah and al-Khuraybah

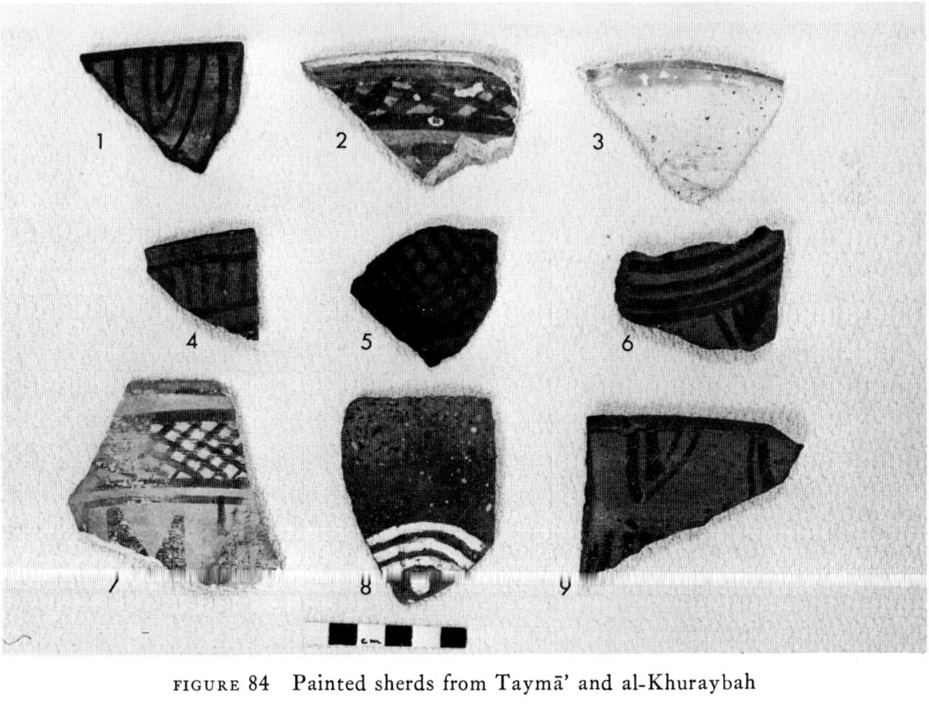

FIGURE 84 Painted sherds from Taymā' and al-Khuraybah

FIGURE 85 Sherds from Taymā'

Appendices

I Glossary

1/MINAEAN

'ḥrm n. fam. or trib. 'Aḥram 11
bwsn n. fam. or trib. Bawsān 9
byt v. "to spend the night" (Ar. *bāta*) 10
grmt n. fam. or trib. Girmat 8
grmnhy n. fam. or trib. Garmanāhy 6, 7
ḥwym n. pr. Ḥuwayyum 2
ḫb't n. fam. or trib. Khabi'at 5
ḫḏn n. pr. Khaḏan 8
ḏ rel. part. 3, 9, 9, 10; rel. pron. 10
s'd'l n. pr. Sa'ad'il 3, 9
'bdt n. pr. 'Abdat 5
'bdwd n. pr. 'Abdwadd 6
ġlb n. pr. Ghālib 11
qḥl n. fam. or trib. Qaḥal 10
mrr n. pr. Marār 4
mrḍ' (?) n. pr. 1
m'ḏ n. pr. Mu'adh b. MRḌ' 1
mn prep. "from" 6
yḥm'l n. pr. Yaḥmi'il 10
yrb n. pr. Yarubb 9
yf' n. pr. Yāfi' b. MRR 4
yf'n n. fam. or trib. Yaf'ān 3, 9

2/TAYMANITE

'b ? 7b
'(bw) n. pr. 34
'tw n. pr. 'Atw 19
'ṯt n. f. "woman" 5
'ḏn v. "to exhort, urge" (Ar. *'aḏina*, IV) – *y'ḏnk*, 3 sg. m. Imperf. IV with 2 sg. f. suf. 5, 6
'sgr n. pr. 'Asgar 17, 18
'ln'm n. pr. 'Ilna'am 29
'ns n. pr. 'Ins, 'Anas 43
'wl (?) n. pr. 'Awāl 45

b n. "son" 1–5, 7, 20, 26, 28, 38, 39, 45
prep. "in" 11, 13, 15–17, 20–23, 33; "in exchange for" 5
bṣdqn s.v. *ṣdq*
bh v. "to lie with" (Ar. *bāha*) 37
bhšrkt s.v. *šrk*

tly n. pr. 30

gml n. "camel" 5

ḥgg n. pr. Ḥaggāg (f. of ḎʼB) 1, 5; (f. of ṢMRF') 14; (f. of FḤK) 7b, 9–11; (f. of Y'ḎRL) 12, 13
ḥdd v. "to be sharp, keen" (cf. Ar. *ḥadda*) 12
n. "vehemence, fury" (cf. Ar. *ḥiddah*) 30
n. pr. Ḥudād 31
ḥrḍ v. "to be sick" (Ar. *ḥaruḍa*) 9
ḥmd n. pr. Ḥamd b'WL ? 45
ḥmn n. pr. Ḥimmān 28

ddn n. loc. Dedan 20–23, 33
dmt n. pr. Dawmat 38

ḏ'b n. pr. Dhi'b 7a; bḤGG 1, 5
ḏt hn'n n. pr. f. Dhāt-HN'N 5
ḏn dem. pron. "this" 3

rb'l n. pr. Rabb'il bRḤM 24
[illegible] n. "riding camel" (Ar. [illegible], [illegible]) 5
rhw v. "to spy out" (cf. Syr. *rᵉhā*, "to watch [from a hiding-place], spy out, be on the look-out") – *yrh* 3 sg. m. Imperf. I 20.

sqʿ n. pr. bMK'L 36
smʿl n. trib. 1, 2

šrṣ n. pr. 4
šrk – *bhšrkt* n. pr. Bi-ha-Shirkat 20
šmt n. "black camel" (Ar. *šāmah*) 5

ṣbr n. pr. Ṣābir, Ṣubayr 46, 47
ṣd n. pr. Ṣadd bḎ'B 7a
ṣdq – *bṣdqn* n. pr. Bi-Ṣidqān 38
ṣlm n.d. Ṣalm 1, 2, (9), 11, 12, 14, 15, 20, 21, 25b, 30, (32), 35, 42
ṣmrf' n. pr. Ṣamrafa' 14
ṣmkfr n. pr. Ṣamkaffar bʿGL 26

ḏr n. "war" – *bḏr ddn* 20, 21, 23, 33; *bḏrr ddn* 22; *bḏr ms'* 16; *bḏr nbyt* 11, 13, 15

ʿgl n. pr. ʿIgl (f. of HB'L) 2; (f. of NṢR) 3; (f. of ṢMKFR) 26
ʿrm n. pr. ʿArim bFSḤ 15
ʿslq(?) n. pr. 29
ʿšmt n. pr. ʿAshmat 39
ʿl'l n. pr. ʿAlay'il b'TW 19; b'SGR 17, 18
ʿyr n. "ass" (Ar. *ʿayr*) 5

fḥk n. pr. Faḥak 8; bḤGG 7b, 9–11

qbb(?) n. pr. Qubāb 43
qṯb v. "present a gift" (?) 34

k prep. "like" (?) 9
k'b n. pr. Ka'b 40
k'l v. "to buy" (Ar. *ka'ala*) 5
krfty n. camel 3
krkr n. pr. Karkar bTLY 30
kfr'l n. pr. Kaffar'il 41
klʿ n. pr. Kulāʿ 5
khf n. "grave" (cf. Ar. *kahf*, "cave") 47

l prep. "to" 20, 30, 34; "by" 11, 12, 15, 15, 32, 35, 42
lwy v. – *ltw* and *ltwy* 3 sg. m. Perf. VIII, "to be bent, twisted, to turn away" (cf. Ar. *'iltawā ʿan*, "to turn one's back on something") 1, 2
lm prep. "by, for" 2, 29
lmḥ n. pr. Lāmiḥ (?) 25a

mt n. pr. Mawt bŠRṢ 4
ms(') n. trib. Massā' 16
msm(*w*) (?) 9
mṣryt n. f. "Egyptian woman" (Ar. *miṣrīyah*) 37
mk'l n. pr. Makk'il (f. of HKDL) 35; (f. of SQʿ) 36
mltw n. pr. Mulātū 44
mn prep. "from" 1, 2
mntt n. pr. 33

nbyt n. trib. Nabayāt (Nebaioth) 11, 13, 15
nṯr v. "to fall" (cf. Ar. *naṯara*, "to fall (leaves)") 17
nḥ(*l*)*t* n. pr. *Naḥ*(*l*)*at* 27
ndr v. "to die" (Ar. *nadara*) – *ndrt* 3 sg. f. Perf. I 5
nṣr v. "to aid," (Ar. *naṣara*) 11, 14–16, 20, 31–35, 42
n. "help" (Ar. *naṣr*) 32
n. pr. Naṣr bḤDD 31; bʿGL 3
nfs n. pr. Nafīs bḤMN 28
nm prep. "by" 1
nml n. "spots, pimples" (Ar. *nimāl*) 9

hb'l n. pr. Habb'il bʿGL 2
hḏb adj. "swift" (Ar. *haḏib*) 32
hšrkt s.v. *šrk*
hkdl n. pr. Hawkad'il bMK'L 35
hlk v. "to perish, die" (Ar. *halaka*) 32
hn'n s.v. *ḏt*
hydʿ n. pr. Haydaʿ bʿŠMT 39

wb' v. "to be plague-stricken" (Ar. *wabi'a*) – *yyb* 3 sg. m. Imperf. I (Ar. *yayba'u*) 10
wṯb v. "to leap, rush, attack" (Ar. *waṯaba*) – *yṯb* 3 sg. m. Imperf. I 30

yṯb s.v. *wṯb*
yrh s.v. *rhw*
yʿḏrl n. pr. Yaʿdhir'il bḤGG 12, 13
yyb s.v. *wb'*

3/DEDANITE AND LIHYANITE

'b n. "father," with 3 pl. m. suf.: *'bhm* 9
'ḫ n. "brother," with 3 pl. m. suf.: *'ḫwhm* 6
'ḫḏ v. "to take possession" (Ar. *'aḫaḏa*), 3rd pl. Perf. I: *'ḫḏw* 6
'rš n. pr. 'Irāsh 15
'(*w*)*s'l* n. pr. 'Uways'il 8
b prep. "in" 9
btt n. "cutting" (cf. Ar. *batt*) 5
bṯ . . . n. pr. 18
bḥš n. pr. Buḥaysh 12
bn n. "son," with Min. 3 sg. m. suf.: *bns* 1; pl. const. *bnw* 6

*ts*ʿ "nine" (Ar. *tis*ʿ) 9
tm n. pr. Taym 1
ṯrqh n. "thieves" (Ar. *saraqah*) 7

grm n. pr. Garm 6
glṯqs n. pr. GLT-Qaws 9

ḥṭlh n. pr. Ḥiṭlah 6, 6
ḥm v. "to defend, protect" (cf. Ar. *ḥamā*), I Perf. pass., 3 sg. m. 7
ḥwl n. "power" (Ar. *ḥawl*) 13

ḫrt v. "to guide" (cf. Ar. *ḫarita*, "to be an expert guide"), IV Perf. 3 sg. m. with 3 sg. m. suf.: *'ḫrth* 16; with 3 pl. m. suf.: *'ḫrthm* 9
ḫrḥḏġbt n. d. Kharaḥ-dhū-Ghābat 9

dln n. pr. 2, 3

ḏt dem. adj. f., "this" 6
ḏrḥ'l n. pr. Dhariḥ'il (f. of MTʿ'L) 13
*ḏm*ʿ*ly* = *ḏ* + *mn* + ʿ*alay*, "He who is on high" 16
ḏh dem. adj. m., "this" 6, 7

r'y n. "reign" 9
rtb v. "to arrange," II Perf. 3 sg. m. with 3 sg. f. suf.: *rtb*(*h*) 12
ršm n. pr. Rashm b. SʿDLH 14
rḍy v. "to favour" (Ar. *raḍiya*), I Perf. 3 sg. m. with 3 sg. m. suf.: *rḍyh* 16; with 3 pl. m. suf.: *rḍyhm* 9
rm n. pr. 3

z dem. pron. m., "this" 3
zdy n. pr. 1

*s*ʿ*d* v. "to bless" (Ar. *sā*ʿ*ada*), III Perf. 3 sg. m. with 3 sg. m. suf.: *s*ʿ*dh* 16; with 3 pl. m. suf.: *s*ʿ*dhm* 9
*s*ʿ*dlh* n. pr. Saʿdallāh 14
snt n. "year" 9

š' n. "thing, wish" (Ar. *šay'*) 6
šm[*'l*] n. "left hand" (Ar. *šimāl*) 7
šnḫ n. pr. 4

ṣlm n. "statue" (Ar. *ṣanam*), dual: [*ṣl*]*mn* 9
ṣlmgd n. pr. Ṣalmgadd 11

ʿ*d'rl* n. angel ʿAdār(')il 13
ʿ*šrn* "twenty" (Ar. ʿ*išrūna*) 9
ʿ*ly* prep. "upon" 7, 7

f conj. "and, so" (Ar. *fa*) 9, 16
prep. "in" (Ar. *fī*) 6
fsy n. pr. 16

qbr n. "tomb" 6, 7
qṭ v. – v Perf.: *tqṭ*, "to inscribe one's name" (?) (cf. Ar. *qaṭṭa*, "to cut") 16, 18

kḥl, n. fam. or trib. Kuḥayl 10

l prep. "by, to, for" 3, 3, 6
llh n. loc. or trib. 12
lw v. "to deny" (Ar. *lawā*) 6

m(*b*)*ṭ* ? 1
*mt*ʿ n. pr. Mataʿ 5
*mt*ʿ*'l* n. pr. Mataʿ'il b. ḎRḤ'L 13
mr'lh n. pr. Mar'allāh 10; b. ṢLMGD 11
mrr n. "perpetuity" (Ar. *murūr*) 6
mrrh n. pr. Murārah 6, 6
*m*ʿ prep. "with" 16
mn prep. "from, against" 7, 12

n's n. pr. Nu'ās 6
*ntnb*ʿ*l* n. pr. Natanbaʿal b. WNY 7
ndd v. (cf. Ar. *nadda*), *maṣdar* v, with def. article: *htndd*, "the (day of) assembling" 13
nšr n. pr. Nashr bBṮ. . . 18
nḍr n. pr. Naḍr 17
nṭr n. pr. Nāṭir 6
*n*ʿ*m* v. (Ar. *na*ʿ*ama*), IV Perf.: *hn*ʿ*m*, "to make pleasant, bestow favours on, be graciously disposed towards" 13

hḏ(*h*)*n* dem. pron., dual m., "these" 9
hm pers. pron., 3 pl. m., "they" 6
hn def. art. 7
*hn*ʿ*m* n. pr. Ha-Naʿam b. MTʿ 5
hnfy n. pr. Ha-Nafy 6

wny n. pr. Wany 7; b. FSY 16

yṯmt n. fam. or trib. Yathmat 1
ymn n. "right hand" (Ar. *yamīn*) 7

4/THAMUDIC

'b n. "father," with 3 sg. m. suf.: *'bh* 12, 84
'b'ns n. pr. 'Ab'anas 97
'g' n. pr. 'Aga' b. DYRT 15
'ḫ n. "brother," with 3 sg. m. suf.: *'ḫh* 8, 82
'ḫt n. "sister," with 3 sg. m. suf.: *'hth* 81
'db(?) n. pr. 'Adīb b. NʿRT 81
'dbn (?) n. pr. 'Adbān 92
's n. pr. 'Aws b. ḪL(F) 104

'srtn s.v. *'krtn*
'sf v. "to grieve" (Ar. *'asifa*) 51
'smnt n. pr. 'Awsmanāt 85
'sn n. pr. 'Awsān b. G(F) 103
'ṭlmn n. pr. 'Aṭlamān 61
'ff n. pr. 'FF 3
'fl n. pr. 'Afil b. 'WS 101
'krtn n. pr. 'Akratān (or read *'srtn*) b. ŠRQT 79
'l def. art. 19, 25
n. "family, tribe" (Ar. *'āl*), s.v. *ḏ'l*
prep. "for" 19, 39, 39, 40
'lt n. d. 'Allāt 13
'lh n. d. 'Allāh 14
n. pr. 'Alih 93
'mt n. pr. 'Amat b. MLK 31
'n pers. pron. "I" 1, 34a, 36, 74
'nʿm (?) n. trib. 'Anʿam 81
'nmr n. pr. 'Anmar b. ʿFR 9
'hl n. "family" (Ar. *'ahl*) 48
'ws n. pr. 'Uways 101
'ys n. pr. 'Iyās 81, 81, 83, 84

b prep. "in, through" 17, 76; with 2 sg. m. suf.: *bk* 25
bt n. "daughter" (Ar. *bint*) 76
bgt n. pr. Baggat b. GDYN 94
bḫyr(t) s.v. *ḫyr*
bddlld ? 24
bdn n. trib. Badan 18
n. pr. 34a
bz adv. "here" 21
bsrq s.v. *srq*
bkrtn n. dual, "two young she-camels" 45, 72
bn'l n. pr. Bin'il 73
bhš n. pr. Buhaysh 83

t'm n. pr. Ta'm 19
tqd n. pr. Taqudd 66
tms n. pr. Tamuss 76

ṯdy n. "breast" (Ar. *ṯady*) 11
ṯry n. pr. Thuray 7
ṯmt n. "old man" (Ar. *ṯimmah*) 65

gdyn n. pr. Gadyān 94
grf n. trib. Girāf 48
n. pr. Garf b. ḤN'L 96
grm n. trib. Garm 84; b. ĠR 42
G(F) n. pr. 103
gf(f) n. trib. Gaf(īf) 48a
gl n. pr. Gall 50
gls v. "to set up" (Ar. *gallasa*) 104
glṭ v. "to shave" (Ar. *galaṭa*) 41
glm n. pr. Galm b. 'B'NS 97
gmr v. "to roast" (Ar. *gammara*) 71

ḥb'l n. pr. Ḥabb'il 81
ḥbb n. pr. Ḥabīb or n. "loved one" 2; *mḥb*, "lover", 56; n. pr. Muḥibb 58
ḥbyb n. pr. Ḥubayb 73
ḥ(gn) v. "to bend, crook (a staff)" (Ar. *ḥagana*) 94
ḥgy n. pr. Ḥaggay 40
ḥdr n. pr. Ḥādir 62
ḥrb v. "to pillage" (Ar. *ḥaraba*) 64
n. pr. Ḥarb 80
ḥrg n. pr. ḤRG 28
ḥslt n. pr. 49
ḥṣd n. fam. Ḥaṣad 11
ḥfy n. pr. Ḥāfi 69
ḥmz n. pr. 55
ḥmlt n. pr. Ḥāmilat 15
ḥn n. pr. Ḥann 81
ḥn'l n. pr. Ḥann'il 96
ḥnnt n. pr. Ḥanānat b. SKRN 78
ḥyt n. pr. Ḥayyat 57

ḫbbt n. pr. Khubaybat 35
ḫrm n. pr. Khuraym 36
ḫff n. pr. Khufāf 39
ḫld n. pr. Khālid 41
ḫldt ? 19
ḫl(f) n. pr. Khal(af) 104
ḫmy v. "to stink" (cf. Ar. *ḫamma*) 63; Act. Ptcp. *ḫm* 63
ḫyr – *bḫyr(t)* n. pr. Bi-Khayr(at) 64

d' n. "illness" (Ar. *dā'*) 62
db n. pr. Dubb 90
dd n. s.v. *sqm*
dr n. "camping-place" (Ar. *dār*) 100
drḥ n. pr. 60
dfy n. gent. 82
dyrt n. pr. Dayrat b. ḤMLT 15

ḏ'l "of the family (or clan) of" 11, 18, 81, 82, 84
ḏ'hl "of the family of" 48
ḏʿ(r) n. pr. Dhuʿ(r) b. ḤYT 57
ḏkr v. "to remember" (Ar. *ḏakara*) 3 sg. m. Perf. 14; 3 sg. f. *ḏkrt* 13
ḏn dem. pron. m., "this" 66

r' n. pr.; bMWG 43a; bnMWG 43b
rḥ n. "fart" (Ar. *rīḥ*) 63
rḥl n. pr. Raḥḥāl 34a
rḫm n. pr. Rakhīm 8
rdd n. pr. 33

rš n. pr. Rasha' 2, 11
rḍw n. d. Ruḍā 3, 21–23, 25
rʿy v. "to shepherd" (Ar. *raʿā*) 55, 59
rqm n. pr. b. ḤMZ 55
rmy v. "to shoot" (Ar. *ramā*), I Perf. pass. 97
rhw b. "tranquillity" (Ar. *rahw*) 25
rwḥ (?) n. pr. Rawāḥ 29

z dem. pron. m. sg., "this" 62, 65, 67, 70
z'g n. pr. 63
zbn n. pr. Zaban 48b
zt dem. adj. 63
ztrft n. pr. Zāt-RFT (?) 58
zd n. pr. Zayd 81; b. MLK 47
zʿm n. pr. Zaʿm b. T'M 19
zfry n. pr. Zufray 63
zmm n. pr. 60
zn dem. pron. m. sg., "this" 6, 34a, 56–58, 68
zn v. "to commit adultery" (Ar. *zanā*) 63

s'lt n. "petition" (Ar. *su'alah*) 21
sby v. "to take prisoner" (Ar. *sabā*), I Perf. pass. 82
strt n. "shelter" (cf. Ar. *sutrah*, "covering, veil") 69
srrt n. pr.; b. QḤF 51
srṭ v. "to draw" (cf. Syr. *s*^{e}*raṭ*) 46
srq – *bsrq* n. pr. Bi-Sirq 53a
sṭrt n. "wish" (Ar. *suṭrah*) 13
sʿd v. "to help" (Ar. *saʿada*), III, Impv. with 1 sg. suf.: *sʿdn* 23
sqm v. "to be sick" (Ar. *saqima*) – *sqm dd*, "to be sick with love" 34a
skrn n. pr. Sakrān 78
slḫ ? 99
slm n. pr. Sālim 14, 20, 83; b. SNH 17; b. ʿBD 30
sn v. "to tend camels" (Ar. *sanna*) 99
n. pr. Sīn 83
snh n. pr. Sanih 17
sy n. pr. Siyy 16

šrqt n. pr. Shariqat 79
šzt n. pr. 65
škr n. pr. Shākir 39
škyt n. pr. Shakiyat 45
šm v. "to wait for, be on the look-out for" (Ar. *šāma*) 73
šwr n. pr. Shawir 44
šwq v. "to fill with longing" (Ar. *šāqa*): I Perf. pass. 48a; V Perf.: *tšwq*, "to long for" 12, 18, 19, 33, 39, 40, 92
šwql n. pr. Shawq'il b. Mʿ . . . 52

ṣll n. pr. Ṣalāl 81

ḍm v. "to embrace, hug" (Ar. *ḍamma*) 65

ẓʿn n. pr. Ẓāʿin 40

ʿbd n. pr. ʿAbd 30, 81
ʿbr n. pr. ʿAbr b. ḪLD 41
ʿbš n. pr. 38
ʿt n. pr. ʿAtī 72, 74
ʿtrsm n. d. ʿAttarsam 23
ʿty n. pr. ʿAtī b. NṮ 25
ʿgg n. pr. ʿAggāg 26, 27
ʿḏrf n. pr. ʿUdhārif 75
ʿr v. "to smite" (Ar. *ʿarā*) 11
n. "disgrace, shame" (Ar. *ʿār*) 3
ʿrk n. pr. ʿArak 66
ʿzz n. pr. ʿAzīz 95
ʿṣm n. pr. ʿĀṣim 77
ʿf v. "to restore to health, cure, guard" (Ar. *ʿafā*, III) 72
ʿfr n. pr. ʿIfr 9
ʿfrn n. pr. ʿFRN b. SY 16
ʿqrb n. pr. ʿAqrab 83
ʿkbl n. pr. ʿAkab'il 4; b. MGNN 82
ʿl prep. "on account of, concerning, for" 11, 23, 62, 81, 82, 84
ʿlqmt n. pr. ʿAlqamat 39
ʿmrt n. pr. ʿAmirat 48
ʿmrl n. pr. ʿAmar(')il 71
ʿn n. "eye" 76
ʿh v. "to be plague-stricken" (Ar. *ʿāha*) 22
ʿw n. pr. ʿUwā b. RŠ 2
ʿwḏ n. "protection" (Ar. *ʿawāḏ*) 22
ʿwṣ n. pr. ʿUwayṣ 22

ġṯ n. pr. Ghawth b. ʿZZ 95
ġr n. pr. Ghayr 42
ġwṯ n. pr. Ghawth (or Ghuwayth) b. ZDL 19
ġyr n. pr. Ghayr or Ghayyar 83
ġyr'l n. pr. Ghayr'il or Ghayyar'il 84

f conj. "and, so" (Ar. *fa*) 19, 74
n. "mouth" (*fa*, accus. of *fam*) 2, 8, 33, 36, 50, 54
fgn n. trib. 82
frš n. pr. 37
fšwl (?) 44
fʿl n. "deed" (Ar. *fiʿl*) 63
fln n. "So-and-So" (Ar. *fulān*) 74
fm n. "grain" (Ar. *fūm*) 64

qḥf n. pr. 51
qdr n. pr. Qudār 98

qsy n. pr. Qasī 18
qf v. "to follow (the tracks of)" (Ar. *qafā*) 44
qhr n. pr. Qāhir b. ’SMNT 85

ktm v. "to conceal" (Ar. *katama*), I Perf. 1 sg.: *ktmt* 74, 77
kḥd n. pr. Kaḥad 67
kḥsmn n. pr. Kaḥaysumān 81
kd n. pr. 44
ks[*ṭ*] n. pr. Kāsiṭ 1
kʿm n. pr. 65
klb n. pr. Kalb 21
kll pron. indef. "every" (Ar. *kull*) 13
km n. pr. Kamm 81
kny n. pr. 36
khl n. pr. Kāhil 83

l prep. "to, for, by" 3, 12, 18, 27, 33, 38, 73
lṯq n. pr. Lathiq 70
lḥy n. pr. Luḥayy 56
lḫb v. "to lie with" (Ar. *laḫaba*) 67
ldd n. pr. Ludād or Laddād 5
l(*r*) ? 67
lsn (?) 99
lʿṣ n. pr. Laʿiṣ b. MRWḎ 46
lmʿ v. "to polish" (Ar. *lamaʿa*, II) 5
ln n. pr. Lawn b. SY 16
lwzn n. pr. Lawzān 67

m prep. 63
mṯġr n. "gate" (?) (cf. Ar. *ṯuġrah*, "crack, opening") 17
mgnn n. pr. Magnān 100
mḥb s.v. *ḥbb*
mḥlm n. pr. Muḥallim 84
mr n. pr. Murr b. MḤLM 84
mrṭ v. "to pluck out hair" (Ar. *maraṭa*) 42
mrn n. pr. Murrān 68
mrwḏ n. pr. 46
ms n. pr. Mass 76
mḍ n. "pain" (Ar. *maḍḍ*) 3
mʿn n. pr. Maʿn 81
mġṯ n. pr. Mughīth 81
mġyr n. pr. Mughayyir 98
mlk n. pr. Mālik 31, 47, 81
mwg n. pr. Mawwāg 43a, 43b
myṯn s.v. *wṯn*

nb v. (cf. Ar. *lāba*, "to thirst") 25
nbhn n. pr. Nabhān 83
nṯ n. pr. Nathth 25
nṯl v. "to empty (a quiver)" (Ar. *naṯala*) 17
nḥt v. "to cut" (Ar. *naḥata*) 60
ndm v. "to grieve" (cf. Ar. *nadima*, "to repent, regret") 81
nsr n. pr. Nasr 6
nʿrt n. pr. Naʿrat b. ZD 81
nʿmt v. Perf. 3 sg. f. + *ʿn* = "to favour" 76
nm prep. "by" 26
nmr (?) n. pr. Nimr 80
nhy n. d. Nuhay 23

hb s.v. *whb*
hn’ n. pr. Hāni’ 11

wṯm v. "to mourn" (cf. Ar. *waṯama*, "to paw the ground, pound, wound") 11
wṯn (cf. Ar. *wasina*) – *myṯn* (cf. Ar. *mīsān*, "sleepy") 62
wgz n. pr. Wagz 59
wgm v. "to grieve" (cf. Ar. *wagama*, "to be silent, speechless, dejected") 82, 84
wdd v. "to love" (Ar. *wadda*) 2, 8, 33, 36, 50, 54; Perf. 1 sg.: *wddt* 74, 75, 77
n. "love" (Ar. *wadād*, *widād*, *wudād*) 22, 25, 29; with 1 sg. suf.: *wddy* 23
wrt ? 19
wrtt ? 19
wʿd n. pr. Wāʿid 32, 33
whb v. "to give" (Ar. *wahaba*), I Impv. 2 sg. m.: *hb* 3
n. pr. Wahb 12

ydʿ n. pr. Yadaʿ: b. WGZ 59; b. WHB 12
yšb n. pr. Yashibb 54
yʿly n. pr. Yaʿlay b. RŠ 11
yġṯ n. pr. Yaghūth 84

5/NABATAEAN

’tr’ n. "le lieu" 92 – *b’tr* prep. "après" 79:3, 5
’glḥ n. pr. ’Aglaḥ 107:2
’ḥ n. "frère" pl. av. suf. 3 sg. m.: *’ḥwhy* 30
’ḥd v. "prendre en possession" 57:2; 92
’ḥr n. "postérité," 79:4, 6; av. suf. 3 sg. m.: *’ḥrh* 16:2; av. suf. 3 pl. m.: *’ḥrhm* 79:2
’dynt n. pr. ’Udainat 77
’rybs n. pr. ’Arîbas 92
’srtg’ n. "stratège" 57:3
’spsn’ n. pr. ’Aspasinâ 41
’swd’ n. pr. ’Aswadâ 121
’šdw n. pr. ’Ašadû 118
’šlm n. pr. ’Ašlam 75
’ftḥ n. pr. ’Aftaḥ br ʿBDʿBDT 104

’fklw n. pr. ’Afkallû br HNY’W 34
’fls n. pr. ’Aflos br HN’T 96
’kys n. pr. ’Akios 41
’l n. "tribu" 130:2
’lt n. d. ’Ilat 42
’lʿz n. pr. al-ʿAzz (ou ’Il-ʿazz) br BʿTW 42
’lf "mille" 79:7–8
’lh’ n. "le dieu" 79:7; 101; 11:3
’lht’ n. "la déesse" 79:8
’m n. "mère" 89:2
’mry n. pr. ’Amray 117
’myw (?) n. pr. 20
’nw (ou *’bw*) 97
’hdly n. pr. ’Ahdalī 80:2
’w conj. "ou" 79:3
’wš’lhy n. pr. ’Auš’ilāhî br ʿWYDW 2
’wšw n. pr. ’Aušû 51
’yty adv. "il y a" 79:4–6

br n. "fils, enfant," *passim*; sg. av. suf. 3 sg. : *brh* 23; pl. cstr. *bny* 79:1; pl. av. suf. 3 sg. m. : *bnwhy* 16:1
brt n. "fille" 47, 107:1, 3; 121
brdw n. pr. Burdû br ʿBDW 8
bʿtw n. pr. Baʿatû 42
blw n. pr. Balû 63
bly interjection "O" 17:3; 51, 65, 75, 85
bn n. voir *br*
bnt n. pr. Banat br ŠḤRW(?) 33
bnh v. "bâtir" 16:1; 3 pl. m. : *bnw* 89:2
bny’ n. "le constructeur" 89:1

tdy n. pr. Tadday 78, 126
tfṣ’ n. pr. fem. Tafṣâ brt ŠLM(W) 47
tltyn "trente" 16:2
tlmwn n. pr. Talmôn br TDY 126
tmmt n. pr. Tammāmat 15
tyrw n. pr. Tairû 106
tym’lhy n. pr. Taim’ilāhî br ’. . . 87
tymmnwtw n. pr. Taimmanôtû 71, 72
tymw n. pr. Taimû 35, 36(?), 44, 111:1 (deux fois); 119

gd’ (ou *gz’*) n. pr. 7
gdw n. pr. Gaddû 32
gryšw n. pr. Guraišû br ʿNMW 4
gšrwn n. pr. 22
gmyrw n. pr. Gamîrû 74

ḥbr n. "compagnon," pl. av. suf. 3 sg. m. : *’ḥbrwh* 89:1–2
ḥbyw (?) n. pr. 21
ḥd "un" 79:7, 8
ḥrtt n. pr. Ḥāritat (Aretas) 16:2; 79:7, 10
ḥrty adj. "arétienne" 79:7–8
ḥrg v. "être sacré, interdit," ptcp. pass. : *ḥryg* 79:4, 6; voir *nḥrg*
ḥrmw n. pr. Ḥarmû 130:2
ḥ(f?)l[w] n. pr. Huffālû br ʿBDW 99
ḥlṣt n. pr. Ḥaliṣat 73
ḥlfw n. pr. Ḥalafû 55, 111:2
ḥlq n. "part," av. suf. 3 sg. m. : *ḥlqh* 79:4 (deux fois), 79:5
ḥmš "cinq" 16:2
ḥmš m’h "cinq cents" 79:9
ḥmlgw n. pr. Ḥamlagû 62, 93
ḥnṭln n. pr. Ḥanṭalān 38, 85
ḥwrw n. pr. Ḥûrû br ’WŠW 51
ḥwy’ (?) 94
ḥy[. .] 111:4
ḥyn n. pr. Ḥayyān 58, 100
ḥyw n. pr. Ḥayyû 54; br ŠʿD’LHY 52, 76; br MQT 95

d’ adj. dém. fem. "cette" 79:5 (deux fois), 9; 90:2
dbrh (ou *ʿbdy*) n. pr. 122
dkrt v. "se souvenir de," Perf. 3 sg. fem. 42; *dkyr* Perf. pass. 6, 7, 9, 10, 12, 17:3; 18:2; 22–24, 27, 44, 51, 52, 58, 61–65, 67, 71, 89, 90, 94–96; *dkyrt* sg. fem. 121; *dkyryn* pl. m. 73
dmsps n. pr. Damasippos 3, 57:4
dnh pron. dém. m. "ceci" 16:1; 17:2; 57; 79:1 3, 6; 92; 111:1
dnyḥw (?) n. pr. 108:3
dwšr’ n. d. Dûšārâ 54, 79:6
dy pron. rel. "celui qui" 16:1; 57:2; 79:1–3; 89:2; 91:8; 111:1; 130:1, 2
dygns n. pr. Diogenes br HN’W 31
dyn[ys] n. pr. Dionysios (?) 25

rbyb’l n. pr. Rabîb’el 45; br DMSPS 3
rḥm v. "aimer," ptcp. act. *rḥm* 16:2
ršw n. pr. Rašû (?) 17:1

zbdw n. pr. Zabdû br ’ŠDW 118
zbr (ou *zbd*) n. pr. 122
zbn v. "vendre," Imperf. 3 sg. m., th. intensif; *yz[b]n* 79:3; ptcp. *mzbn* 79:6
zbynw n. pr. Zabînû (?) 10
zydmnwtw n. pr. Zaidmanôtû : br D . . . 24; br DYN[YS] 25
zydw n. pr. Zaidû 70; br (TYMN) 44; br ZYDW 26; br MʿNW 67

slʿ n. "drachme" pl. *slʿyn* 79:7–9
sywn n. de mois Siwān 16:2

šbw n. pr. Šabbu (?) 111:1, 2
št "six" 79:10
šḥrw n. pr. Šaḥrû 33
š'..w n. pr. br 'MRY 117
š'd'lhy n. pr. Ša'd'ilāhî 52, 76
šltw n. pr. Šalitû br MNY 16:1 (deux fois)
šlm n. "paix" (ou adj. verb. "que soit sain et sauf") 1, 3–5, 14, 16:3; 28–31, 35, 36, 38, 40, 45, 46, 49, 50, 53–55, 59, 67, 69, 70, 72, 74–78, 85, 98, 99, 109, 112, 114–116, 118, 119, 122, 127; *bšlm* 42, 73, 90:2
n. pr. Šalim br 'BDMNWTY 86
šlm' n. pr. Šalmâ 124
šlmt n. pr. fem. Šalimat brt W'LW 107:1
šlmn n. pr. Šalāmān (ou Šalmān) 5, 9, 15, 18
šlmw n. pr. Šalimû 6, 47; br ŠLMN 9, 18; br 'NMW 13
šly n. pr. Šullay 46, 125, 127
šlytw n. pr. Šulaitû br ŠLTW 16:1
šlymw n. pr. Šulaimû 17:4
šmšw n. pr. Šamšû 115
šnt n. ét. cstr. sg. "année" 16:2; 17:2
šnnw n. pr. 19; br 'MYW(?) 20
šnyfw n. pr. Šanîfû br NḤŞ 43
šybw n. pr. Šaibû br ŠMŠW 115
šy''lqwm n. d. Šai''alqawm 101

ṣ'bw n. pr. Ṣa'bû br 'DYNT 77
ṣ]'bw n. d. – [*'lh ṣ*]*'bw* "dieu de Ṣa'bû" (?) 111:3

ṭb adj. "bon" – *bṭb* "en bien" 51, 63, 67, 73, 90:2, 96, 98

'bd v. "faire" Perf. 3 sg. m. 17:1; 87, 88, 130:1; 3 pl. : *'bdw* 79:1; 111:1; inf. *m'bd* 79:5
'bd' n. "l'esclave" 130:1
'bd'ysy n. pr. 'Abd'îsî br WHBW 53
'bdt n. pr. 'Ubdat 111:5
'bdrb'l n. pr. 'Abdrabb'el 116; br ŠBW 111:2
'bd'bdt n. pr. 'Abd'ubdat 104; br 'RYBS 92
'bdmnkw n. pr. 'Abdmalikû 109
'bdmnwty n. pr. 'Abdmanôtî 86
'bdw n. pr. 'Abdû 8, 60, 99; br 'ṢBW 98
'bwdw n. pr. 'Abûdû 59
'd prép. "jusqu'à" 16:2
adv. "en plus" 90:1
'drw n. pr. 'Adrû : br TYMW(?) 36; br 'MNW 108:1; br NḤŠṬB 112
'šr wšt "seize" 79:10
'šyny s. v. *qyny*
'ṣbw n. pr. 'Aṣbû 98
'l prép. "sur" 111:4

'lm n. "éternité" – *l'lm* "pour toujours" 67; *'lm 'd 'lm* "éternellement et pour l'éternité" 16:2
'lh v. "mettre au-dessus," Perf. causatif : "*'ly* 91:9
'lym n. ét. cstr. sg. "serviteur" 55
'm n. "peuple" av. suf. 3 sg. m. : *'mh* 16:2; 79:10
prep. "avec" 79:6
'mrw n. pr. 'Amrû 23
'mryw n. pr. 'Amrayû 30
'mnw n. pr. 'Amanû 108:2
'mw n. pr. 'Ammû 39
'myrt n. pr. 'Amîrat br WHBW 79:1
'nmw n. pr. Ǵānimu (Ghānimû) 1, 4, 13(?), 14, 29, 96; br GRYŠW 4; br DMSPS 57:2–4; br ZBYNW 10
'nytw n. pr. 'Unaitû (ou *'lytw*) br MYD'W 66
'wtw n. pr. Ǵautû (Ghautû) br MN'T 61
'wydw n. pr. 'Awîdû 2; br ŠLYMW 17:3
'wh v. "tenter" ptcp. act. emph. : *'wyh* 79:3

f conj. "alors, dans ce cas" 79:4, 5
f'rn n. pr. Fa'rān br ŠLY 127
fsl' n. "le sculpteur" 62, 93, 104 (deux fois), 109

qbr n. "tombeau" ét. cstr. sg. 126; sg., en orthographe arabe, *qbrw* 89:2; ét. emph. sg. *qbr'* 16:1
v. "enterrer" Imperf. 3 sg. m. : *yqbr* 91:9
qbylw n. pr. Qubailû (?) 11
qdrw n. pr. Qadarû br ŠLMN 15
qdm n. pr. Qadm br MYD'W 65 – *mn qdm* "devant" 54
qmyrw n. trib. Qumairû 130:2–3
qynw n. pr. Qainû 108:2; br W'LT 107:3
qyny n. pr. (ou 'ŠYNY), br 'MRW(?) 23

ktb v. "écrire" 90:2
n. *ktb'* "l'inscription" 90:2
ksf n. "somme" 79:7, 8 (deux fois)
k'bw n. pr. Ka'abû 89:2
kfr' n. "le tombeau" 79:1, 4
kl pron. indéf. "tout, chacun" 79:6
khn' n. "le prêtre" 17:5
kwt adv. "pareillement" 79:5, 8

l' interjection "O" 16:3; 58

m'h n. "cent" 79:9
mḥršw n. pr., br ḤBYW(?) 21
mr'n' "notre seigneur" 79:7

msgd' n. "le lieu de culte" 111:1
mškn v. "mettre en gage" Imperf. 3 sg. m. : *ymškn* 79:3
mškb' n. "le lieu des banquets (sacrés)" 57:1
m'nw n. pr. Ma'nû 67
m'yrw n. pr. Muǵairû (Mughairû) 40
mqt n. pr. Māqit 95
mlk n. "roi" 16:2; 79:10
mlkw n. pr. Malikû 49; voir *mnkw*
mn prép. "de" 54; 79:4, 9; 130:2; av. suf. 3 sg. fem. : *mnh* 91:9
pron. rel. "qui" 90:1; 91:9
mn't n. pr. Mun'at 61; 79:3, 6; 94; br 'MYRT 79:1
mnkw n. pr. Malikû 102; br ŠLMN 5
mnwtw n. d. Manôtû 79:8
mny n. pr. Mannay br ŠLTW br MNY br ... N br MNY 16:1
myd'w n. pr. Maida'û 65, 66

nbṭw n. trib. "Nabatéens" 16:2; 79:10
nḥrg'(?) n. "esclave sacré, hierodule (?)" 67
nḥṣ (ou *nṭṣ*) n. pr. 43
nḥšṭb n. pr. Naḥašṭab 112
nšrw n. pr. Našrû br ḤRMW 130
nšlw n. pr. Našlû 27, 28

nfš n. av. suf. 3 sg. m. : *nfšh* "lui-même" 16:1; av. suf. 3 pl. m. : *nfšhm* "eux-mêmes" 79:2
nwl' n. "le tisserand" 125

hgrw n. pr. fem. Hagarû 79:1, 4, 5; br 'MYRT 79:1
hn conj. "si" 79:2, 5
hn't n. pr. Hāni'at br 'NMW 96
hn'w n. pr. Hāni'û 31; 89:1
hny'w n. pr. Hunai'û (?) 34
hw pron. 3 sg. m. "ce" 79:4
hw' v. "être" Perf. 3 sg. m. 90:1; Imperf. 3 sg. m. : *yhw'* 79:3, 5

w'lt n. pr. Wa'ilat 107
w'lw n. pr. Wa'ilu br 'GLḤ 107:2
wtrw n. pr. Witrû br 'NMW 1, 4, 14
whb'lhy n. pr. Wahb'ilāhî br BLW 63
whbw n. pr. Wahbû 53; 79:2

yt note d'accusatif, av. suf. 3 sg. m. : *yth* 79:6
yt'w n. pr. Yita'û 113
yrḥ n. "mois" 16:2
yld n. av. suf. 3 sg. m. : *yldh* "sa progéniture" 16:2; av. suf. 3 pl. m. : *yldhm* "leurs enfants" 79:2
ywm n. "jour" 79:9

6/PALMYRENE

bgšw n. pr. Bagešû
sywn n. mois Siwān
š'd n. pr. Ša'd
ṭb – bṭb "en bien"
f[s]l v. "graver"
qml' n. pr. Qāmilâ

7/HEBREW

'byšlw[m] n. pr. 'Abišalôm (?) 1
brkh n. "bénédiction" 2
dh pron. dém. "ceci" 1
rb n. "rabbi" 2
šwšnh n. pr. Šošannah 1
'ṭwr n. pr. 'Aṭûr (?) 2
mnḥm n. pr. Menaḥem 2
yrmyh n. pr. Yeremiah 2

II Concordance of the Inscriptions

1/MINAEAN

JS	*RÉS*	WR	JS	*RÉS*	WR
47	3721	2	59	3733	6
48	3772	3	61	3735	8
53	3727	4	62	3736	7
58	3732	5	64	3738	9

2/TAYMANITE

Ph. 266	WR	Ph. 266	Jamme, *TS*	WR
a	20	aa		28
b (1–3)	1	ab		31
d (1–3)	35	ac		15
f	38	ad (1–2)		32
m	7	ag		11
		ah		18
n	6	ah (2)		36
o	26	ai (1–2)	p. 75, n. 37	34
p (4)	24	al (1h3)		37
t (1–2)	14	am		39
u, v	8	ao		3
w (2)	44	ao (2)		9
x	2	ap		4
y (1–2)	30	at (?)		27
z (1–2)	29	au (1–5)	nn. 26, 32 and p. 37	5

3/DEDANITE AND LIHYANITE

JS	Caskel	WR	JS	Caskel	WR
79	76	6	186	3	13
81	17	7	314		11
83	30	9	318		14

4/THAMUDIC

Hu.	Eut.	Ph.	Jamme, *TS*	JS	WR
506 (373, 6)	968				66
511 (374, 11)					65
512 (374, 12)					64
513 (374, 13)	706 + 704	272f	p. 14		63
514 (374, 14)					62
515 (374, 15)					61
516 (375, 16)	712	272k	p. 33		60
517 (375, 17)	709 + 710	272l	p. 14		59
521 (376, 21)	718	273a	p. 14		58
522 (376, 22)	717	273b	p. 14		57
573 (425, 2)	788			5	76
574 (425, 3)	789			4	75
575 + 576 (425, 4, 5)	790 + 791			3 + 2	74
577 (425, 6)	792			lbis	73
578 (426)	786 + 787			7 + 6	77

5/NABATAEAN

CIS	JS	MS	*CIS*	JS	MS
200	30	79	263	72	101
204	27	81	264, 1	50	51
205	12	83	264, 2	51	52
213	24	82	264, 3		53
221	20	56	264, 4	52	54
222	37	80	264, 5	53	55
223	26	29	266	44	85
225	35	128	271	17	91
226	13	84	278, 1	62	93
234	40	57	278, 2–3	63	94
237	48	86	279	64	95
			281 = 261		
239	73	96, 97	282	94	74
240	69	106	283	93	72
257		126	285		75
259	81, 82	111	286	87	77
260	80	115	299	78	112
261		122	300	79	118
262		121	301		117

Doughty	MS
Doc. épig., pl. v, fol. 8	109

JS	MS	JS	MS	JS	MS
12	83	56	92	93	72
13	84	62	93	94	74
17	91	63	94	122	58
18	89, 90	64	95	123	61
20	56	69	106	124	59
24	82	71	104	125	62
26	29	72	101	126	63
27	81	73	96, 97	208	39
30	79	74	98, 99	209	40
35	128	77	107	211	41
37	80	78	112	212	42
40	57	79	118	214	43
44	85	80	115	215	44
48	86	81, 82	111	216	45
50	51	87	77	217	46
51	52	90	78	218	47
52	54	92	71	222	49
53	55				

6/HEBREW

JS 223 nab. = MS 1

Plates of Inscriptions

Table of scripts (transcription of glyph forms not representable as text).

	TAYMANITE	JAWFIAN	DEDANITE	LIHYANITE EARLY	LIHYANITE LATE	THAMUDIC NAJDI	THAMUDIC HIJAZI	THAMUDIC TABUKI	
ʾ									ء
b									ب
t									ت
ṯ									ث
j									ج
h									ح
ḥ									خ
d									د
ḏ									ذ
r									ر
z									ز
s									س
ś									
š									ش
ṣ									ص
ḍ									ض
ṭ									ط
ẓ									ظ
ʿ									ع
ġ									غ
f									ف
q									ق
k									ك
l									ل
m									م
n									ن
h									ه
w									و
y									ي

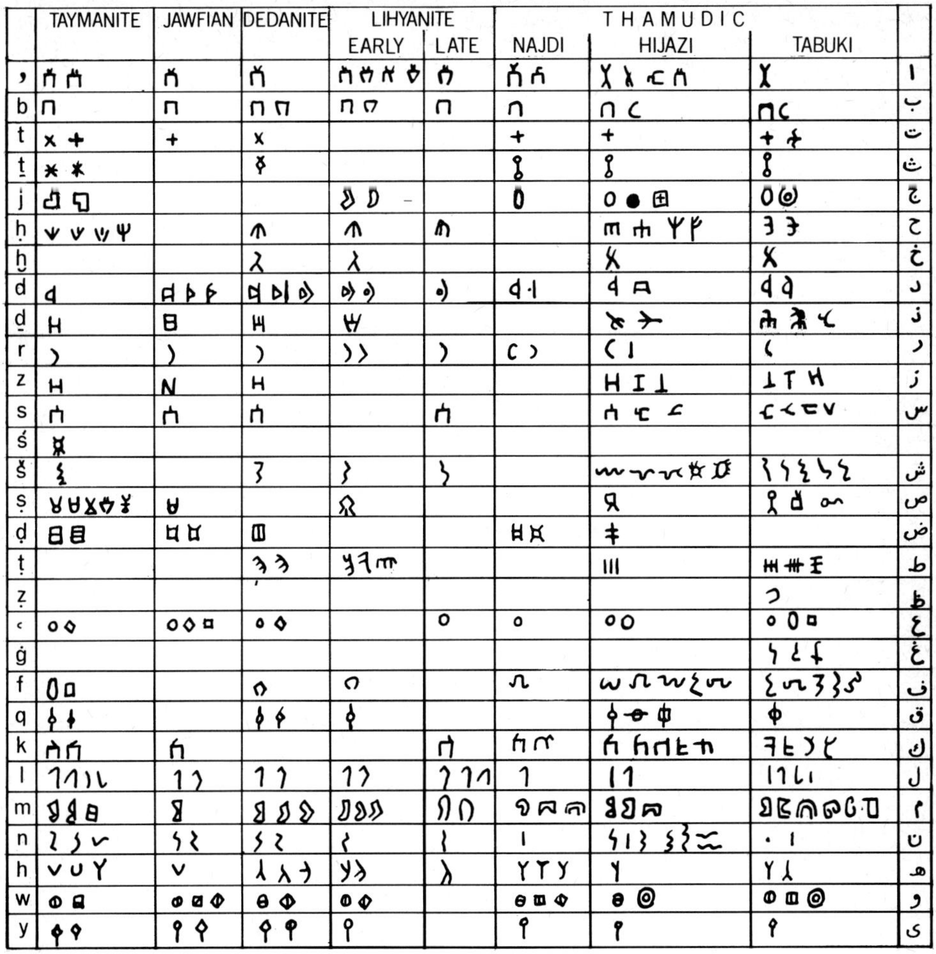

1   Table of scripts

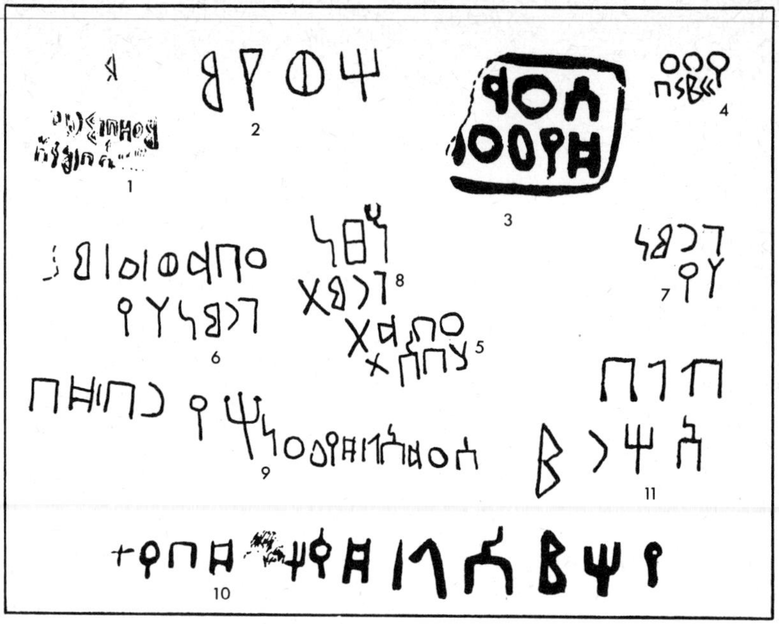

5, 8, 9 (also Dedanite and Lihyanite no. 15)

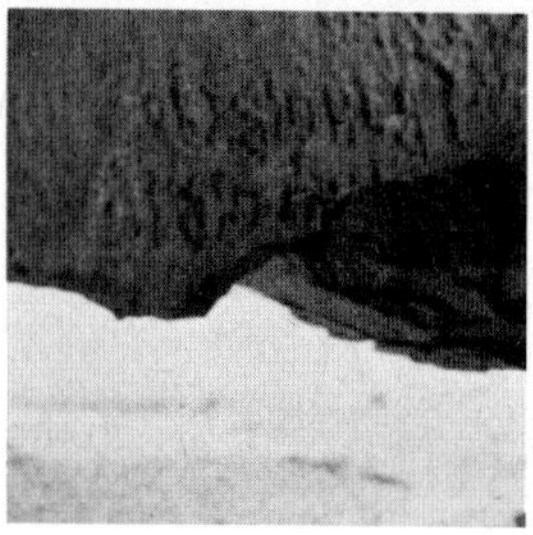

1

2 Minaean inscriptions

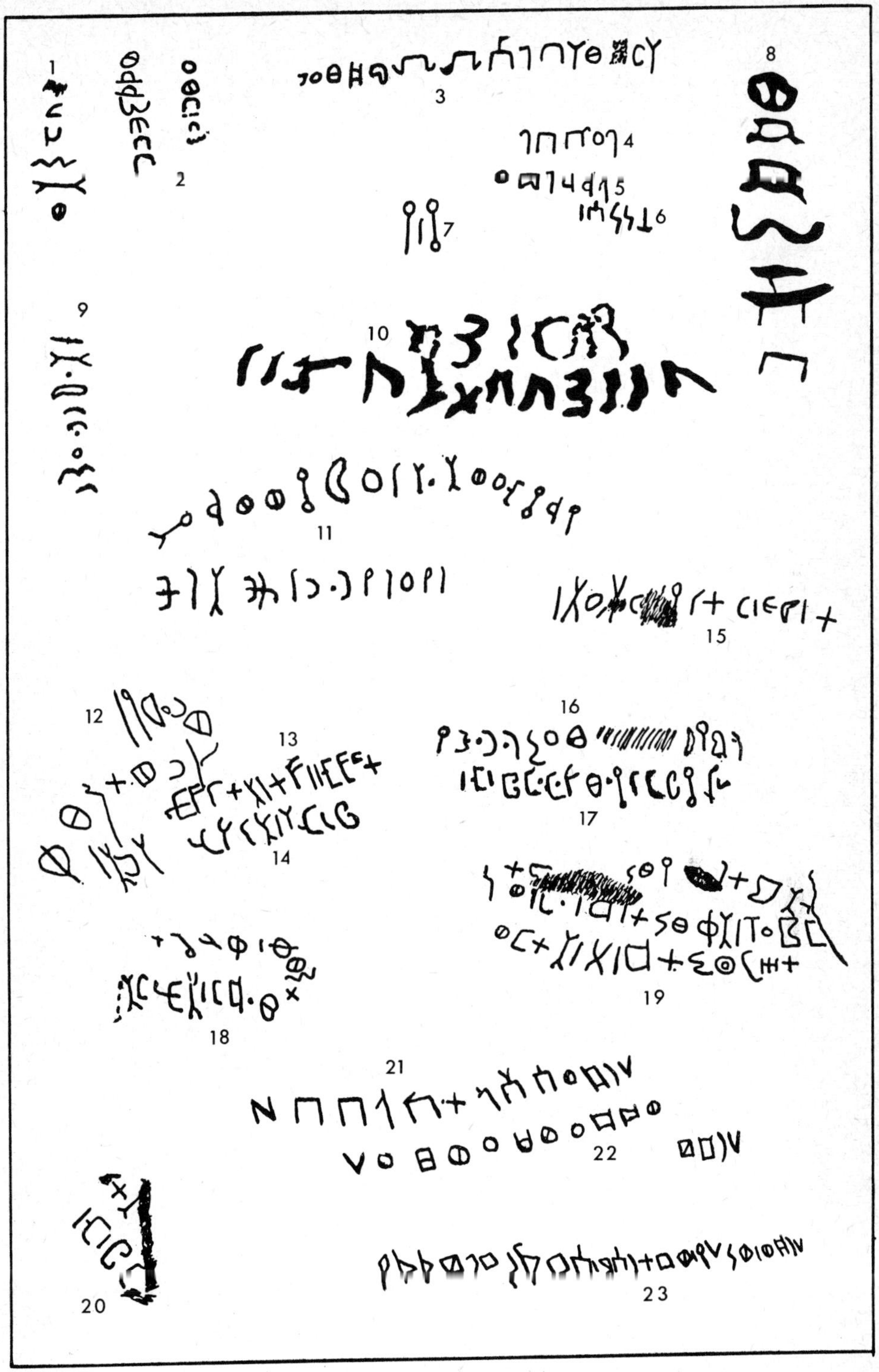

3 Thamudic inscriptions

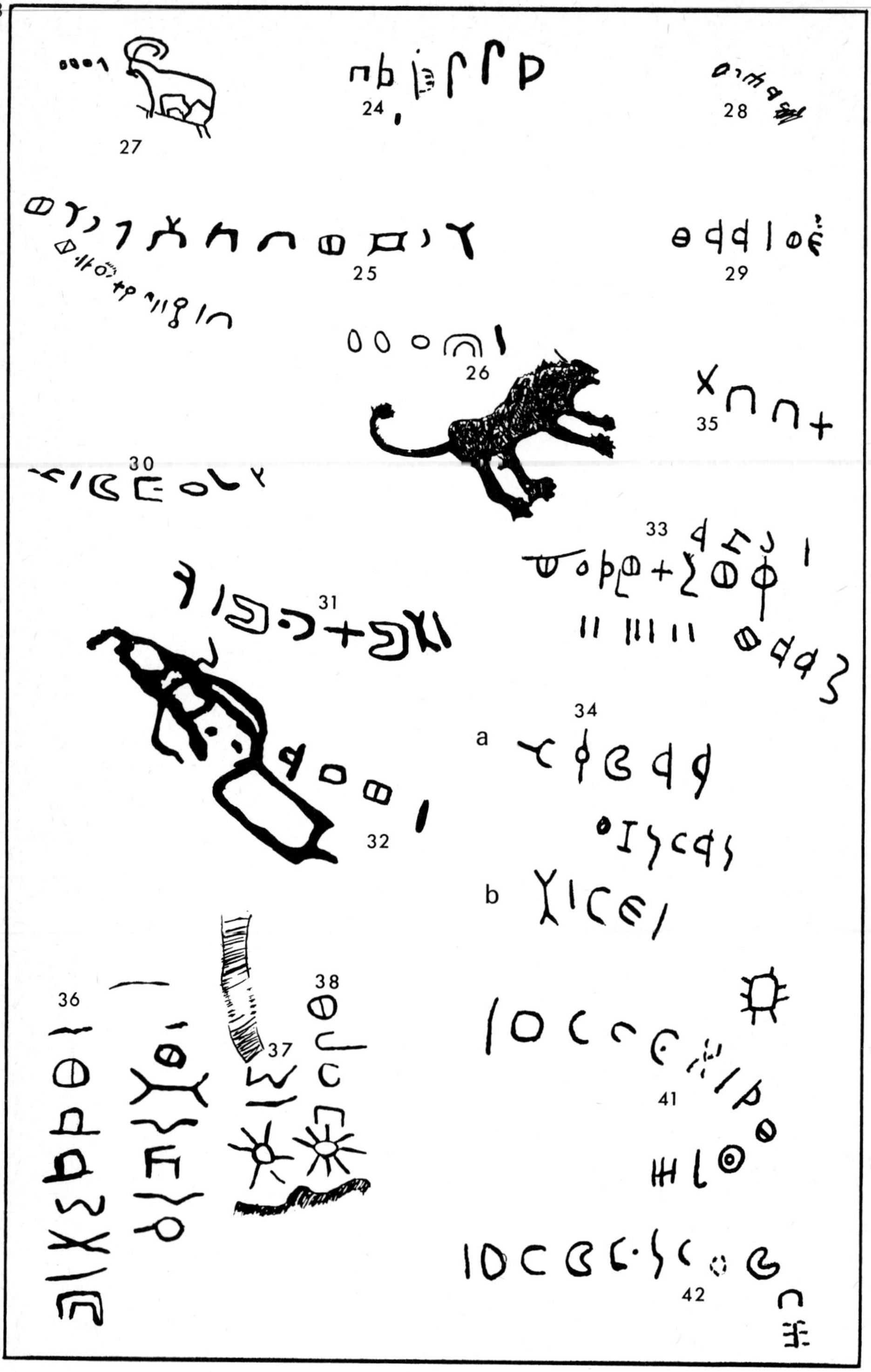

4 Thamudic inscriptions

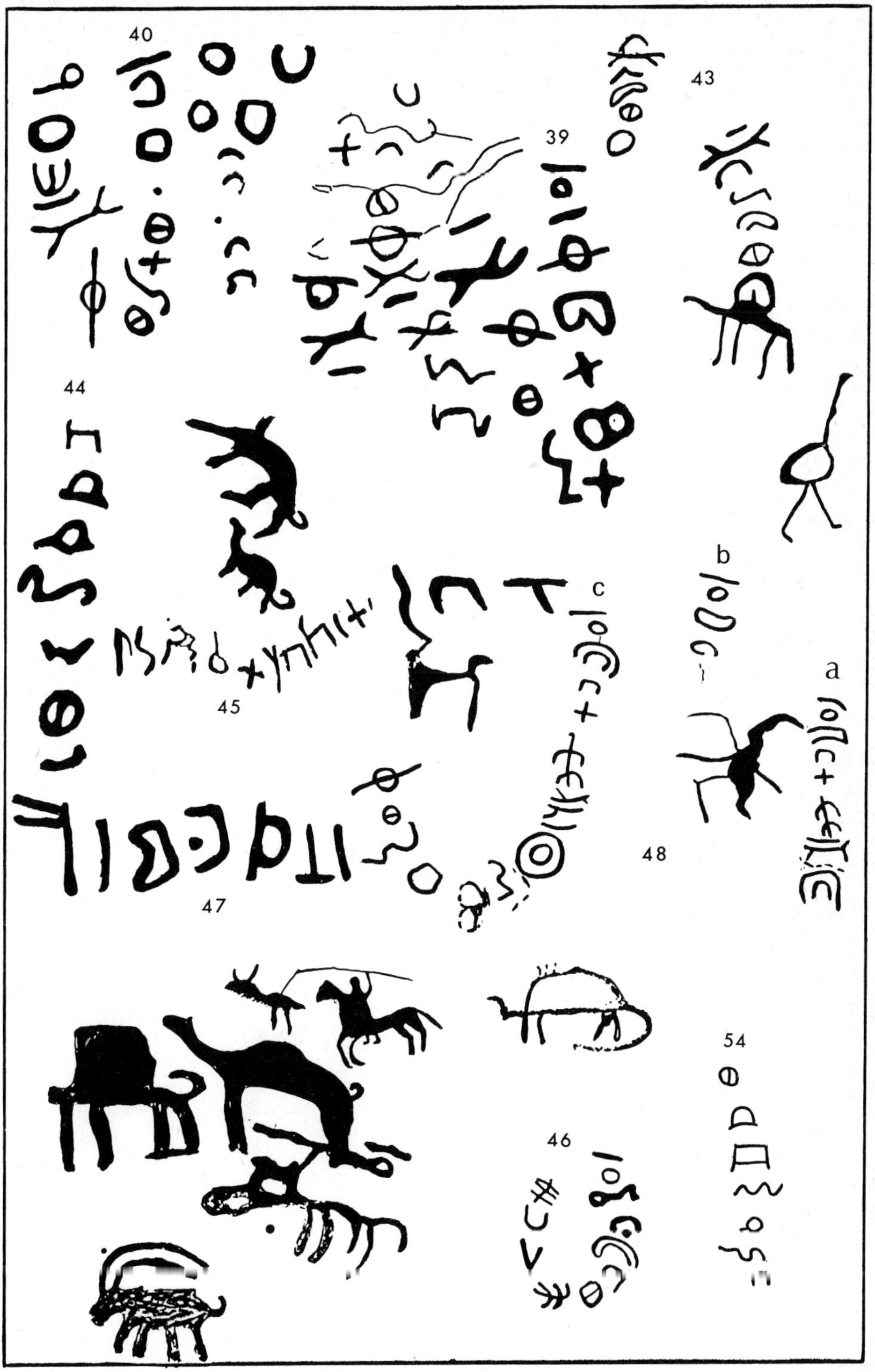

5 Thamudic inscriptions

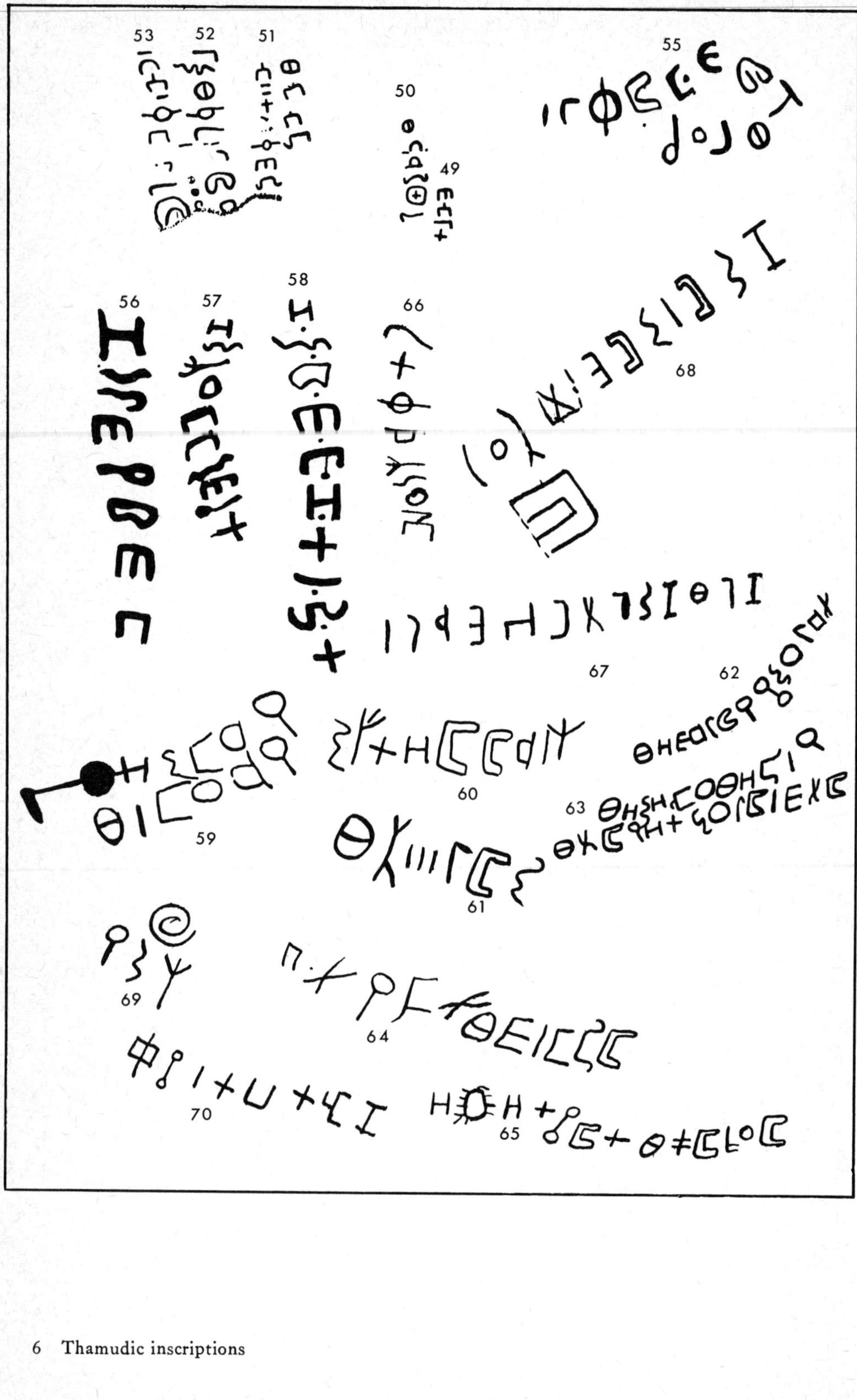

6 Thamudic inscriptions

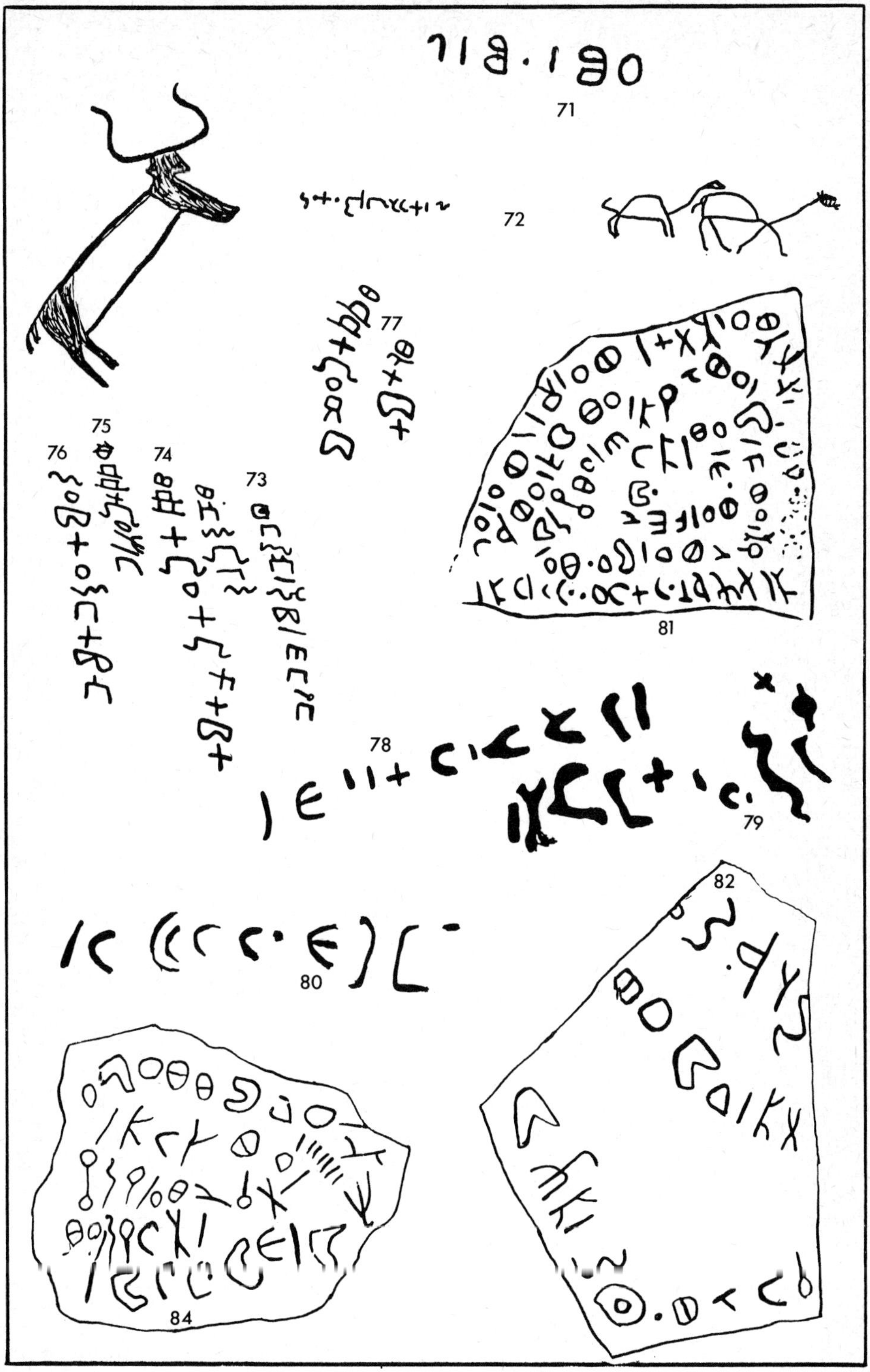

7 Thamudic inscriptions

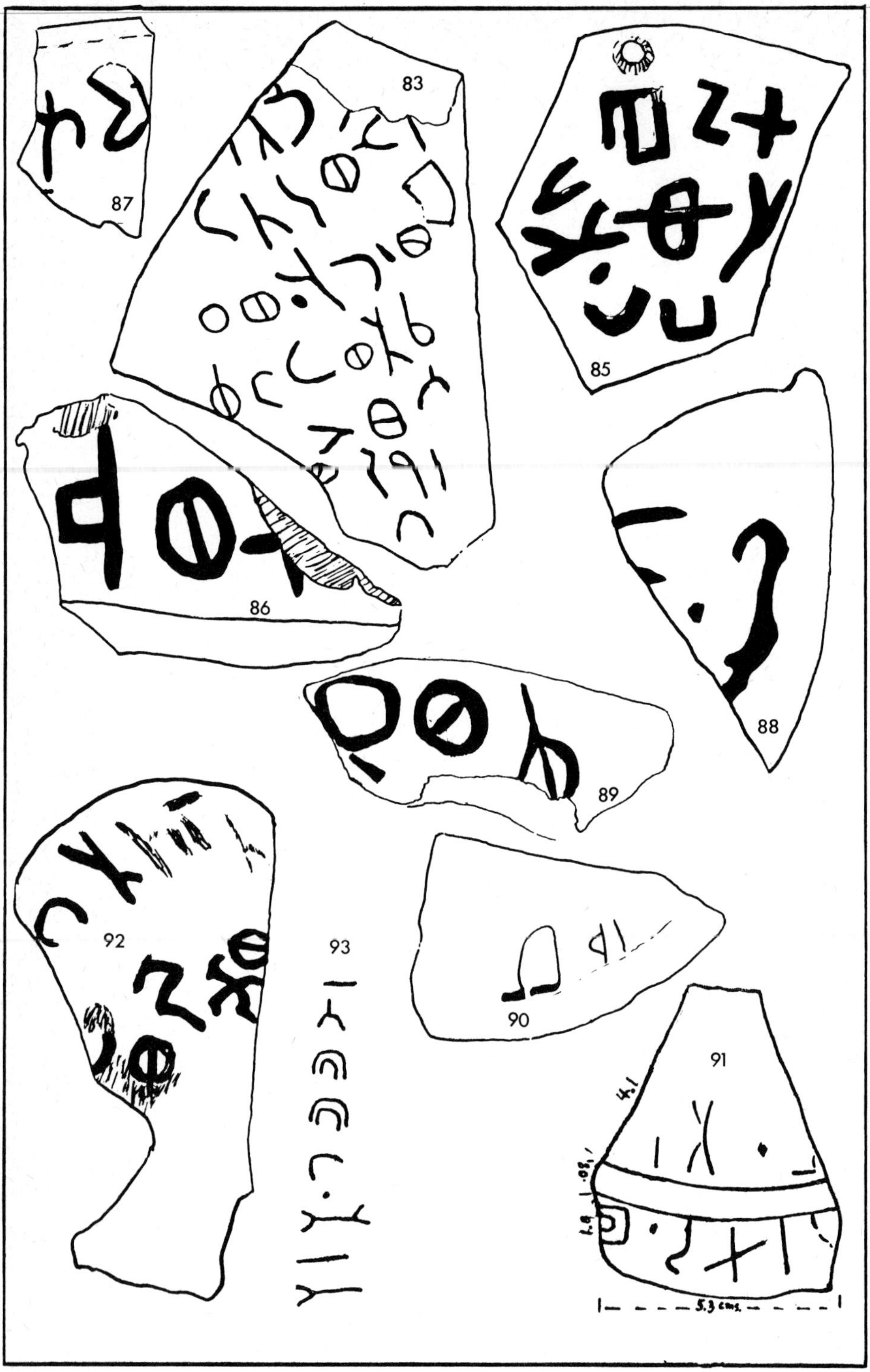

8 Thamudic inscriptions

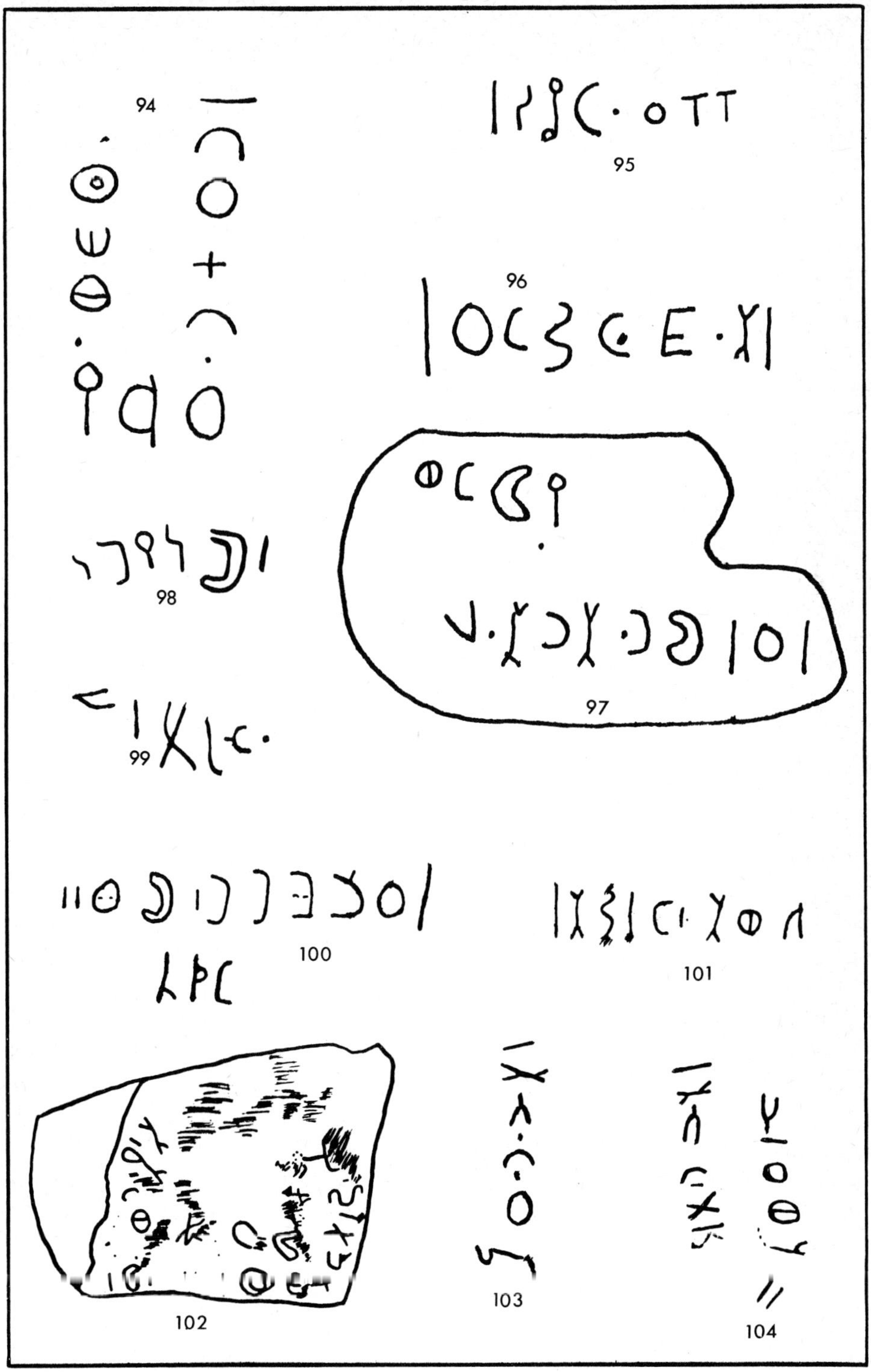

9 Thamudic inscriptions

3–7

8–11 (also Nabataean nos. 1–5)

10 Thamudic inscriptions

12–17 (also Nabataean no. 15)

13–17

19

11 Thamudic inscriptions

21, 22

21, 22

23

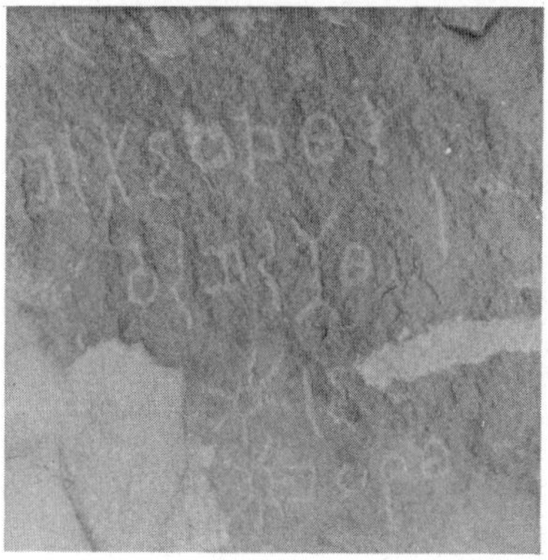

36–38

12 Thamudic inscriptions

24

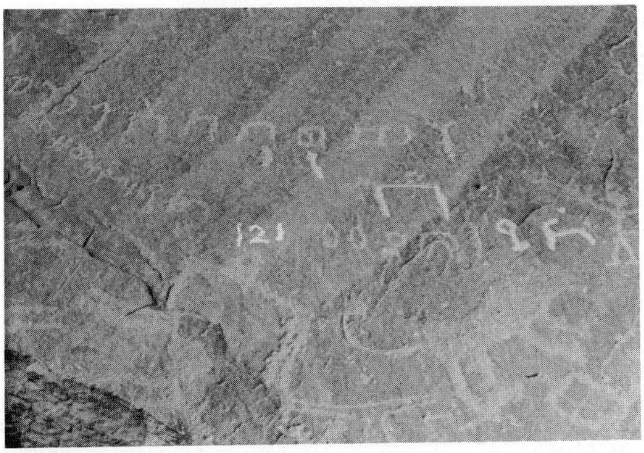

25, 26

27

29

13 Thamudic inscriptions

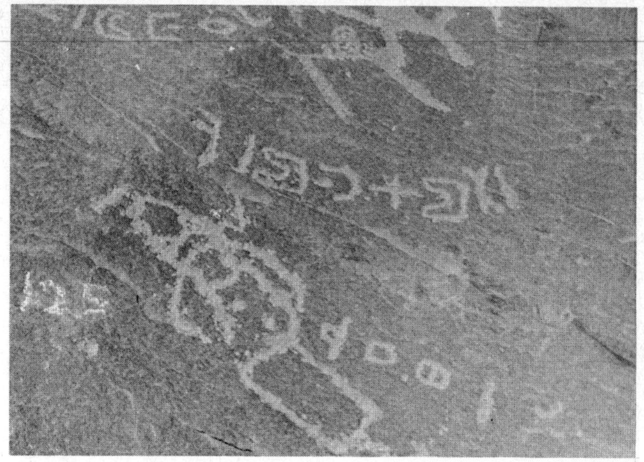

30–32

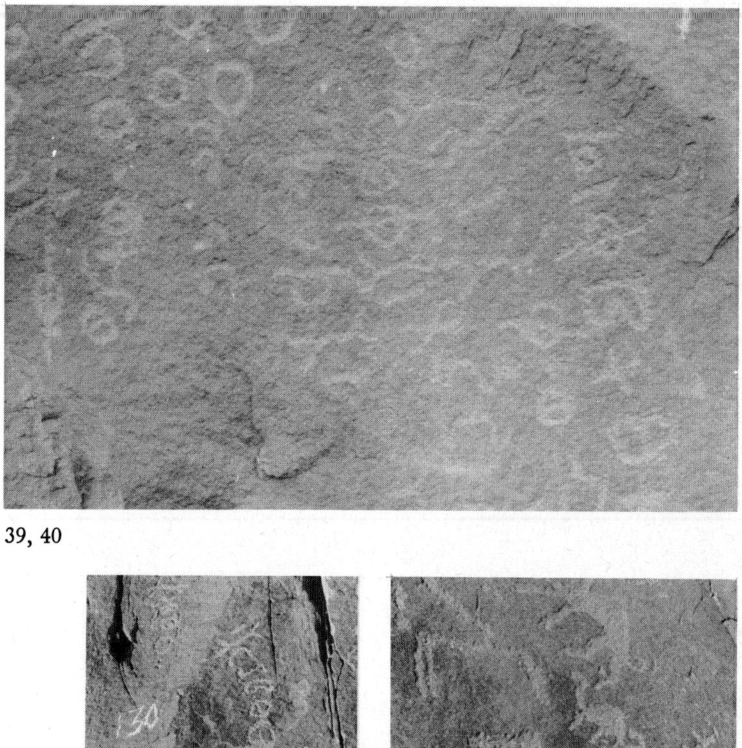

39, 40

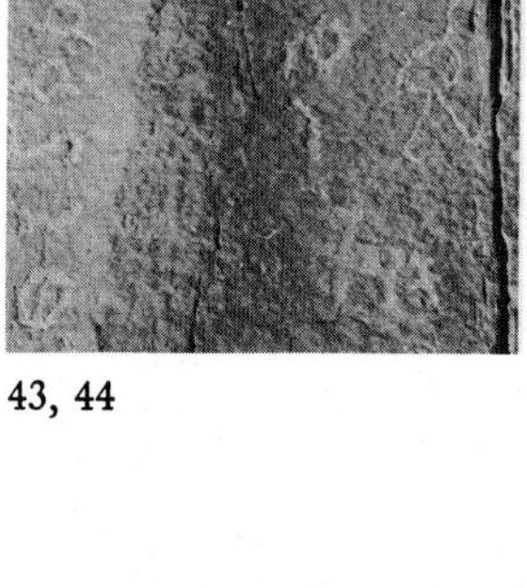

43, 44

45

14 Thamudic inscriptions

47

55

57

46

48

15 Thamudic inscriptions

49–53

56

60, 62, 63, 65

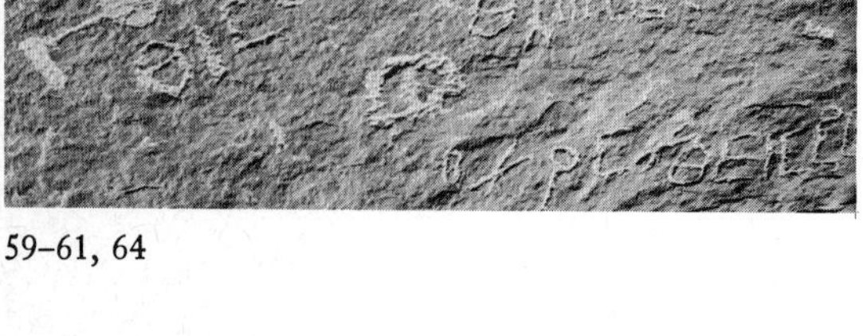

59–61, 64

61, 64, 65

58

16 Thamudic inscriptions

81

84

86

88

78, 79

90

85

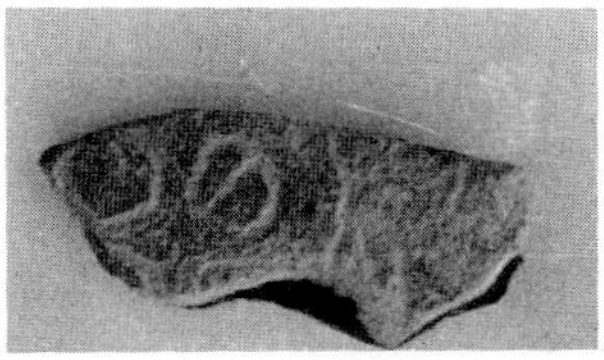
89

87

83

91

92

17 Thamudic inscriptions

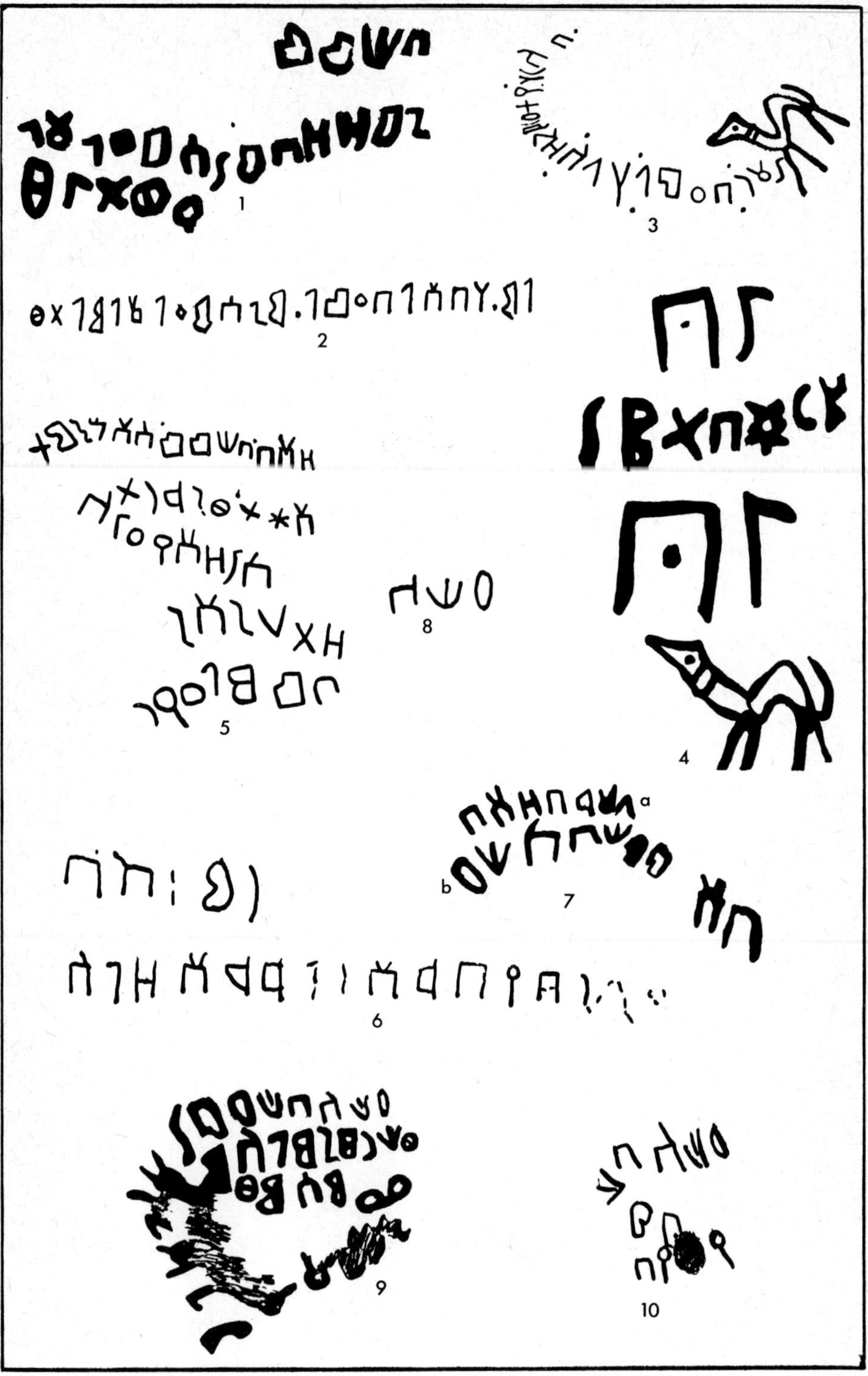

18 Taymanite inscriptions

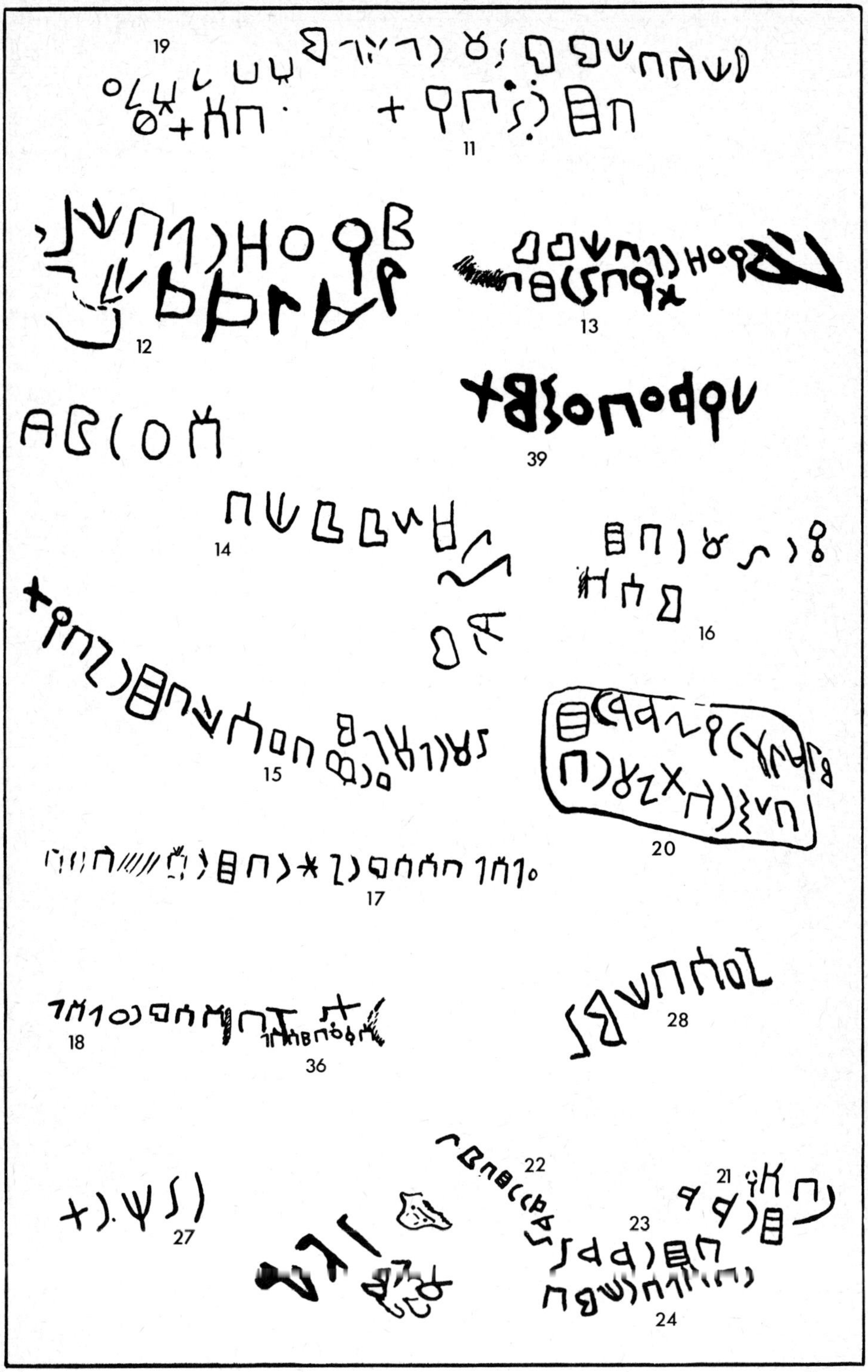

19 Taymanite inscriptions

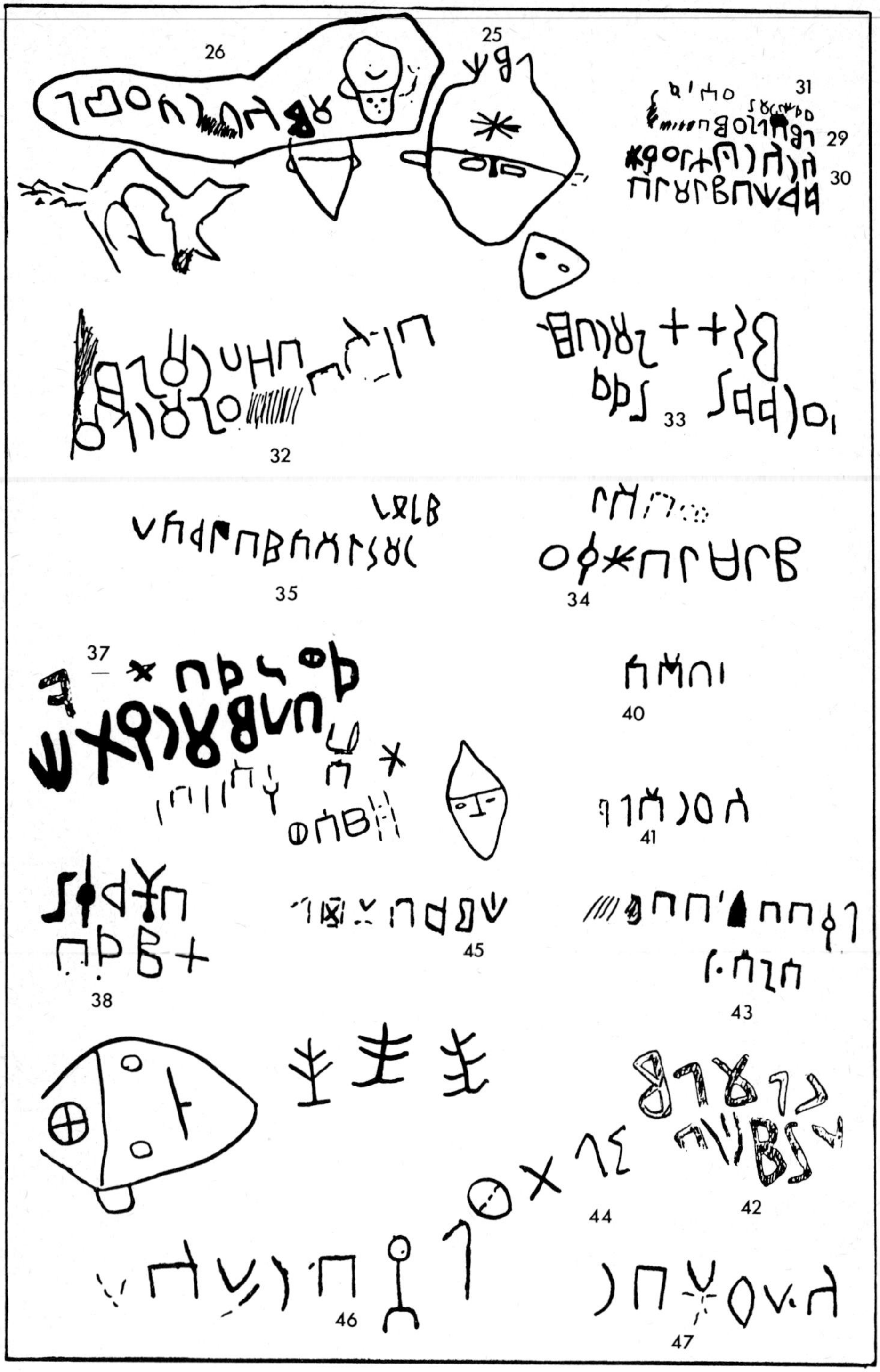

20 Taymanite inscriptions

1

3

4

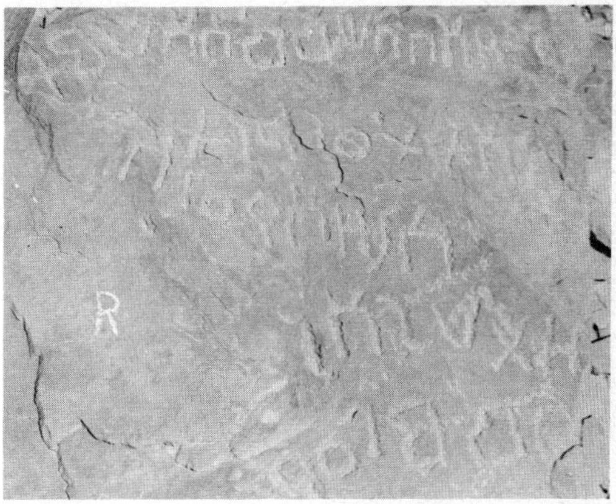
5

7

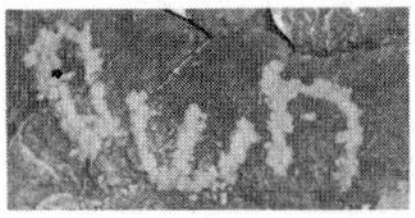
8

12

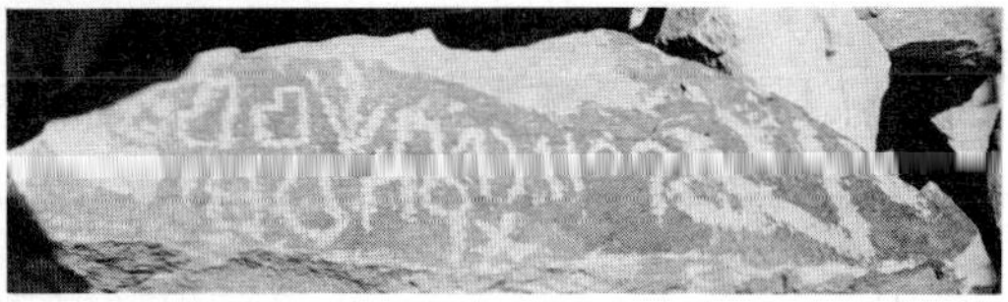
13

10, 15

21 Taymanite inscriptions

9

20

25–27

28–30

32

18, 36

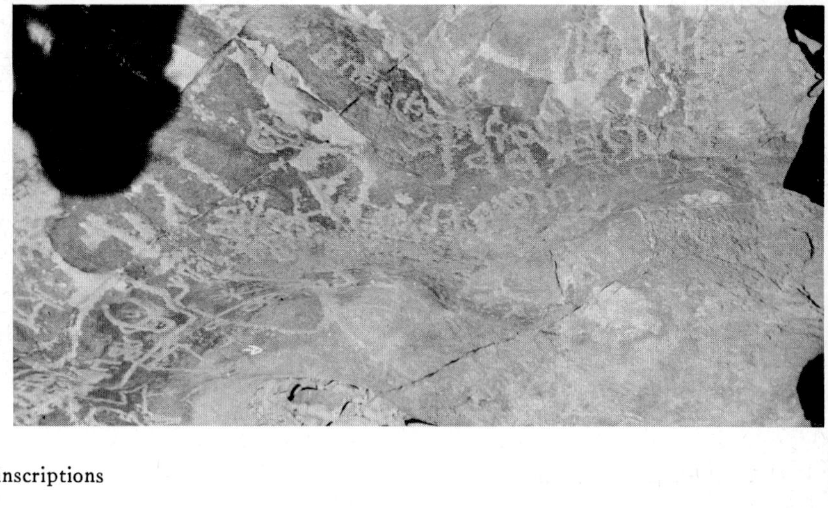

21–24

22 Taymanite inscriptions

34

39

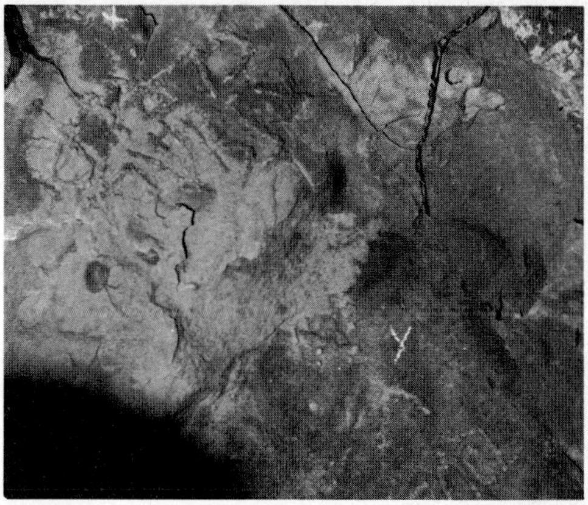

42

37

48

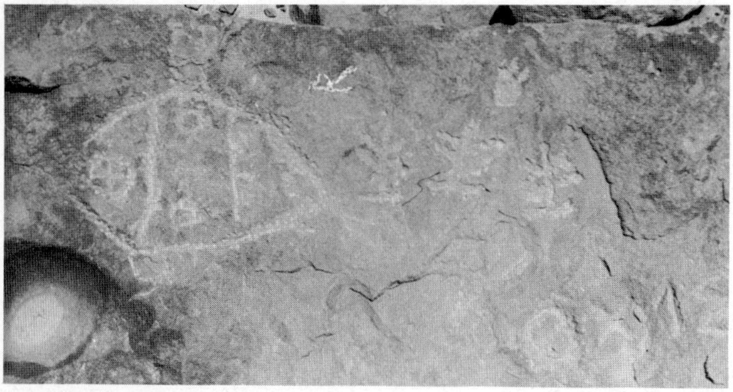

44

38

33

23 Taymanite inscriptions

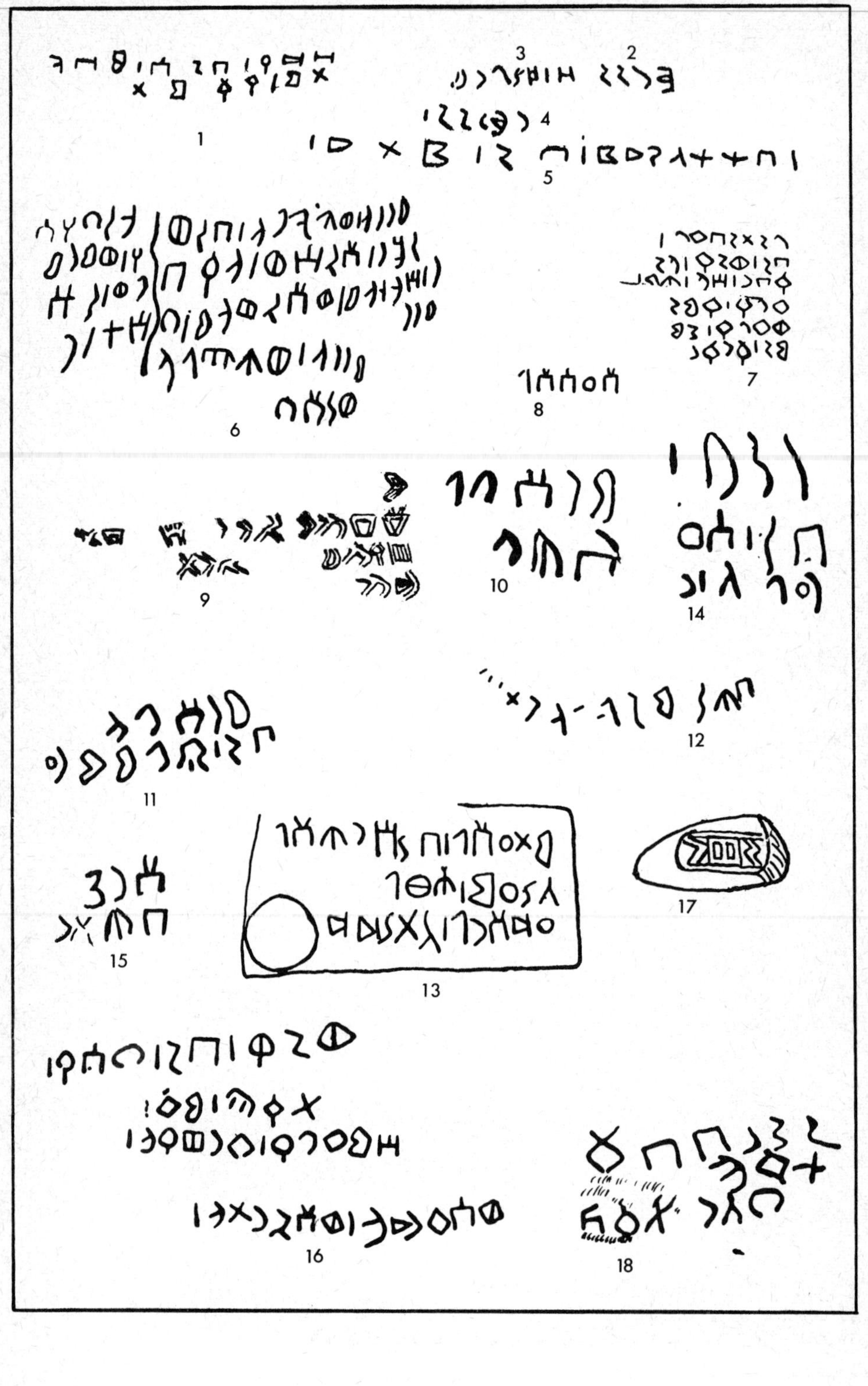

24 Dedanite and Lihyanite inscriptions

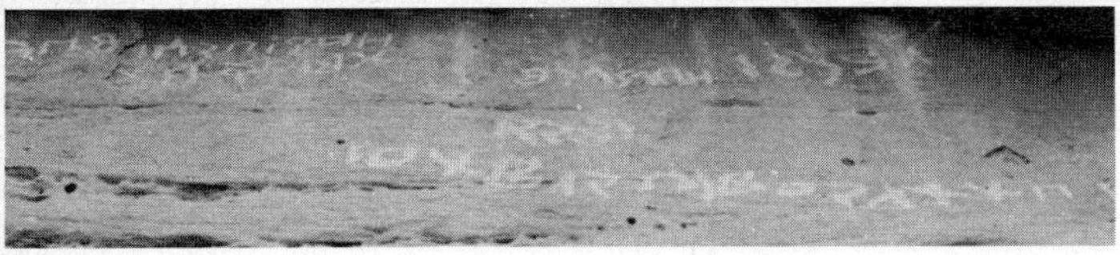
1–5

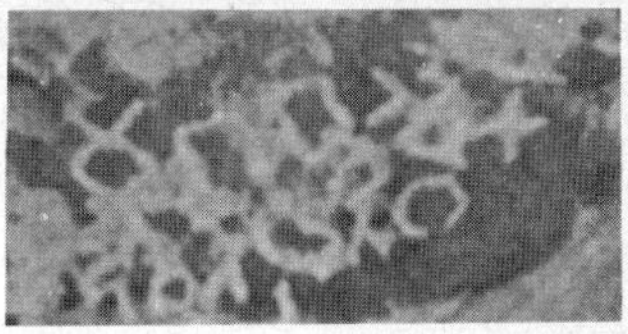
18

6

9

11, 12

16

13 (also Minaean no. 4)

25 Dedanite and Lihyanite inscriptions

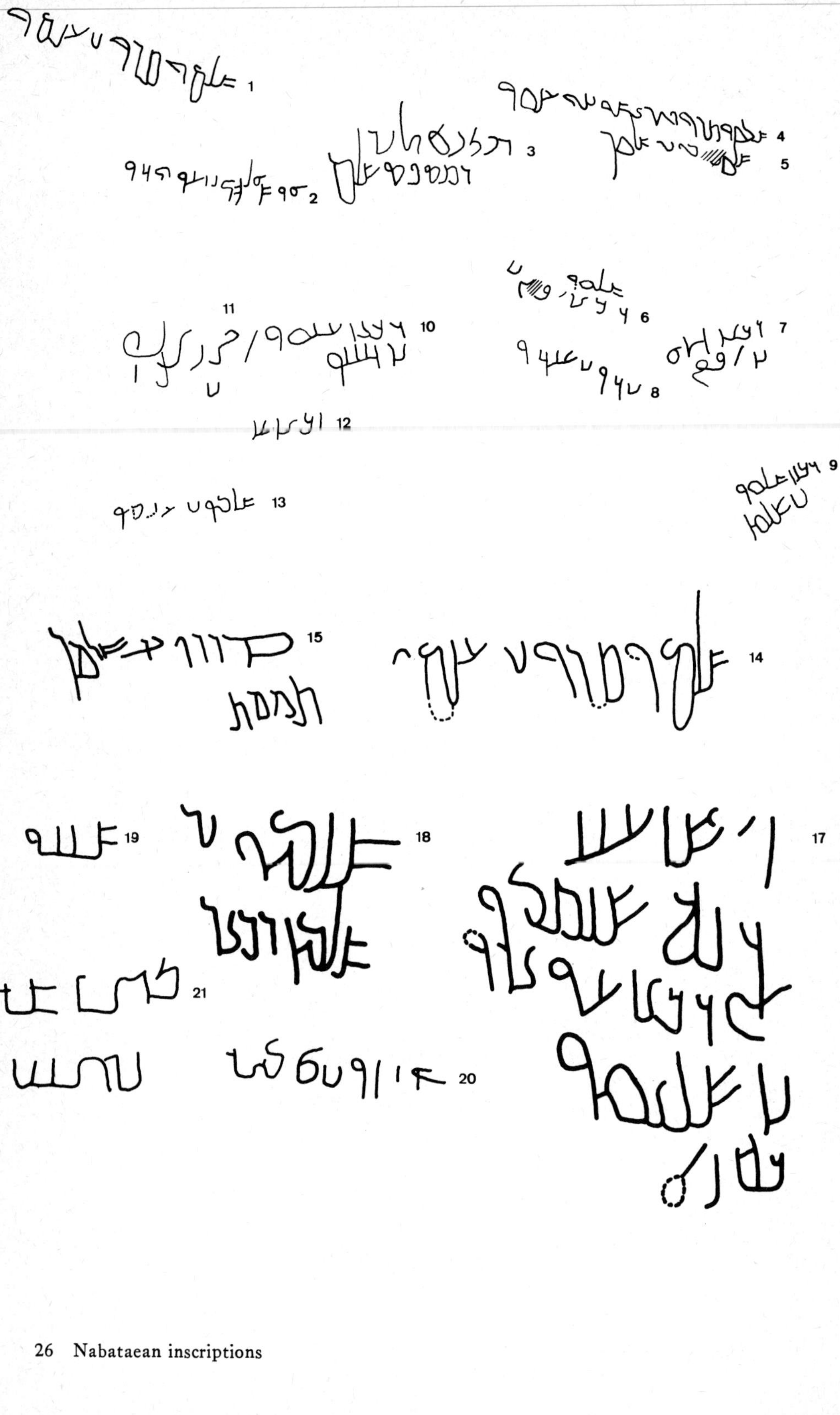

26 Nabataean inscriptions

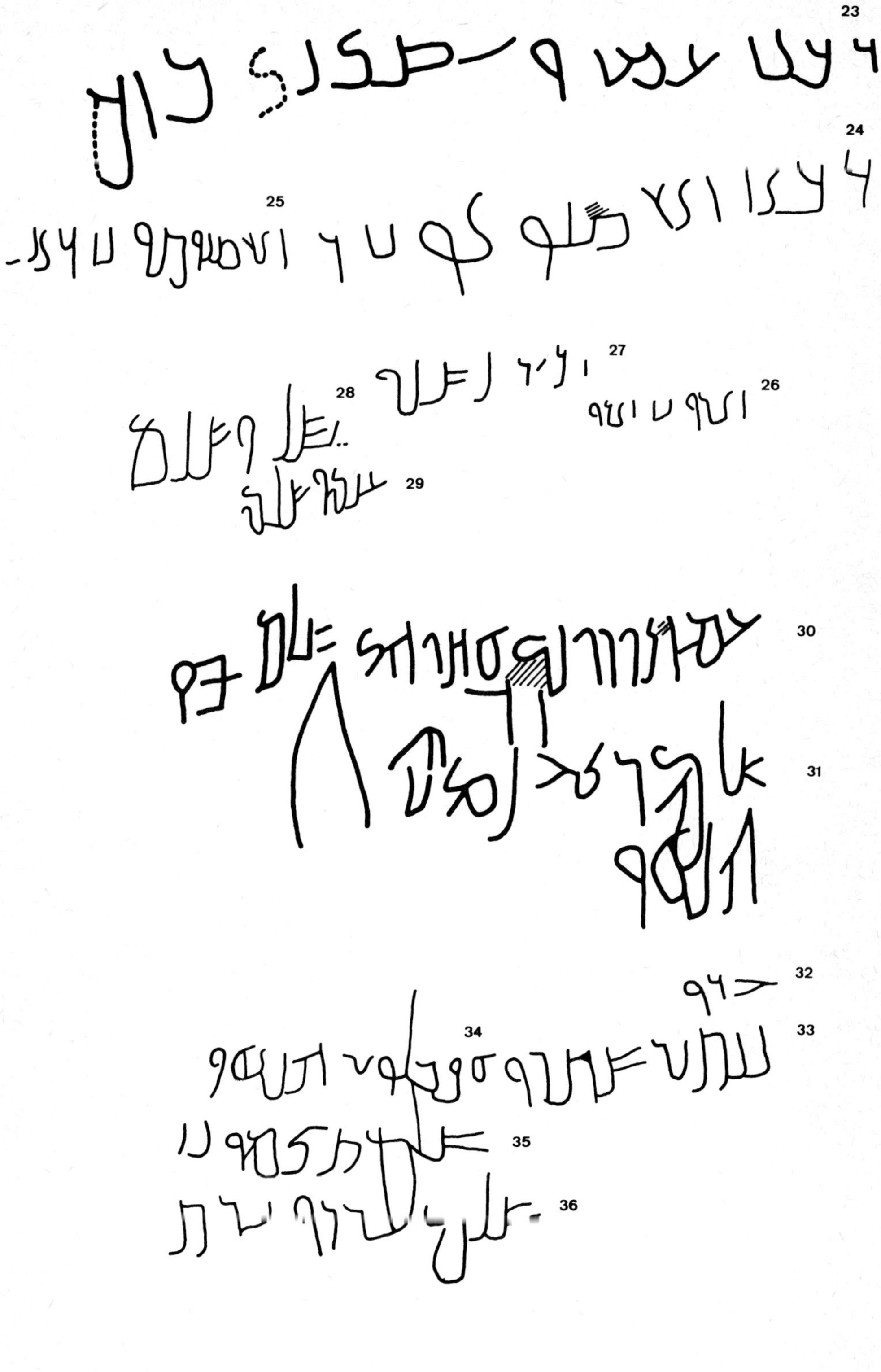

27 Nabataean inscriptions

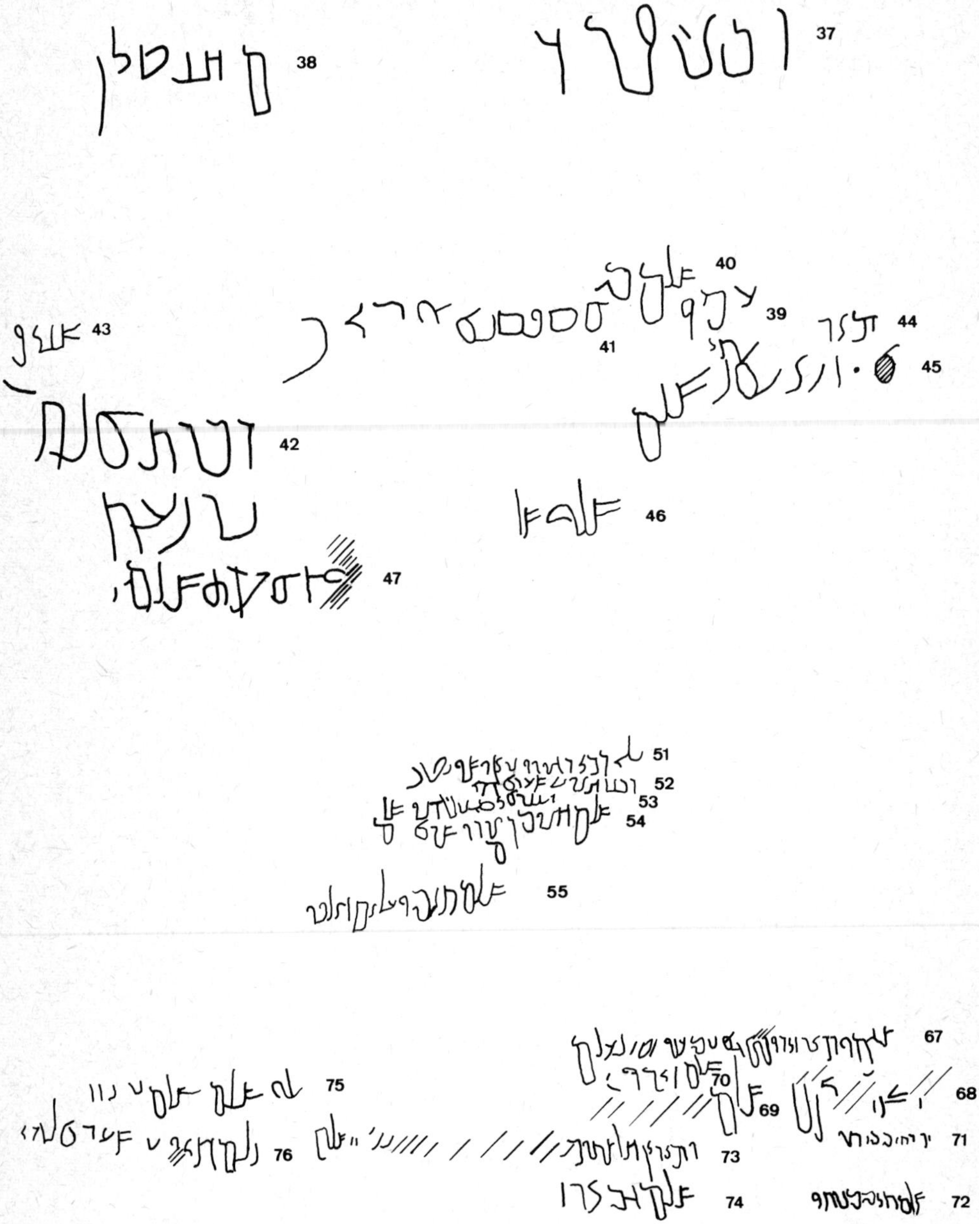

28 Nabataean inscriptions

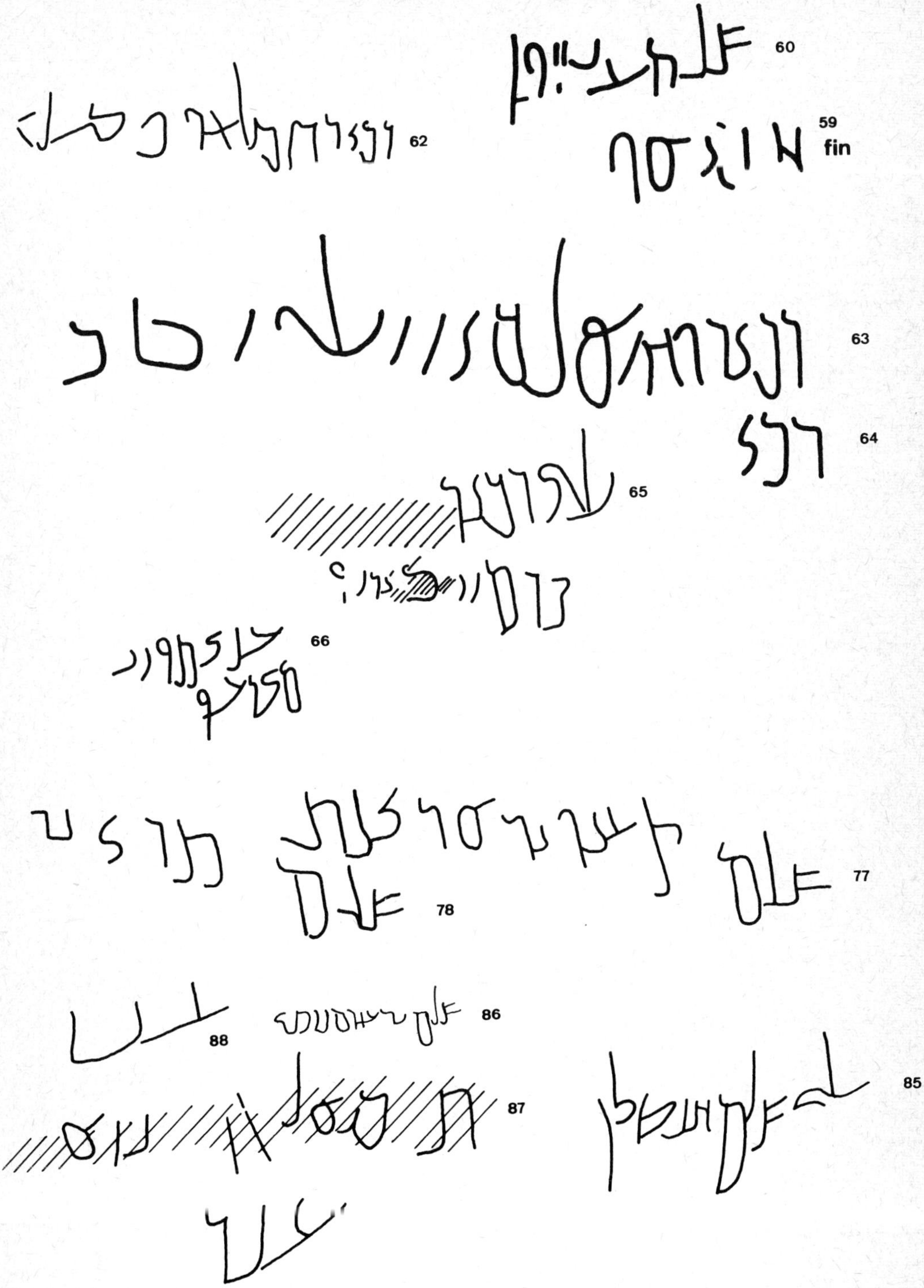

29 Nabataean inscriptions

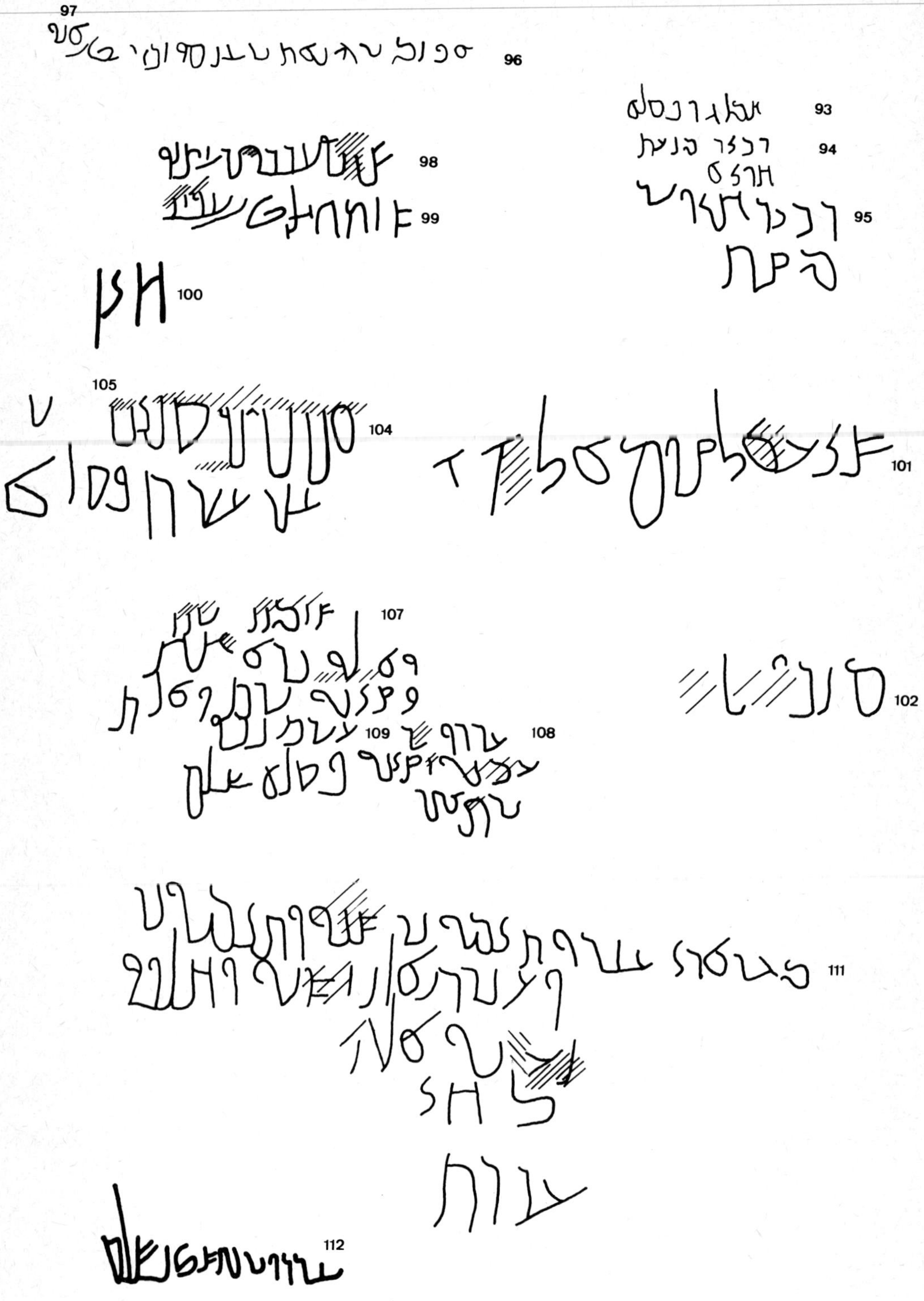

30 Nabataean inscriptions

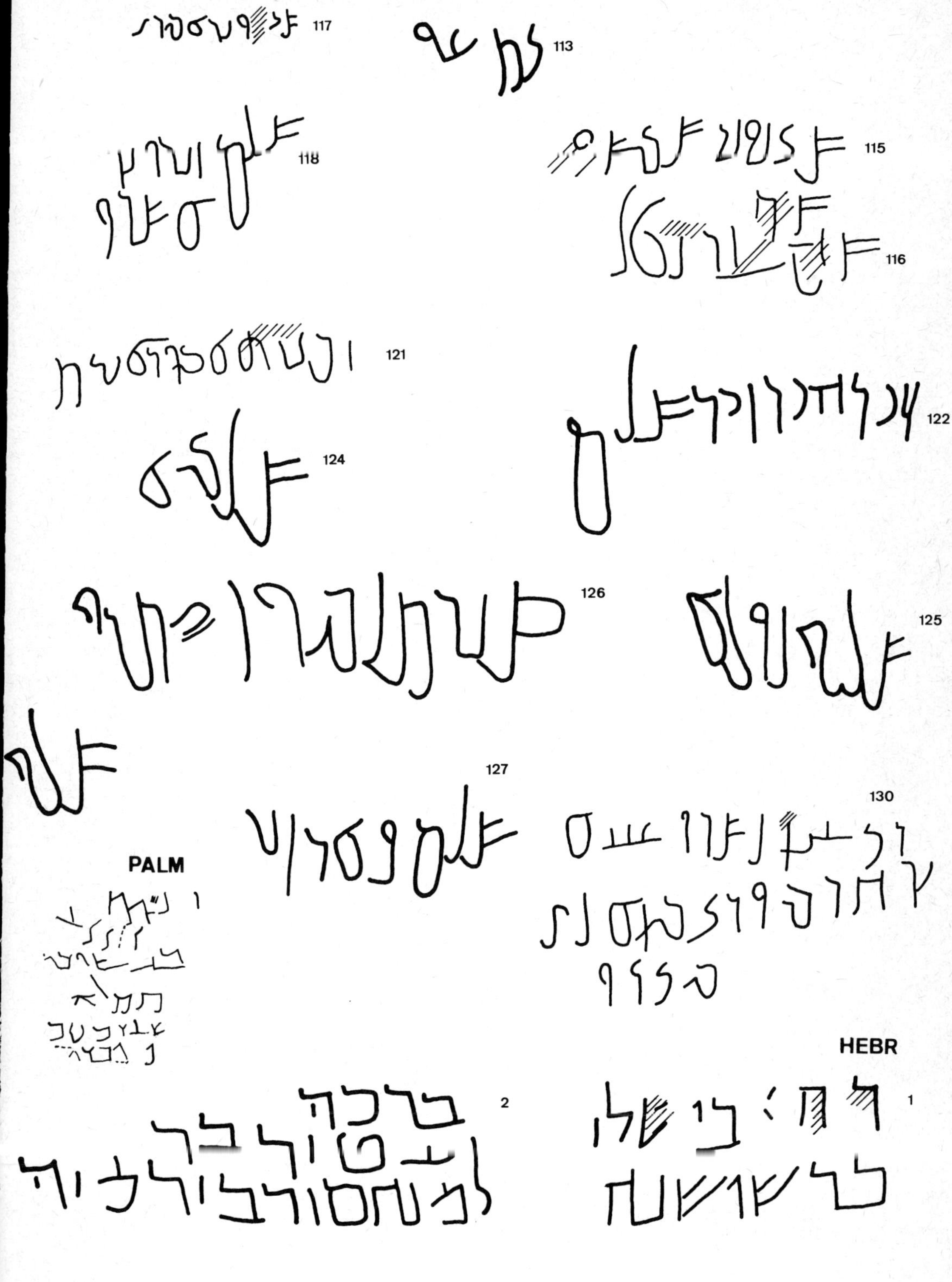

31 Nabataean, Palmyrene, and Hebrew inscriptions

236

16

22

57

30, 31

67–76

32 Nabataean inscriptions

79

91

237

101, 102

130

33 Nabataean inscriptions

1

2

34 Hebrew inscriptions

Index

When reference is made to an illustration, the page number is given in italics